EUNUCHS AND CASTRATI

A CULTURAL HISTORY

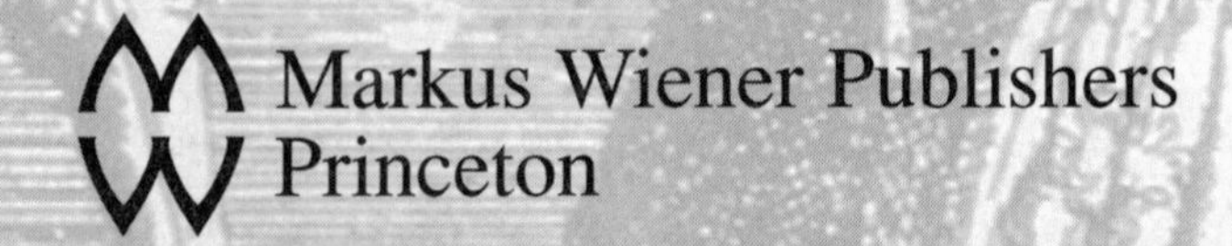
Markus Wiener Publishers
Princeton

Eunuchs and Castrati

A Cultural History

PIOTR O. SCHOLZ

Translated from the German by
John A. Broadwin and Shelley L. Frisch

Chapters 1 to 5 translated from the German by John A. Broadwin
Chapters 6 to 10 translated from the German by Shelley L. Frisch

Illustrations: Archive of Piotr O. Scholz

For information write to: Markus Wiener Publishers
231 Nassau Street, Princeton, NJ 08542

Library of Congress Cataloging-in-Publication Data

Scholz, Piotr O.
[Entmannte Eros. English]
Eunuchs and Castrati: a cultural history/Piotr O. Scholz;
translated from the German by John A. Broadwin and Shelley L. Frisch.
Translation of: Der entmannte Eros.
Includes bibliographical references and index.
ISBN 1-55876-200-0 hardcover
ISBN 1-55876-201-9 paperback
1. Eunuchs I. Title.
HQ449.S364 2000
306.76'2—dc21 00-063415

Printed in the United States of America on acid-free paper.

Contents

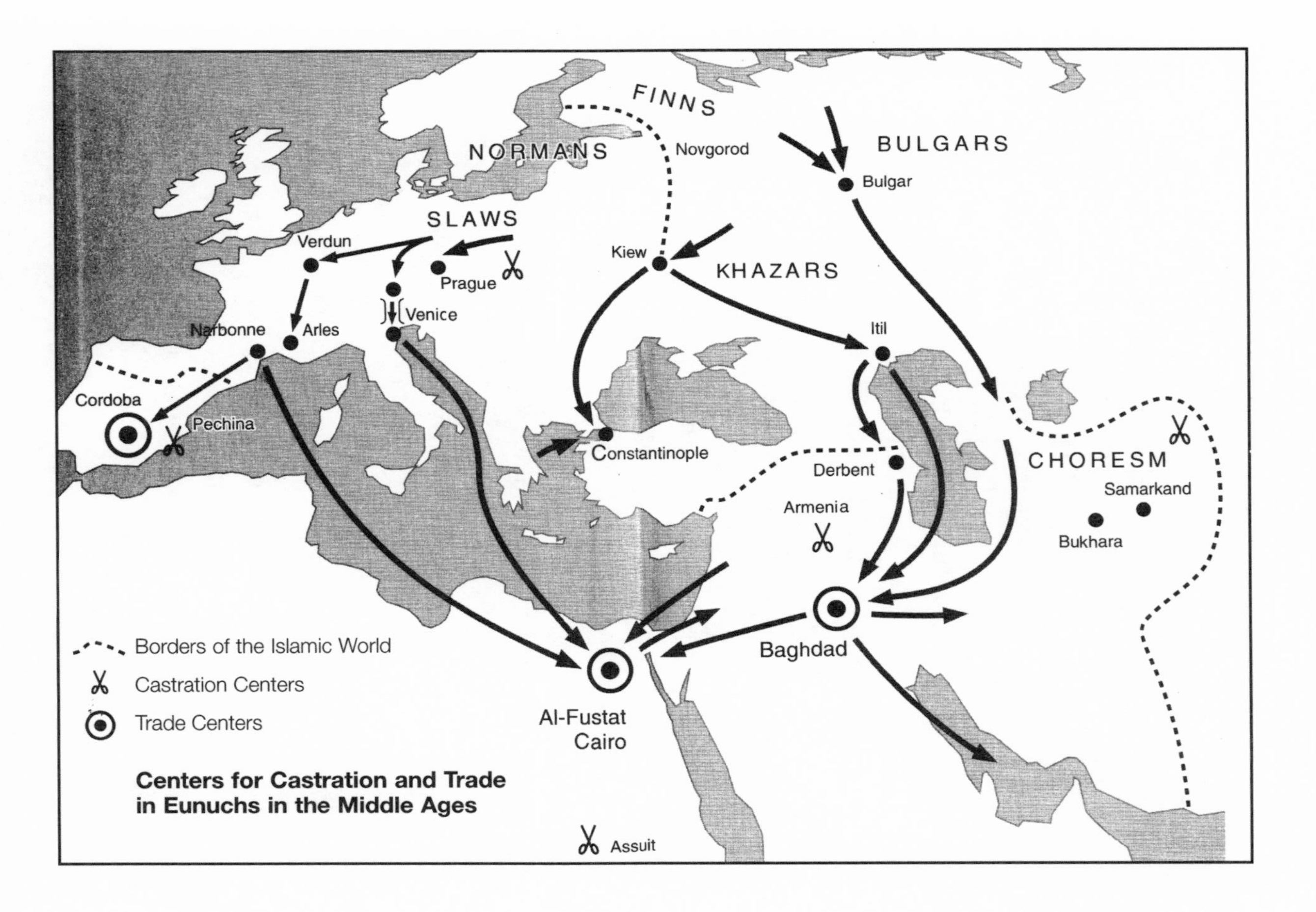

Centers for Castration and Trade in Eunuchs in the Middle Ages

Preface

At the 13th International Congress of Archeology held in Berlin in 1988, I found that a number of the attendees were surprised at the distinction drawn between "castrati" and "eunuchs." Even professional scholars often equate eunuchs with men who have been emasculated or castrated. Yet there is no inherent reason why a eunuch has to be a castrato. I noted a similar reaction to the term *gallos* when used to describe an "ecstatic, frenzied mystagogue" who had mutilated himself. Even though the cultic reasons for the ritual of castration were not always well understood, they nevertheless became a source of inspiration in the Roman period and late antiquity for a series of monuments and their associated iconography (the cult of Attis and Cybele). Some of the leading references on classical antiquity lack entries for *eunouchos*.[1] This is what impelled me—after studying the concept of the *eunouchos* and its use in the Bible—to investigate this neglected subject in greater depth. It was Peter Guyot's dissertation (1979) that first drew the attention of historians to this topic, even though it ultimately failed to have any long-term impact on historical research. It was not until I had begun to study ancient Egypt and the cultures along the Red Sea that I once again came across evidence linking eunuchs and the practice of emasculation to so-called "marks of kingship." It is instructive in this regard to note the sandstone pillar statue of the apostate pharaoh Akhenaton, which depicts the naked Egyptian king as an "emasculated" (or merely asexual, androgynous?) being. Usually just the head and torso are shown; only rarely is the entire figure presented. This is a graphic illustration of how a subject becomes taboo.

The many books dealing with oriental courts, in which eunuchs are portrayed as harem guards, together with the revival of interest in the celebrated castrati of Italian opera that was sparked by the resurrection of the role of the countertenor (Gérard Corbiau's 1994 film *Farinelli* and, for German-language readers, Hubert Ortkemper's 1993 book *Engel Wider Willen: die Welt der Kastraten*[2] also made an important contribution in this regard) paved the way for the present study. Even John Irving's 1994 novel *A Son of the Circus* contributed by focusing attention on the little-known *hijra*s of India, castrated men who might be compared to transsexuals in the West. Taken together, these things represented a challenge to approach the subject from a historico-cultural and psychohistorical perspective, albeit while stressing only certain major themes. In the spirit of Josef Strzygowski, who conceived of art history as the history of ideas, I availed myself of tools from hermeneutics, iconography, and semiotics, branches of knowledge that concern themselves with the interpretation of works of art, works that are clearly as expressive and evocative as any literary texts.

The history of eunuchism and the practice of castration date back to ancient times and were associated with the *Sitz im Leben* or characteristic life settings of various religions and cultures. Since much of the evidence of that past relates to religious rites and myths that are no longer celebrated and were kept secret largely because of their sacred character, it is sometimes difficult to trace them back to their origins. These ritual acts were closely tied to the idea of sacrifice and were regarded—in the mythic sense—as a kind of "insurance policy" to make certain that wishes expressed would in fact be fulfilled. There was a commonly held belief, for example, that one could assure that the earth would be fruitful and people prosperous if one sacrificed one's own capability to procreate. Castrating an individual (which was tantamount to his death) was one way to fertilize the Earth Goddess, the giver of all life. These paradoxical ideas and the rituals that derived from them led to the creation of institutions that survived to some extent into the modern era. More than 2,000 eunuchs, for example, were employed at the court of the last emperor of China (whose memory is preserved for many in Bertolucci's film *The Last Emperor* [1986/87]). The range of nations within whose diverse cultures eunuchs and castrati are found is so varied that it is impossible to depict every aspect of the subject.

Eunuchs were not simply "bedchamber attendants," as the Greek term suggests. Nor were they always slaves, as some authors stress. They could just as well be ascetics, priests, magicians, scholars, physicians, military commanders, admirals, or senior officials at the courts of both eastern and western rulers. In the Byzantine Empire in particular they managed to rise to the highest levels of the imperial hierarchy. The only office they were precluded from attaining was that of emperor.

I hope that my brief historical survey will guide my readers as they travel through various lands and periods familiarizing themselves with the duties and responsibilities, the unspeakable torments, passions, and joys of these individuals. The rich and varied forms of religious, social, and sexual life associated with eunuchs and castrati embrace a wealth of myths relating to gods and demons, initiation rites, rituals, and magic.

They touch on the history of law and medicine, various systems of government, and secret societies. And they are presented to us in terms of the cruelest punishment and tortures. On the one hand, they facilitated unique developments in the evolution of vocal music, and on the other they gave rise to a multiplicity of human behavioral patterns that reflect every aspect of good and evil. Readers will become acquainted with various forms of sexuality, such as androgyny, transvestism, transsexualism, and homosexuality, and learn about the historical, religious, and social issues associated with their characteristic "life settings." Whether out of a sense of shame or because of moral considerations these phenomena appear only on the margins of the history of customs and mores.

In an age when carnality is easily confused with sexuality, the Platonic idea of love seems to be increasingly a relic of the past. "And besides justice, he [Eros] has the biggest share of moderation. For moderation, by common agreement, is power over pleasures and passions, and no pleasure is more powerful than Love! But if they are weaker, they are under the power of Love, and *he* has the power; and because he has the power over pleasures and passions, Love is exceptionally moderate." (Plato, *Symposium*) In the spirit of the ancient myths I dedicate this book to the "martyred Eros."

According to Iwan Bloch, eunuchs and the practice of castration are unique phenomena, for there are "only two sexes upon which all true cultural progress is founded: the genuine male and the genuine female. All the rest are ultimately fantasies, monstrosities, or vestiges of primitive prehistoric sexuality."

The German language has had problems incorporating the

terminology and etymology of castration. In their famous dictionary, the Brothers Grimm listed "mutilation" (*Verstümmelung*) as a term to be used on an equal footing with "emasculation" (*Entmannung*). It may have been useful to stress the original meaning of the word [to cut or maim], if what one had in mind was Amfortas and Klingsor. In the present day a shift of meaning has extended the semantic range of the term. During the Middle Ages, as the Brothers Grimm noted, two other words came into use that were more in line with the vernacular: *mönchen* "to monk" or "make a monk of" (castrate); and *kapaunen* "to capon" (emasculate, neuter, literally castrate a cock, geld). The noun capon therefore became a euphemism for a castrato or eunuch. Anything else pertaining to the practice was either suppressed or kept secret. Thus the works of ancient writers published in German translation—the epigrams of Martial, for instance—were usually fragmentary. Many passages dealing with the issue were for no apparent reason left in the original language. The terms contained in these passages ended up being used only by physicians and lawyers as part of their technical vocabularies. Even specialists who dealt with the study of religion, the ancient Middle East, art history, or archeology over the course of decades either omitted discussion of certain subjects or mentioned them only under the rubric of "fertility cults." It was inevitable that people became oblivious to or did not know how to categorize phenomena that "sullied" the idealized and perfect picture of a bygone civilization painted in the spirit of the great archeologist Winkelmann.

To Prof. Roland Hampe (1908–1982), my teacher at Heidelberg University, goes the credit for having made ancient

Greek civilization come alive again in such a way that we, his students, were touched by its real and natural charm. It is to his memory that I gratefully dedicate this book. I would also like to take this occasion to remember my friends from the archeology roundtable at Heidelberg. Finally, I wish to express my thanks to all those who encouraged and contributed in word and deed to the writing of this book.

Wiesbaden
Piotr O. Scholz

Sexuality and Emasculation—or Longing for Paradise

> "And the exquisite coloring of his skin! The way the god consorts with flowers shows that. For he never settles in anything, be it a body or a soul, that cannot flower or has lost its bloom. His place is wherever it is flowery and fragrant; there he settles, there he stays."
>
> —Plato, *Symposium*

For centuries human sexual behavior has been subject to religious and moral taboos. In the West it was impossible before the advent of Sigmund Freud (1856–1939) to discuss sexuality openly in the natural sciences and humanities. Not until Iwan Bloch published the results of his research at the end of the 19th and the beginning of the 20th centuries did scientists and scholars begin—albeit with great reservations and reluctance—to discuss sex. And even then they made their findings accessible only to specialists within their own fields. New disciplines emerged, including ethnology, archeology, psychology, the science of religion (*Religionswissenschaft*), sociology, and sexology.

Library shelves gradually began to fill up with the publications of Bronislaw Malinowski (1882–1942) on sexual practices in "savage" societies, the studies of Ludwig Friedländer, Gaston Vorberg, Hans Licht, and Theodor Hopfner on the life and customs of ancient civilizations, the works of Walter Schubart on religion and Eros, and the books of Iwan Bloch and Magnus Hirschfeld on sexuality. These works were often privately printed or made available "solely for the purposes of scholarly research" and kept in "locked cages." They nevertheless came to be recognized as pioneering efforts in the study of sexuality as a socially relevant discipline.

German theologians and Orientalists—primarily Hermann Gunkel (1862–1932) and Hugo Greßmann (1877–1927)—rightly called for an inquiry into the *Sitz im Leben*, the life settings or situations in life that are characteristic of every manifestation of humankind.[3] Their efforts added a new dimension to the study of cultural history.

For quite some time emasculation by castration and the physical and psychological damage associated with it were considered matters of peripheral importance or extreme, exotic manifestations of bygone civilizations that aroused only the curiosity of the voyeur. It now turns out that the custom is being practiced even today in some countries, in India for example, where emasculated men called hijras often perform an important function as entertainers at weddings and at festivities celebrating the birth of a [male] child. As John Irving has sought to describe in his novel *A Son of the Circus*, they also play a major role in the subcontinent's seamy underworld:

"He detested the all-too-womanly gestures of most hijras and zenanas; he thought the mischief with which they dressed indicated an all-too-womanly frivolity. As for the traditional powers of the hijras to bless or to curse, Rahul had no belief that they possessed such powers; he believed they tended to parade themselves, either for the smug amusement of boring homosexuals or for the titillation of mere conventional homosexuals."[4]

Emasculated men, usually described incorrectly as eunuchs, can now be found among transvestites, transsexuals, and the members of various sects and associations claiming to have found the way to remain completely celibate. It is not only a question of ascertaining whether castrati, i.e., emasculated men, still exist in this place or that (e.g., singers who choose to be castrated to preserve the soprano or contralto range of their voices), but of determining how at the very dawn of humankind castration became a religious, cultural, and socially desirable practice.

Human beings became aware of their sexual determinedness just when they thought that they had become the masters of their own sexuality—only to discover that they were in fact its servants. Clearly, sex was essential not only for procreation but to sustain a certain unconscious force that expressed itself in various and often uncontrollable ways. Society thus put a stigma on sexuality; it was regarded as a numinous mystery impossible to comprehend rationally and viewed as an integral part of religiosity, because "sexuality and the sacred readily coincide . . . First, the polarity of the sexes furnishes sometimes the model and sometimes the basis for the dichotomizing of nature and society into complementary and antagonistic principles that, in justifying taboos and directing exchanges, are at the heart of the 'sacred as respect.' Second, since sex determines reproduction, it is inevitable that it be associated with the rites of fertility and, successively, puberty and initiation."[5]

This religious determinism led those endowed with a "mythical consciousness" (E. Cassirer) to think in terms of patterns that, in accordance with their immanent logic, generated creation myths. It is not surprising therefore that—as a result of this determinism—certain individuals sought to triumph over sexuality by embracing androgyny, in which the characteristics of both sexes are united, or becoming asexual, even if it involved the application of brute force. Between these two poles (neither of which necessarily requires abstention from sexual intercourse), various forms of sexuality evolved that, after being divested of their original *Sitz im Leben*, degenerated into bizarre if not cruel practices. The deeper meaning of the myths and rites was lost. The original reason for castration in cult practice was forgotten as well. Only by seeking the causes that underlay the emergence of eununchism and the practice of castration can we arrive at a deeper understanding of a phenomenon that has often been suppressed, hidden, denied or simply gone unacknowledged. The most important aspects of castration ultimately concern the private and social as well as the religious and cultural spheres of life; they are part of both the eastern and western traditions and appear in primitive societies and advanced civilizations where they reflect every imaginable facet of good and evil.

Dss doppelte Geschlecht: Studien zur Bisexualität in Ritus und Mythos (1955), the classic work by the ethnologist Hermann Baumann (1902–1972), introduces us to the beliefs of primitive peoples and ancient cultures where androgyny came to symbolize mankind's eternal longing for perfection. The hope was that androgynes would be, if not the equal of the gods, at least blessed with some of their omnipotence. Androgyny appears to have been considered a highly desirable goal. What is unclear, however, is whether it also involved the idea of liberation (through the achievement of sexual independence). In its various manifestations—shamanism, mythical narration, and the practice of cults—religion made possible a form of Eros that transcended sexuality. Plato distinguished between sexuality, with its biological and carnal desire to procreate, and Eros or love, a loftier passion that elevates the soul. In *The Symposium* he indicated that only a woman could tell the truth about love and so he had Diotima say:

> Love . . . is giving birth in beauty, whether in body or in soul. All of us are pregnant . . . both in body and in soul, and, as soon as we come to a certain age, we naturally desire to give birth. Now no one can possibly give birth in anything ugly; only in something beautiful. That's because when a man and a woman come together in order to give birth, this is a godly affair. Pregnancy, reproduction—this is an immortal thing for a mortal animal to do, and it cannot occur in anything that is out of harmony, but ugliness is out of harmony with all that is godly. Beauty, however, is in harmony with the divine. Therefore the goddess who presides at childbirth . . . is really Beauty. That's why, whenever pregnant animals or persons draw near to beauty, they become gentle and joyfully disposed and give birth and reproduce . . . [6]

All reflections on the nature of Eros seemed to center on the subject of sex, and sex was originally considered solely in terms of procreation and conception. As these discussions became more differentiated, there was a realization that the psychological and emotional aspects surrounding the physical part of sex should not be disregarded, for doing so could lead to aberrations such as "coitophobia," the idea of the presumed uncleanliness of women or their otherness compared to men, i.e., to an ambivalent attitude that would only intensify the irrational and unconscious striving for an all-liberating androgynism.

We speak in general terms of feminine, masculine, and neuter genders, the latter being of limited duration with regard to physiologial sexual development. Before reaching puberty and becoming an adult male or female, a child is sometimes referred to as a "neuter" in terms of the development of secondary sex characteristics, including changing of the voice. By castrating boys and suppressing such changes before they reach sexual maturity, one could preseve the "angelic" quality of their voices. Strictly speaking one cannot classify neutered individuals as a "third sex," although they have in fact been regarded as such since antiquity, as shown in the following story related by Flavius Philostratus (c. A.D. 200). A man who had been castrated by a tyrant later killed his tormentor in revenge. When he was about to be convicted of murder, the presiding judge declared that since according to the law he was neither male nor female, he could not be punished. So his life was spared and he escaped punishment.[7]

Wherever religion and culture are interwoven people realize the inadequacy of dividing human beings into just two or even three sexes. In addition to the "classical" sexual groups there developed the idea of androgyny, i.e., the union of the physical characteristics of male and female in one being, and the notion of asexuality, a characteristic of spiritual beings, especially angels. Myths, legends of the saints, and fairy tales are filled with androgynous and asexual beings, and fairy tale logic tries to account for the seeming irrationality and supernaturalism of religious manifestations.

As the historian of religion Joachim Wach (1898–1955) stressed time and again, all cultures, however diverse, are shaped by religion and the institutions that give expression to it. Thus the attitudes that helped to reinforce the cultic and ritual aspects of religious activity are mirrored in the ambivalence toward omnipotence, androgyny, and asexuality as possible ways of rising completely above the things of this earth. The seminal influence of this ambivalence on our own culture is clearly reflected in the visual arts, music, and literature. Examples range from the macabre works of Alfred Kubin (1877–1959) through the lush sensuality of the female figures in the paintings of Gustav Klimt (1862–1918) and the numinous hermaphrodites on the canvases of Gustave Moreau (1826–1898) to the ethereal and almost sexless figures in the works of Pierre Puvis de Chavannes (1824–1890). Poised on the threshold of modernity, these currents also found expression in literature (Stéphane Mallarmé) and music (Richard Wagner) as writers and musicians tried to appropriate anything of an empirical or mystical nature that mythology had to offer. These currents gave rise to a new "gnosticism," an attempt to transcend materialism and naturalism. "The Year of the Soul," as poet Stefan George called it, was ushered in. The human imagination alternated between Mnemosyne and Hope in the quest for some illusory transfiguration or deliverance. Some individuals had recourse to "flowers of evil" (Charles Baudelaire), others to the poetic alchemy of Rainer Maria Rilke's "unfolding of objects":

> Who, if I cried, would hear me among the angelic
> orders? And even if one of them suddenly
> pressed me against his heart, I should fade in the
> strength of his
> stronger existence. For Beauty's nothing
> but beginning of Terror we're still just able to bear,
> and why we adore it so is because it serenely
> disdains to destroy us. Each single angel is terrible.
> And so I keep down my heart, and swallow the call-note
> of depth-dark sobbing. Alas, who is there
> we can make use of? Not angels, not men;
> and already the knowing brutes are aware
> that we don't feel securely at home
> within our interpreted world. There remains, perhaps,
> some tree on a slope, to be looked at day after day . . . [8]

In the closing years of the 19th century, people endeavored to unveil the meaning of earlier civilizations, different religions, and unfamiliar customs. They once again became aware of things that had long been buried and forgotten, and opened the doors to a world in which the polarities of heaven and earth, reflecting as it were the dualities of sex and love, were continually seeking to unite and disentangle themselves at the same time.

Early human beings had to come to terms with the mystery of creation. They understood the function of the menstrual cycle and its relation to fertility, the purpose of procreation, and the fact that men and women—the archetypal symbols of duality—had to be brought together to reproduce. So long as their specialized sex organs functioned properly and they both remained fertile, male and female could produce offspring and ensure the continuity of life. However since either a man or a woman could become sterile or otherwise incapable of reproducing, cults early used magic in an effort to preserve or restore fertility and the capability to procreate. In ancient Egypt the rejuvenating ritual of the Sed festival took place in the thirtieth year of a pharaoh's reign in order to ensure that the aging king would retain his reproductive powers. Unfortunately, we do not have complete knowledge regarding these rituals based on myth or of their place in the context of ancient religion. They have generally come down to us in scholarly mythological versions rather than their original mythical form. Since the ancients believed that everything had been created by the gods, they felt obliged to thank and pay homage to them on a regular basis.

Later ideas regarding the use of sacrificial offerings to win the favor of the gods were a natural outgrowth of these myriad sacrificial rites. In consequence the belief took root that human beings were different from the gods and not quite perfect. The gods' perfection manifested itself, among other things, in their bisexuality; they were self-generated beings and therefore monistic in nature. The proof that such phenomena were in fact possible existed in the all-encompassing world of nature. We might mention the "Tree of Life," a metaphor for the union of the sexes, the snake, the symbol of continual regeneration, the cosmic bird and its famous egg out of which creation emerged, and finally the earth which regenerated the microcosm every year in order to sustain it. All these things were viewed as examples of dual sexuality and therefore deified. These ancient ideas have survived to the present day in the form of archetypal images.

These beliefs can be found not only in the great civilizations of antiquity, which were familiar with the phenomenon of hermaphroditism, but also among primitive peoples who wished to possess the powers of the hermaphrodite or transform themselves into different beings and forms to resemble or be on a par with the gods. Good examples of this practice are the shaman's use of ecstasy to change his sex or form during the performance of various rituals and his use of magic to enter the bodies of other beings. Yoga, a product of Hindu philosophy, is a further example of the employment of these kinds of techniques. It comprises a system of exercises for transcending or interiorizing the duality of the sexes. In many cultures music and dance are used to intoxicate people or whip them up into a state of ecstasy and so enable them to stand outside of or transcend themselves. Dance can serve as a vehicle to enable people to cross the threshold of sensory experience and cognition and create space in their imaginations where principles different from those that define the orderly structures of more enlightened societies can operate. This is why the adherents of the cult of Cybele performed the rite of castration in a state of frenzy, when they were carried away by music and dancing.

Reports of magic fertility rites performed by shamans are particularly instructive since they show the continuity of magical and ritual acts from the days of ancient Egypt and classical Greece to recent times. The German ethnologist Andreas

Dancing Maenad. Part of an Isis sculpture (ivory work from Alexandria in late antiquity) in the Cathedral of Aix la Chapelle

Lommel has described one of these shamanic fertility rites:

On his journey to the Earth Mother the shaman was accompanied by three times nine maidens and the same number of youths. These virgins and youths carried birch branches and danced with the shaman. The shaman put on his robe and also had his drum with him. During the seance he went dancing to the Earth Mother and asked her to bestow *jalyn*, sexual passion. With the drum and the drumstick in his hand he began to neigh like a horse and turn around in a circle, shouting *'Koruu, koruu!'* as though calling a herd of horses.

> At this moment the assembled women broke out into loud cries and began to whinny like mares: "*Innä-sasakh!*" Whinnying, they hurled themselves on the shaman and performed wildly erotic movements of the body over him. They are said even to have thrown him on the ground . . . Three times the shaman performed this rite, each time with the same accompanying circumstances. We hear that the excited women actually threw themselves on the shaman completely naked. This rite is also called the "taking of sexual passion for the spirit of the earth for men and beasts" or "the bringing down of the power of procreation."[9]

These shamanic rituals, which were said to have effected a gender change in some cases, helped give rise to the idea of dual sexuality, which is not to be confused with the bisexuality of hermaphroditism. Hermaphroditism became a popular subject in classical and Baroque art as well in the works of various Mannerists. Despite the obvious similarities between these phenomena in primitive societies and advanced civilizations, they must be considered differently in the case of each.

Nevertheless the sexual libido of antiquity may have found expression in these advanced civilizations—sublimated into the artistic device known as *discordia concors*—and may also account for the mystery surrounding the art of Leonardo da Vinci (1452–1519). In fact, if we are prepared to grant the existence of both a male and a female component in the make-up of every human being, we could begin to theorize about Leonardo's latent homosexuality. It is not generally understood that what motivated Leonardo was nothing less than the desire to reveal through art the cosmic symbolism of polar opposites uniting, which to him was synonymous with God. Within these polarities one might find confirmation of the archetypal image of Janus, represented as a head looking in opposite directions, which is encountered in almost all cultures with which we are familiar. That image touches on every branch of knowledge that deals with an understanding of the universe. Androgyny became a favorite metaphor for alchemy. Those who speak of hermaphroditism in this context clearly misunderstand the fundamental differences that come to the fore when it is compared to androgyny. Androgyny represents a mystical manifestation of the existence of God, whereas hermaphroditism may be regarded as nothing more than the fantasy of a perverted sexuality.

Out of this welter of sexuality, bisexuality, and carnality there emerged asexual beings, the soul and its "angelic" counterpart. As celestial beings, angels represent the polar opposite of human vices. Although they are aware of the power that sex exercises over humans, angels can show them how to liberate themselves from the bondage of sex, at least in the afterlife. In primitive societies and advanced civilizations the afterlife became an integral part of existence, either in images depicting escape from the clutches of carnality or in liberation through asexuality.

Beginning in ancient times people felt impelled to find an answer to the question whether dance, meditation or trances were the only ways in which to communicate with higher beings, i.e., the gods. It became apparent that certain symbols (written, numerical, and pictorial) could facilitate this communication. Because they contained hidden messages from the gods, many of these symbols, called hieroglyphs or "sacred carved letters," acquired magic and religious, oracular meaning. Consider, for example, the *I Ching*, trigrams and hexagrams, runes, numerology, and various games that originally had a sacred character and served as the basis of divination, only to undergo a subsequent process of secularization. Holy men and women who seem to have been asexual possessed the gift of foretelling the future. These seers were either "virginal boys" (used as mediums) or old men and old women or in some cases castrati, who ranked among the most well-known magicians and astrologers of antiquity and in the East.

These ideas help to give us an understanding of the religious motivation behind castration. Castration, which refers principally to emasculation (an ovariectomy is also sometimes called castration), can be performed using various methods that were well known in prehistoric and ancient times. Proof of this has come down to us in the form of ancient instruments that were used to carry out the procedure.

When viewed in medical terms, the procedures used can be described as surgical interventions and studied from a physiological perspective. In principle the procedures involve the

Buddha statue, 5th century A.D., showing a castrato. The transparent cloth highlights the missing genitals. (Archaeological Museum, Mathura, India)

intentional removal of the testicles, creating "semi-castrati" or impotent persons, called *spadones* in antiquity. In contrast to the *spadones* were the "full castrati" who had undergone surgical removal of the penis as well. Medical doctors devoted increased attention to castration in the late 19th and early 20th centuries when they were confronted with the *skoptsy* in Russia who were attracting particular attention at that time. The *skoptsy* were members of an ascetic religious sect that practiced castration as a precondition for achieving salvation. In this sense they may be viewed as modern precursors of the Heaven's Gate disciples in the United States. Our attention, however, is directed not to the medical indications for castration, but to castration as either an enforced or a voluntary, self-conscious act. Originally castration was performed using very primitive means and the mortality rate was correspondingly high, especially when little attention was paid to hygiene, as for example in the Coptic monasteries of Egypt that supplied the Turks with castrated black eunuchs. According to figures collected in the region at that time, only every fourth person forced to undergo castration survived the brutal procedure.

The results of the operation varied according to the age of the castrato, i.e., the degree of his sexual maturation. If the surgery was performed before puberty, it could lead to gigantism and mild to moderate obesity. What it preserved was a boy's high-pitched voice which became an important asset for the castrati who figured in the world of opera during the 17th and subsequent centuries. Their sexual development was of course incomplete, thereby extending the period of childhood and adolescence while allowing them to give the impression of remaining eternally young. In adults, on the other hand, castration produced rather different side effects. In the case of "semi-castrati" the sex drive was not completely suppressed but body and facial hair grew sparsely if at all.

The different types of castration varied according to locale and were selected with an eye to the various intended functions the "victims" were supposed to perform. Originally emphasis was probably laid on voluntary emasculation for religious or moral (i.e., legal), medical or psychological reasons. From time immemorial, however, castration was also used as a form of punishment; this aspect of the practice is reflected in the Code of Hammurabi (c. 1700 B.C.). Enthusiastic adherents of the cult of Cybele and Attis, especially those who later became priests (called *galli*), emasculated themselves with a sharp stone or knife in the course of frenzied, orgiastic festivities that celebrated the memory of the self-emasculation of Attis. Many ascetics in the pagan, Buddhist, Christian, and Islamic worlds peformed self-castration in their quest for chastity and their longing for redemption.

Mainly in antiquity but in the modern period as well castration was considered a medically appropriate treatment for dealing with certain pathologically motivated sex crimes. It was also approved, by the way, for treating hernias. Transsexualism, a much-discussed topic today, was regarded in ancient times as reason enough to emasculate an individual, although it may be presumed that the idea of castration still filled many men with the hope of preserving their youthfulness or fulfilling some pathological sexual desire to experience androgynous or homoerotic sensations, which Petronius satirized as follows:

> Come and get it! Come quickly, you bum-boys outrageous!
> Get it on! Giddyup! Try to follow!
> All you ace organ-grinders, dude-buggies, glad-handers
> old and fey, caponized by Apollo![10]

Given their preference for smooth, hairless, hermaphroditic bodies, the ancients developed ideas of what was sexually and aesthetically pleasing that fitted in nicely with the practice of castration. The story of Hermes and a son of Aphrodite—one of the later Greek myths—gave rise to the idea of a being with characteristics of both sexes. The *Anthologia Palatina* contains a graphic description of one of these creatures:

> An hermaphrodite, a lovely one, was also present,
> Half man, half woman, a wondrous union of the two,
> You see in him his mother, Venus, and his father, Hermes:
> He has the voluptuous heaving breasts of a young maiden,
> Yet displays the contours of the male organ of procreation—
> Behold how he combines the charms of both sexes.[11]

The ideas associated with hermaphroditism were widespread in the Greco-Roman world reflecting sexual fantasies that can be found in the art and literature of the modern period as well. *The Man without Qualities*, Robert Musil's (1880–1942) unfinished novel, contains the following excursus:

> You know that myth Plato tells, following some ancient source, that the gods divided the original being into two halves, male and female? . . . Nobody knows which of so many halves running around in the world is his missing half. He grabs one that seems to be his, vainly trying to become one with her, until the futility of it becomes

> hopelessly clear . . . It's not only the myth of the human being divided in two; we could also mention Pygmalion, the Hermaphrodite, or Isis and Osiris—all different forms of the same theme. It is the ancient longing for a doppelgänger of the opposite sex, for a lover who will be the same as yourself and yet someone else, a magical figure that is oneself and yet remains magical, with the advantage over something we merely imagine of having the breath of autonomy and independence. This dream of quintessential love, unhampered by the body's limitations, coming face-to-face in two identical yet different forms, has been concocted countless times in solitary alchemy in the alembic of the human skull . . . [12]

The longing for fulfillment "in one's own imagination" (Leonardo) articulated by Musil may be related to the myriad explanations of the human condition that appeared in antiquity. Deeply embedded in these ancient explanations, however, were other hopes, in fact even the hope of reaching paradise. In mythical visions of paradise, human beings were eternally young; hence there was no aging. It was even believed that the combination of fecundity and virility ran counter to the idea of paradise. Wherever people procreate, life dwells alongside death, the two characteristic features of that transitoriness of human life that can be overcome only through the process of reproduction. From this perspective, visualizing eternity through the eyes of asexual beings may have a certain logic, because when there is no sex there are no births or deaths. This is an idea common to many religions. Consider for example the pharaoh Akhenaton, whom the ancient Egyptians considered a god, or the founder of Buddhism in far-off India or, finally, Christ. Each of them is frequently depicted as sexless so as to emphasize the idea of the timeless within time, wedged between this life and the one that lies beyond death, while at the same time pointing to paradisiacal life after death in which earthly desires are non-existent.

Visions such as these, however, do not govern all religious representations of paradise. In the Islamic view of the afterlife, for example, virility plays an important role and *huri*s, described in the Koran as chastely amorous virgins, must be eternally prepared to satisfy men's desires. This is the reason that castration is forbidden by Muslims. Every Muslim has to have the wherewithal to be able to dream of the promise made in the Koran (Sura 2:25): "Proclaim good tidings to those who have faith and do good works. They shall dwell in gardens watered by running streams: whenever they are given fruit to eat they will say: 'This is what we used to eat before,' for they shall be given the like. Wedded to chaste virgins, they shall abide there for ever." This pleasure-filled vision is in stark contrast to the ideal of celibacy espoused by other religions, but it is not unique. The Chinese also hoped that the dead would live in a similar style to that of the living; castrati in fact believed that their manhood would be restored in the afterlife. For this reason they kept their severed penises in ornamental cases so that they could take them to their graves and thence to the afterworld.

On the one hand, members of radical gnostic sects strove to remain chaste and abstain totally from sexual activity (which in the case of Origen [ca. 185–254] led him to castrate himself), while on the other there were those who indulged an insatiable appetite for debauchery and believed that they

Origen castrating himself (Engraving, 1791)

would most likely continue to live their dissolute lives in the afterworld. It was between these two extremes that principles of ethics and religion developed that helped to establish the concept of sin. And it was the idea of sin, which almost always involved victims and forgiveness, that determined how sexuality and the practice of castration associated with it—prohibited in both Judaism and Islam—were to be judged. There is, by the way, much to suggest that circumcision, among the most important religious rites in the Semitic world, may actually have been one of the sources of this ancient practice.

Among other ethnic groups and in different cultures people not only dreamed of hermaphroditic beings (whom they identified with emasculated and womanish ephebes called *effeminati*), but even hoped to be able to have sex with them in the afterlife. Paintings on the walls of Etruscan graves clearly indicate as much. These dream thoughts about the afterlife were stimulated by the ritual of castration—sometimes forced—practiced in real life to help satisfy desires such as those mentioned above.

Since time immemorial, enforced castration has been used as a sign of punishment or as a token of victory over an enemy (whose genitalia would then be carried as trophies of war). And it was used to "produce" lucrative "products," products that were in great demand as guardians of sanctuaries, attendants at the courts of various rulers, and keepers of harems. Even now castrati can be found serving as highly-paid guards and bedchamber attendants performing traditional functions that clearly do not belong to the past alone.

What power structures promoted the practice of castration? In both primitive cultures and advanced civilizations, the exercise of power possessed a sacred quality that had a lasting and determining effect on a number of different things. These included many signs and symbols of power manifested in institutions that could look back on long traditions that were rooted largely in myth. These included, among other things, the office of "bedchamber attendant" (*eunouchos*) and the harem (in Semitic languages the word *haram* refers variously to a sacred place, a sanctuary, or a royal palace, a place that one is generally forbidden to enter) which for historical reasons has come to be applied mostly to the apartments in oriental palaces allotted to females. These aspects of "sacral kingship" make eunuchism the focus of a much-neglected manifestation of power in kingdoms stretching from the Far East to the Mediterranean. Since the sacred quality of kingship (haram/sacred enclave) is inextricably bound up with divinity—the king was directly equated with god or he at least ruled by the grace of god—the "sacred kings" would tolerate only those in their immediate presence whom they deemed their peers or knew to be passive, neutered creatures modeled on angels who were but manifestations of the workings of divine power. Without god they would not exist. In this sense "sacred kingship" provided a breeding ground, as it were, for eunuchism. Indeed, eunuchism was and is to be found wherever such power structures form part of a state's self-image. In their capacity as devoted servants and slaves, court eunuchs represented both the "third sex" and the extended arm of the monarch by whose grace they had become executors of his royal power. In fact, they owed their existence and their positions to the king's favor. Even though they had been deprived of their manhood, they had at least not been killed. Hence they offered their lives to the king as a sign of "thanksgiving."

In the ancient Near East and Egypt as well as in medieval Europe, castration (which often resulted in death) was used to punish men who had committed adultery or had been convicted of raping a free-born noblewoman.[13] In ancient Egyptian teachings and court records castration is mentioned time and again. Adultery, it was said, was to be punished by cutting off the "ears" and "nose" of the offender—an obvious allusion to castration. This was also the case in classical antiquity, which we can infer from a remark made in a comedy by Terence (c. 195/190–159 B.C.): " . . . and now he's threatening him with the usual treatment reserved for adulterers."[14]

The lawful use of castration as a punishment is probably of very ancient origin and dates back to a time when men fought for a woman's favor, a rivalry that often ended with the castration of the defeated party. Whether this hypothesis is still valid in view of the many opposing opinions voiced by various ethnologists must remain an open question. One thing is certain, however: It was common practice to castrate a vanquished enemy in order both to maintain his "commercial value" and his capacity for work and not to have to be concerned about the risk of his producing "alien" offspring who might someday want to avenge their forebear's defeat. The triumphal removal of an enemy's sexual organ to celebrate victory in battle was a custom that had a long and venerable tradition. Indeed, it was practiced as recently as the Battle of Adowa (1896), which saved the empire of Menelik II (1814–1913) and resulted in the deaths of thousands of Italians. The fact that the Ethiopians actually practiced the custom was confirmed by the Swiss Alfred Ilg, who had been in the employ of Menelik II, and the

German explorer Max Grühl, who wrote as follows: "Enemies slain in battle were subjected to castration [*sälläbä*] . . . The genitalia that were taken as booty would be filled with straw and stuck on the tip of a spear. Later they were hung over the door of a person's house."[15] Among the Konso of southwestern Ethiopia, the severed male sex organs of the vanquished were dried in the sun and worn as bracelets; in the province of Kafa (an independent kingdom until as late as the 19th century) an imitation phallus made of silver—originally it appears to have been the stuffed and specially treated penis of a defeated warrior—adorned the emperor's formal dress, his crown. To the great shame of the entire nation it was captured by the Amhara in 1897.

It would be a mistake, however, to believe that these customs were practiced only by so-called "uncivilized" peoples. One might recall, for instance, the Battle of Culloden (1746) in which so-called "civilized" Englishmen cut off the penises of fallen Scottish Highlanders—not to mention other battles and revolts in the past such as the War of the Sicilian Vespers (1282).

The mass castration of large numbers of individuals as punishment for the commission of political crimes was a common practice not just in antiquity, but also in the modern age in various areas of the western world—as a means of torture, in cases of adultery and rape, and in revolutionary times when the severed genitalia of representatives of the ancien régime were put on display as trophies of the people's victory in the name of "liberty, equality and fraternity." The situation was much the same in the East where castration—intimidating as it was cruel—came into wide use whenever drastic measures were called for.

In the Near East, especially at the Persian court, castrated boys were in great demand as articles of commerce. The practice of castrating kidnapped male children and selling them into slavery was a secure source of income for centuries in an area stretching from China to Gibraltar. Although the Chinese established a special facility for performing castrations—a virtual monopoly that "turned out" literally thousands of court eunuchs—the sale of castrati remained a flourishing branch of the slave trade, which is practiced to this day in various countries bordering the Red Sea. And even though U.N. resolutions have proclaimed the illegality of slavery, kidnapping for the purpose of trafficking in human beings still takes place in crisis spots around the world, e.g., in the southern Sudan and southern Ethiopia. It should not be forgotten that the first antislavery laws in the Ethiopian Empire were promulgated only in 1919 and extended by Emperor Haile Selassie (1892–1974) in 1935. However, despite all the various laws, slavery has not yet been eliminated in some countries. In certain Middle Eastern and African societies it is often difficult to tell the difference between a servant and a slave. For fear of their master the latter generally keep silent. The large number of castrated eunuchs still in the employ of Islamic rulers as guardians of the harem have been recruited from the ranks of slaves. In addition, Muslim holy sites, the graves of the sultans and caliphs in Cairo, the Ka'bah in Mecca, the sacred shrine in Medina (the tomb of Muhammad in the Prophet's Mosque), and the Dome of the Rock in Jerusalem were and sometimes still are guarded by eunuchs. As late as 1990 there were 17 eunuchs in Medina and 14 in Mecca who had the "honor of serving at holy sites." Most are quite wealthy, according to a report in 1990 by one of their number, Salim Farid, in the Saudi newspaper *al-Yamama*. Although he stressed that he and his fellow eunuchs had been accorded a great honor, he did not neglect to call those who had castrated him "bestial criminals."

Since in the past the mortality rate was quite high following castration, slaves who survived the operation commanded correspondingly high prices. In the Middle Ages there were well-known centers for castration in both East and West, for example in Assiut in Egypt and Verdun in France. In Assiut—according to a 17th-century account by the French traveler Jean Chardin (1643–1713)—Coptic monks carried out the shameful procedure; if their victims survived, they generally sold them to the Turks. In Verdun, Jews supplied the markets of the Caliphate of Cordova with Slavic and Frankish slaves. The situation continued virtually unchanged until the collapse of the Ottoman Empire.

As a result of studies in the professional literature and reports in newspapers, not to mention John Irving's novel *A Son of the Circus* that I referred to above, a phenomenon in India, that of the castrati called hijras, has become known throughout the world. The hijras combine all the characteristics associated with castration. They are transvestites who work as prostitutes and are usually homosexual. They carry on traditions and customs associated with Hindu festivities and ceremonies and serve in the temples of the various mother goddesses (especially the goddess Bahuchara Mata). And they are deeply involved in cult practices that are closely related to those of ancient civilizations. Finally, one sees in them the "sacral" personification of the "modern" world of transsexualism and realizes that the question of the "martyred Eros" involves more than just castration alone.

The Jews, Greeks, and Romans disapproved of castration and emasculation. The practice was considered inhumane and forbidden by God (Deuteronomy 23:1). A characteristic example of this attitude is reflected in the following passage from Herodotus, who believed that human dignity was sacred and that those who violated it should be punished accordingly:

> With the children he sent Hermotimus as guardian, who was by birth a Pedasian, and among the eunuchs second to none in the king's favour. The Pedasians dwell above Halicarnassus; and among these Pedasians the following occurrence takes place: when within a certain time any calamity is about to fall on the different neighbours who dwell round their city, then the priestess of Minerva has a large beard. This has already happened twice to them. Hermotimus, then, was sprung from these Pedasians; and of all the men we know, revenged himself in the severest manner for an injury he had received. For having been taken by an enemy and sold, he was purchased by one Panionius, a Chian, who gained a livelihood by most infamous practices. For whenever he purchased boys remarkable for beauty, having castrated them, he used to take and sell them at Sardis and Ephesus for large sums; for with the barbarians eunuchs are more valued than others, on account of their perfect fidelity. Panionius, therefore, had castrated many others, as he made his livelihood by this means, and among them this man: Hermotimus, however, was not unfortunate in every respect, for he went to Sardis with other presents to the king; and in process of time was most esteemed by

Xerxes of all his eunuchs. When the king was preparing to march his Persian army against Athens, and was at Sardis, at that time having gone down, on some business or other, to the Mysian territory which the Chians possess, and is called Atarneus, he there met with Panionius. Having recognised him, he addressed many friendly words to him; first recounting to him the many advantages he had acquired by his means; and secondly, promising him how many benefits he would confer on him in requital if he would bring his family and settle there; so Panionius, joyfully accepting the proposal, brought his children and wife. But when Hermotimus got him with his whole family in his power, he addressed him as follows: 'O thou, who of all mankind has gained thy livelihood by the most infamous acts, what harm had either I, or any of mine, done to thee, or any of thine, that of a man thou hast made me nothing? Thou didst imagine, surely, that thy machinations would pass unnoticed by the gods; who following righteous laws, having enticed thee, who has committed unholy deeds, into my hands, so that thou canst not complain of the punishment I shall inflict on thee.' When he had thus upbraided him, his sons being brought into his presence, Panionius was compelled to castrate his own sons, who were four in number; and being compelled, he did it; and, after he had finished it, his sons, being compelled, castrated him. Thus the vengeance of Hermotimus overtook Panionius.[16]

In the Beginning Were the Gods

"The gods have many shapes.
The gods bring many things
to their accomplishment.
And what was most expected
has not been accomplished.
But god has found his way for
what no man expected."
—Euripides, *The Bacchae*

Using their own special language, many ancient myths, the majority of which survive only as fragments, recount stories in which the gods practice castration among themselves. They depict this unique act not only as punishment for losing a battle and a means for taking revenge but as a symbol of cosmic forces. Graphic descriptions of the procedure can be found among the peoples of the ancient Near East, India, and Egypt as well as in various Greek and Roman sources. Many of these mythological traditions warrant our attention, especially the Osirian cycle in which the sexual behavior of the Egyptian gods brought the draconian act of emasculation into the center of the story of Osiris, Isis, Horus, and Seth. Besides providing a key to understanding the ancient Egyptian power structure, the myth illustrates how Isis managed sometimes to assume the role of mother and sometimes that of wife of both Osiris and Horus. Nor were Isis's relationships limited to these two "positive" heroes; they also included the latters' antagonist Seth, who, after having killed Osiris, became the sworn enemy of Osiris's son, Horus.

According to the myth that has come down to us, the Egyptian gods Osiris and Seth had both been castrated. Although the devastating effects of their emasculation were miraculously eliminated and reversed (with some help from Isis), no one disputes the fact that both of them were nevertheless victims of dismemberment. The myth also tell us that Isis replicated Osiris's phallus. Later, similar replicas were consecrated and carried in a procession instituted at the festival of Pamyles to memorialize Isis's deed. In fact, many in ancient Rome seem to have been familiar with the custom. On July 26, for example, Roman women would carry the replica of a penis (*fascinum*) in solemn procession to the temple of Venus and place it on the goddess's breast. Whether there was a direct connection to the Egyptian tradition is still in dispute. What seems certain, however, is that comparable traditions of ancient origin can be found in all the cultures of the Mediterranean and continue to be observed even though they are not immediately recognized for what they in fact are.

In the first part of the ancient Egyptian cycle of myths, two brothers—Osiris and Seth—were opposed to each other. The Greeks later identified Seth with the god Typhon. Osiris was the good ruler and Seth a wily evildoer whom the Egyptians represented as an ass. Seth continued to be depicted as an animal, in greatly distorted form, down to the time of Apuleius (c. 125–170) and his *Metamorphoses* (also known as *The Golden Ass*) and seems to have lived on in Shakespeare's *Midsummer Night's Dream* and the proverbial—and not particularly flattering—metaphorical use of the term.

Unfortunately the mythical narratives of the Nile Valley have come down to us in only fragmentary form. Some derive from the Pyramid Texts of the third millenium B.C.; others, dated later, were preserved in a problematical Hellenistic version that sought to bring them into conformity with Greek mythology. In any case, until new, less incomplete texts of the myths are brought to light, the sometimes contradictory story of Osiris, Isis, and Seth related by Plutarch (ca. 46/49–125) remains the authoritative version. Theodor Hopfner (1886–1946), a scholar of ancient history who was born in Prague, wrote a comprehensive commentary on Plutarch's treatise in which he covered all the ancient Egyptian materials known up to the 1930s.

Plutarch recounted a creation myth[17] about the origin of the gods, integrating them into various cosmological events. This gave rise to a seemingly bewildering variety of relationships. Thus Plutarch speaks of the "children of the Titans" (in this instance the parallel with Greek mythology is obvious): ". . . Isis and Osiris, being in love with each other even before they were born, were united in the darkness of the womb. Some aver that Aroueris [Horus] was the fruit of this union." The birth of the gods took place in a succession of five remarkable days. On the first day Osiris was born, on the second Aroueris ("some aver that he is called the elder Horus"), on the third (and in violent fashion) Typhon [Seth], on the fourth Isis, and on the fifth Nephthys, Seth's future consort (whom the Greeks alternately identified with Aphrodite and Nike). The ancients used the five days during which the gods came into existence to complete the true 360-day solar year and demonstrate the logic of the myths as explanations for the creation of the world.

Considering these family relationships, one realizes that the element of incest was not something peculiar to the ancient Egyptians. Rather, it was a characteristic of nearly all known creation myths. In fact, it was the norm in mythology for brothers and sisters to marry—and even for sons to marry their mothers. This is why it is so difficult to distinguish between brothers and cousins, to say nothing of the fact that the unnatural mother-son relationship, which one might describe as a prototype of the Oedipus myth or Oedipus "complex," was also a source of great bewilderment. Together Osiris, Isis, and Horus embodied the so-called "Kamutef principle" of continual self-regeneration, Isis representing the eternal feminine—now as mother and now as consort—with a correspondingly determining influence on the role of the male of the species.

Born a god, Osiris in the course of time became the king of Egypt. During his 28-year reign he devoted himself to civilizing his subjects and instructing them in various crafts and skills. This made his evil brother Seth envious and resentful, leading him to conspire against Osiris. Seth was intent on eliminating Osiris and actually succeeded in doing so for a time. By a ruse he induced Osiris to lie in a chest, whereupon Seth and his cohorts closed the box and threw it into the sea.

"They say that all these events occurred on the seventeenth day of the month of Athyr [13 November], when the sun passes through the scorpion." When the report of this treachery reached Isis, she set out to find her consort and husband, traveling as far as Byblos, where we find parallels between this myth and representations of Cybele and other mother goddesses in Asia Minor. Thus it is not surprising that the coffin containing Osiris grew up into the Tree of Youth near the shrine of Astarte. Isis's love was so great that she overcame every obstacle to find the body of her husband and bring it back to Egypt where she left it unattended for a short time while she went to see Horus. Meanwhile: " . . . Typhon [Seth], when he was hunting by night in the moonlight, came upon it. He recognized the body, and having cut it into fourteen parts, he scattered them [all over Egypt]." In a deep state of mourning Isis began to collect the dismembered parts and restore them. "The only part of Osiris which Isis did not find was his male member; for no sooner was it thrown into the river than the lepidotus, the phagrus and oxyrhynchus ate of it, fish which [the Egyptians] most of all abhor. In its place Isis fashioned a likeness of it and consecrated the phallus, in honour of which the Egyptians even today hold festival."[18] We may therefore assume that the tied-on beard with which Osiris is usually portrayed symbolizes Isis's deed.

After presenting the first part of the Osirian cycle, Plutarch focused his attention on Horus [Horosl, who began to assume a leading role in the myth appearing as his parents' avenger:

> Afterwards Osiris came to Horus, it is said, from the underworld, and equipped and trained him for battle. Then he questioned him as to what he considered to be

> the finest action, and Horus said, "To succour one's father and mother when they have suffered wrong." .... The battle then lasted for many days and Horus won. When Isis came across Typhon [Seth] tied in bonds, she did not kill him, but freed him and let him go. Horus did not take this at all calmly, but laying hands on his mother he ripped off the crown from her head. Hermes [Thoth] however put on her instead a cow-headed helmet. When Typhon brought a charge of illegitimacy against Horus, Hermes [Thoth] helped Horus, and the latter was judged by the gods to be legitimate. Typhon was defeated in two other battles, and Isis, having had sexual union with Osiris after his death, bore Harpocrates, prematurely delivered and weak in his lower limbs.[19]

Using earlier sources, we can now add a number of details to the abbreviated Hellenistic account of the ancient Egyptian myth. These additions are of interest as they include certain passages—including ones dealing with the peculiar sexual habits and customs of the gods—that were deliberately suppressed by Plutarch, behaviors that are deserving of our attention in this context.

The family relationships involving Horus and Seth are quite complex. Reflecting the inseparable polarities that make up all aspects of life, both are regarded alternately as tutelary gods watching over the pharaoh, as mirror images of cosmic forces, and as symbols of the dualities that characterized much of ancient Egyptian religion and society.

The myth on which the Egyptian monarchy was based is crucial to an understanding of Egyptian sacred kingship. It tells the story of the claim made by two combatant gods to the throne of the "two kingdoms"—as Egypt was known at that time—and the series of momentous and often incomprehensible (to us) confrontations between the two heirs apparent during which they inflicted devastating injuries on each other. Ultimately it was incumbent on the high council of the gods—the so-called family of the nine—to declare whose claim was valid. In the ensuing battles Horus lost an eye and Seth his penis. The *Pyramid Texts* of the third millennium B.C. provide documentation for this version of the battles: "Hor [Horus] complained of the loss of an eye; Seth complained of the loss of his phallus. Hor's (plucked-out) eye drifted along until it dropped on to the other side of the lake . . . (thus saving Hor's eye from being destroyed by Seth)."[20]

Since the *Pyramid Texts* are made up exclusively of a kind of epigram or "utterance" (sometimes with accompanying illustrations), it was only later that we came into possession of more detailed mythological narratives. One in particular from the time of Ramses V describes the nature and outcome of the struggle between Horus and Seth:

> After Horus, with the help of the other gods, recovered the eye which Seth had robbed him of, the two combatant brothers appeared before the high court of the gods which counseled them finally to make peace with each other . . . . Whereupon Seth said to Horus: "Come, let us celebrate this special day in my house." And Horus replied: "Indeed—I accept your invitation." In the evening a bed was prepared for both of them and the two retired together for the night. In the wee hours, however, Seth stimulated himself until his member was hard, after which he thrust it between Horus's thighs. Horus placed

> his hands between his thighs and just managed to catch Seth's seed. Horus then went to see his mother: "Come here, Isis my mother; come and see what Seth tried to do to me." He opened his hand and showed her Seth's seed, at the sight of which she let out a cry of outrage, grabbed her copper knife, cut off Horus's hand, threw it into the river, and caused a new one to grow in its place. Then she brought in a soothing ointment and rubbed it on Horus's member causing it to become hard, whereupon she held it over a jar so that his semen would flow into it. Isis then took Horus's semen and set off in the prime of day for Seth's kitchen garden inquiring of Seth's gardener: "Tell me, what vegetable does Seth eat when he is here?" The gardener answered: "Except for lettuce [a symbol of fecundity and the god Min] he doesn't eat any vegetables here." So Isis poured Horus's semen on the lettuce."[21]

The only reason this strange story detailing Horus's victory over Seth (the high court of the gods, by the way, also decided in Horus's favor) includes this bizarre interpolation of pederasty was to provide yet another example of Seth's wickedness. Thus did good triumph over evil (in the person of Horus) in ancient Egypt. Plutarch supplemented this account of the myth as follows: "This Horus is himself determinate and complete; he has not destroyed Typhon [Seth] completely, but only removed his activity and strength. This is why they say that the statue of Horus in Coptos holds the genitals of Typhon in one hand and they relate that Hermes, having ripped out the sinews of Typhon, used them as lyre-strings, claiming that this denotes that reason regulated the universe and made it harmonious out of discordant parts; and it did not wipe out the destructive element, they aver, but maimed its power."[22]

Archeologists have in fact discovered just such a statue depicting Horus's triumph over Seth. Originally these myths served as metaphors for cosmic events. Later other mythological motifs were added, providing us with a number of starting points for a discussion of the ancient Egyptians' view of various types of sexual behavior. Emasculation, for instance, was regarded by them not only as a legitimate and appropriate means for punishing an enemy but for dealing with homosexuals as well. Pederasty was considered by them to be a grave sin. Thus we read in the *Book of the Dead*: "I have never slept with any of my servants . . . I have never slept with a man . . . I am not a pederast. I am not a fornicator."[23]

The image of Harpokrates as "weak in his male member" is a sign of the boy's failure at birth to develop sexually, a circumstance that gave him his "womanish" character and may have led to his becoming a prototype for the later *effeminati*. We have no definitive explanation for this phenomenon, because the portrayal of Harpokrates (Horus's alter ego) in the cycle of myths is not in accordance with the "Kamutef principle." On the contrary, it may have given rise to the idea of a "third sex." This mythography suggests that emasculation was associated with the idea of restraining the forces of destruction, especially the unbridled sex drive that can degenerate into violent and aggressive behavior. At the same time, however, castration generated something within males that disposed them to behave passively. This may help to explain the later view of eunuchs at oriental courts as non-violent, submissive creatures.

The Egyptian myths fused with other mythical traditions in the Mediterranean world during the Hellenistic era, finding a number of parallels in ancient Near Eastern mythology (most of which derived from Indo-European and Semitic cultures) that likewise included stories of castration as practiced among the gods. Thus the Sumero-Hurrian gods—Alalu the first god, Anu the sky god, Kumarbi the vegetation god (whom one may identify with Kronos), and finally Teshub the storm god—castrated one another at regular intervals.

Like their Egyptian counterparts, the mythical texts that have come down to us from the 13th century B.C. are incomplete. Still, they provide sufficient evidence of the primal gods' mythically conditioned obsession with castration:

> . . . Kumarbi took Alalu's place and did battle with Anu. Anu could no longer withstand Kumarbi's gaze. He escaped from Kumarbi's clutches fleeing like a bird by flying toward the sky. Kumarbi followed in hot pursuit and grabbed Anu's feet and dragged him down to the ground. He bit off his genitals, whereupon Anu's sperm [literally his virility] melted in his belly like bronze (which is an alloy of copper and tin). After Kumarbi had swallowed Anu's sperm he was pleased and laughed, whereupon Anu turned to him and said: "So you are pleased about what you have in your belly, because you have swallowed my sperm. Be not pleased about what you have in your belly, for I have put a heavy weight there. I have impregnated you with three powerful gods. I have impregnated you with the storm god, the River Aranzakh and the great god Tashmishu, three terrifying gods whose seed I have put inside you. And in the end you will smash your head against the cliffs of Mount Tasha!" After having spoken these words Anu rose into the sky and hid there . . . [24]

The many instances of castration that help to make up the story of creation recall the Battle of the Titans in later Greek mythology, which clearly has its roots in the Near East. We might note in this context that Hurrian and Hittite mythology also touched on the subject of androgyny, another characteristic feature of the gods. Many cultures regard androgyny as the sign of an exalted creature. In India, for instance, one of the forms in which Shiva is represented is the composite deity Ardhanarishvara. The so-called Shiva-*linga* (phallus) can be found in every Hindu temple, and Shiva is worshiped as the god who castrated himself, or who lost his *linga* by a curse. Shiva symbolizes the classic dichotomy of desire and self-denial, the polarities that typify existence: life and death, fecundity and sterility.

To round out our discussion of religious concepts in the ancient world and the part played in them by the practice of castration among the gods, we need look only at the civilizations that for thousands of years helped to shape the cultures of the Middle East and provided a rationale for the existence of castrati. In addition to the creation myths, which resemble one another in all Middle Eastern civilizations, there are other mythical narratives that portray castration as an offering to the gods. The basic myth, which exists in a number of different versions, including the Cybele legends, is part of a group of myths that recount tales of descent into the underworld and have been preserved in a variety of different forms. They are best illustrated by the myth of the great goddess Innana/Ishtar and her paramour Tammuz/Dumuzi, whose death was caused by his love of Ishtar. This sacred couple symbolizes the eternal seasonality of vegetable life, a theme that appears almost universally in a number of different versions, for example in the myth of Cybele and Attis. And it is reflected in the widespread Semitic fertility cults of the goddess Tanit practiced by the Phoenicians in Carthage and so eloquently described by Gustave Flaubert (1821–1880) in his novel *Salammbo*:

> At the foot of Byrsa there stretched a long black mass: it was the temple of Tanith, a whole made up of monuments and galleries, courts and forecourts, and bounded by a low wall of dry stones . . . . This first barrier enclosed a wood of plane trees as a precaution against plague and infection in the air . . . . Tents were scattered here and there, in which during the day-time, depilatory pastes, perfumes, garments, moon-shaped cakes, and images of the Goddess with representations of the temple hollowed out in blocks of alabaster, were on sale . . . . Two long porticoes, with their architraves resting on dumpy pillars flanked a quadrangular tower, the platform of which was adorned with the crescent of a moon. On the angles of the porticoes and at the four corners of the tower stood vases filled with kindled aromatics. The capitals were laden with pomegranates and coloquintidas. Twining knots, lozenges, and rows of pearls alternated on the walls, and a hedge of silver filigree formed a wide semicircle in front of the brass staircase which led down from the vestibule . . . . The first room was very lofty; its vaulted roof was pierced by numberless apertures, and if the head were raised the stars might be seen. All round the wall rush baskets were heaped up with the first-fruits of adolescence in the shape of beards and heads of hair . . . . Aedicules of different shapes were visible beneath clusters of turpentine trees. Here and there rose a stone

> phallus, and large stags roamed peacefully about spurning the fallen fir-cones with their cloven hoofs. But they retraced their steps between two long galleries which ran parallel to each other. There were small open cells along their sides and tambourines and cymbals hung against their cedar columns from top to bottom. Women were sleeping stretched on mats outside the cells. Their bodies were greasy with unguents, and exhaled an odour of spices and extinguished perfuming-pans . . . [25]

Control over the temple of Tanit was in the hands of a castrated high priest. In the novel his name is Shahabarim, and Flaubert gives a moving description of him: "His sunken eyes shone like the lamps of a sepulchre; his long thin body floated in its linen robe which was weighted by the bells, the latter alternating with balls of emeralds at his heels. He had feeble limbs, an oblique skull, and a pointed chin; his skin seemed cold to the touch, and his yellow face, which was deeply furrowed with wrinkles, was as though contracted in longing, in an everlasting grief."[26] And further on: " . . . moreover, all that he saw in terrestrial things compelled him to recognise the male exterminating principle as supreme. And then he secretly charged Rabbet with the misfortune of his life. Was it not for her that the grand-pontiff had once advanced amid the tumult of cymbals, and with a patera of boiling water taken from him his future virility?"[27]

Flaubert's narrative was based on descriptions that he found in well-established sources. The only thing that has changed since Flaubert wrote the book is the spelling or transcription of some of the names. Still his achievement remains unsurpassed in its ability to evoke the atmosphere surrounding the shrine of a fertility cult.

The symbolism which he so easily mastered continues to be called into question whenever scholars discuss so-called bottle-shaped idols and cast doubt on the assumption that they represent phallic idols. "Bottles," however, appear time and again as phallic symbols in Persian and Indian miniatures, that is, long before anyone needed a psychoanalysist to tell them what they represented.

Egyptian and Near Eastern myths involving castration among the gods occur again and again throughout Greek literature. Hesiod's (c. 700 B.C.) *Theogony*, for example, which survives only in fragments, recounts the history of the gods and the creation of the cosmos. His cosmogony begins with Chaos from which emerged Earth (Gaia), Tartaros (the infernal regions), and Eros, the god who first provided the impulse to sexual reproduction. In the next generation of the first gods Earth gave birth to Ouranos (Heaven). Then Ouranos united with Gaia to engender the Titans, whom Ouranos so hated that they remained hidden inside the Earth. Incited by their mother Gaia, Ouranos's progeny swore to revenge themselves on their father. In the end, however, all except the Titan Kronos shrank from acting. Helped by his mother, Kronos declared his readiness to attack his father:

> So he spoke, and giant Gaia
> rejoiced greatly in her heart
> and took and hid him in a secret ambush
> and put into his hands
> the sickle, edged like teeth, and told him
> all her treachery.
> And huge Ouranos came on

bringing night with him, and desiring
love he embraced Gaia and lay over her
stretched out
complete, and from his hiding place his son
reached with his left hand
and seized him, and holding in his right
the enormous sickle
with its long blade edged like teeth,
he swung it sharply,
and lopped the members of his own father,
and threw them behind him
to fall where they would, but they were not lost away
    when they were flung
from his hand, but all the bloody drops
that went splashing from them
were taken in by Gaia, the earth,
and with the turning of the seasons
she brought forth the powerful Furies
and the tall Giants
shining in their armor
and holding long spears in their hands;
and the nymphs they call, on boundless earth,
the Nymphs of the Ash Trees.
But the members themselves, when Kronos
had lopped them with the flint,
he threw from the mainland
into the great wash of the sea water
and they drifted a great while
on the open sea, and there spread
a circle of white foam
from the immortal flesh, and in it
grew a girl, whose course first took her

to holy Kythera,
and from there she afterward made her way
to sea-washed Cyprus
and stepped ashore, a modest lovely Goddess,
and about her
light and slender feet the grass grew,
and the gods call her
Aphrodite, and men do too,
and the aphro-foam-born
goddess, and garlanded Kythereia,
because from the seafoam
she grew, and Kythereia because she had gone
to Kythera,
and Kyprogeneia, because she came forth
from wave-washed Cyrpus,
and Philommedea, because she appeared
from *medea*, members.[28]

This story of castration, with its obvious cosmic dimension (the separation of the earth and the sky), furnished the visual arts with an inspiring motif, Aphrodite's birth from the foam, which we can trace from antiquity through the Renaissance (Sandro Botticelli, 1445–1510) to the present day. It also included the element of incest, with all its Oedipal overtones, as reflected in the marriage of Ouranos and Gaia. Clearly this is an archetypal phenomenon and prompts us to ask the same questions George Devereux (1908–1985) posed to the field of psychoanalysis, which sought to explain these archaic mythical images as "human, all too human" phenomena.

It becomes clear that these myths are closely related to each other, even when the images they use have been muted or replaced by others. Thus in the Hurrian version "the penis is bitten and torn off," whereas in the Greek "the members are harvested with a sickle." On the one hand the act of castration symbolizes the total degradation of the victim—as is still the case today among the Afras of the Horn of Africa—and on the other it represents the desire to assume the virility of a vanquished enemy. To this day there are some ethnic groups (e.g., the Scots, Greeks, Arabs, and certain Balkan peoples) in which men consume the testes of castrated animals in the hope of increasing their sexual potency.

By the same token other peoples strictly forbade the consumption of these parts, notably the Jews (Genesis 32:32), who categorically rejected the idea of castrating either human beings or animals. The recurrence of past myths across a range of cultures would seem to suggest similarities in human perception. New myths are merely old wine in new bottles. Thus we might envisage the later Greek pantheon of anthropomorphic gods as grand metaphors for cosmic and anthropological events as they are reflected, for example, in Giorgio Vasari's (1515–1574) monumental fresco on the ceiling of the Sala die Cosimo il Vecchio in Florence, in which the myths of classical antiquity live on in the reality of the visual arts. Scenes of life on Planet Earth are clearly visible in the background; Vasari's painting renders the violent but essential act of creation as does no other work of art with which I am familiar, including Antonio Carneo's (1640–1680) attempt to immortalize the same motif in the Palazzo Caiselli in Udine. The process of recovering classical mythology and history during the Renaissance and Baroque reflects great attention to detail as regards a knowledge of the sources. However it presents a problem so far as their *Sitz im Leben* (life setting) is concerned. So long as only ahistorical events were involved, i.e., those pertaining to the cosmos, this was of no great importance. However, whenever history comes into play, questions arise that have to be dealt with in the same way one deals with counterfeits. Hence the preference for emphasizing enduring mythical modes of expression—of which the myths themselves, of course, are the best examples—over the fleeting realities of the moment.

The castration of Ouranos interrupted the constant, almost violent work of procreation. Kronos's deed brought nature to maturity and completion, giving rise to the cycle of death and rebirth that helped to define it. This is why Kronos is regarded as the father of cyclical, not linear, time. For his evil deed Kronos suffered a similar fate. Fearing that one of the children he had fathered with Rhea (whom one can identify with Cybele) would, as he had been foretold, deprive him of power, he swallowed them all—Hades, Poseidon, Hestia, Demeter, and Hera. Only because Rhea had handed Kronos a stone wrapped in napkins in place of Zeus was the last of his sons allowed to escape. On reaching adult age, Zeus began a 10-year battle with his father, forcing him, with the aid of other Titans (including the Cyclopes), to disgorge his siblings. Despite its gruesomeness, the image of a Titan devouring his children was a popular theme in the visual arts down to the time of Francisco Goya (1746–1828). Whether Zeus in fact castrated Kronos is not certain, but we cannot rule out the posssibility, especially if we take literally the revenge of which Hesiod speaks, and bear in mind the prototypes of this myth in Asia Minor. The fate of Kronos in Greek mythology is unclear and is overshadowed by other events in the world of the

Olympian gods in which Zeus came to play a leading role.

For Zeus was both the son and the grandson of castrated gods as well as the father (though without a "female significant other") of four "sexually impaired" children. First there was Agdistis, the result of Zeus's spontaneous ejaculation, who was born an androgyne, therefore causing the Olympian gods to change him into a woman. Next came Adonis, who was "wounded in the thigh" (castrated). He was followed by Dionysos, who emerged from either Zeus's hip or his thigh and suffered "sparagmos," the loss of his penis while he was being torn asunder. Women would regularly work Dionysos's phallus into a state of erection. This reminds us of Osiris and is one of the reasons that the Greeks identified him with the Egyptian god. And finally there was Athena, who sprang from the head of her father.

These mythical events—and we could easily cite further examples—show Zeus (as illustrated in the above-mentioned "mock births") as a virtual mother, that is to say, they are part of a so-called "hidden" myth in which other, unreal events are used as justification for introducing castration. It was even said that Zeus, after raping his mother Demeter (Gaia), sought to pacify her by claiming he had castrated himself. In fact, all he had done was to castrate a ram and toss its genitals at the feet of the angry goddess. Regardless of how the myth changed, one thing is certain: nobody wished to see the supreme god castrated. This is why he is mentioned only in passing whenever these kinds of events are described. All the various forms of the myth suggest that the loss of a penis had far-reaching consequences, including the unique transformation of a phallus into Aphrodite, whose father's genitals, thrown into the sea, ultimately gave birth to her. This explains why the word "aphrodisios" became a metonym for the male member or for a man having sexual intercourse. The ambiguity that signifies the difference between masculine and feminine becomes clear in myths in which the gods are in a state of continual metamorphosis, ridding themselves of sexual boundaries and thereby drawing attention to the androgynous nature of the divine. Hence, what we see before us is the primal image, dating back many thousands of years, of a bisexual being that seems to indicate that gender roles are constructs not determined by one's biological sex.

The mythology of the Olympian gods comprises an endless series of erotic and sexual adventures, of which castration is only a part. It includes the strange story of the contest between Marsyas and Apollo, which has come down to us only in relatively recent times. Not as straightforward as the Battle of the Titans, it relates in a kind of code the story of the castration and subsequent violation of Marsyas, an intimate of the mother goddess Cybele. The Silenus Marsyas mastered the art of the flute to such an extent that he challenged the great god Apollo to a musical competition. Apollo accepted on the condition that the winner be allowed to do anything he wished to the loser. Apollo played the lyre and was declared the winner as the result of a questionable decision. He then had Marsyas flayed alive. From Marsyas's blood sprang the river in Phrygia, Cybele's home, that bears his name. According to another tradition it has been suggested that Marsyas is part of the mythology surrounding Cybele. He is depicted as her loyal companion, his flute being one of the classical instruments played at festivals honoring her in her various hypostases as the Dea Syria (Goddess of Syria) and the Mater Magna:

> Her followers howled, the maddening flute was blown
> and soft hands struck the cowhide drumskins.[29]

Music played a major role in cults, festivals, and public games that were largely orgiastic in nature. The works of Andrea Mantegna (1431–1506) even portrayed the triumph of Caesar as verging on an orgy. His painting evokes a Rome that was coming increasingly under the influence of the Orient, a fact stressed by Goethe (1749–1832) as well:

> But he also succeeded in conveying the most immediate and individual naturalness in the representation of a great variety of figures and characters. He can depict men as they live and have their being, with all their merits and shortcomings, as they loiter in the market-place or join in processions, or throng together . . . But the nobleman seems to be hurt in an even more abusive way, for a band of musicians is following, composed of the most varied types: a good-looking, even pretty youth in a long, almost feminine dress, sings to a lyre and seems to be jumping about and gesticulating. No triumphal procession is complete without one: his role was to make strange gestures, sing bantering songs, and to mock the conquered captives mischievously. The jesters point to him and seem to comment on his words with their foolish gestures, which may well irritate the nobleman. And that we are not dealing with serious music can be seen at once from the next figure, for immediately behind comes a lanky, sheepskin-coated, high-capped bagpiper, and some boys with a tambourine seem to increase the uproar.[30]

It was the custom in Greek epics of the heroic age for victors to strip the vanquished of their ams and armor and "throw the parts that are secret to the dogs," which was more devastating to the victims than death itself:

> And the dogs mutilate
> the grey head and the grey beard and the parts that are secret,
> this, for all sad mortality, is the sight most pitiful.[31]

Even today the Beja, a nomadic people occupying mountain country between the Red Sea and the Nile River, practice this custom, a custom that occasionally shows a somewhat "more dignified" face: the lopped-off penises of an enemy are worn around the neck as trophies or used to decorate the front door and walls of one's house or tent. Just over a hundred years ago, after the battle near Zula (Adulis), the soldiers of the negus paid the emperor tribute by flinging the severed penises of their enemies at his feet.

The meaning of the verbs "to skin" and "to flay" is equivocal, just as it was in antiquity. This ambiguity is clearly reflected in the ethnographic drawings of oriental subjects by the Late Baroque traveler and illustrator Eberhard Werner Happel (1647–1690). One drawing shows a sculpture of Marsyas bound to a tree, the symbol of everlasting fertility and thus of Attis; on another, dating from the Hellenistic period, Marsyas appears again tied to a tree while a Scythian slave is whetting a knife to skin him. Peter Paul Rubens (1577–1640), José Rebera (1590–1652), and Luca Giordano (1632–1705) use the grisly episode as a metaphor to celebrate the triumph of the Apollonian spirit over untamed nature, the preserve of Pan, a goat-footed god of the fields and woods and inventor of the panpipe. The Greeks fought an unsuccessful battle to ban the introduction of the panpipe or syrinx, a flute-like instrument imported from Asia Minor that eventually became part of the cult of Dionysos and thus a regular feature of Greek festivals.

These myths concerning the gods of antiquity, which survive only in fragments, strongly suggest that castration was a common practice among human beings as well—an archaic practice that continues even to this day if we are to believe reports coming out of Chechnya about the castration of captured Russian soldiers during the recent fighting there.

The story of the emasculation of Dionysos, the joyful god of wine, is likewise disconcerting. The god of vegetation who is often identified with the phallus was as much a victim of castration as his oriental counterparts, Osiris, Adonis, and Attis. Emasculation was not a marginal phenomenon limited to one particular culture. Rather, it represented to the ancients the true secret heart of the cult—a fact that becomes even more significant when we consider that even Christian theologians such as Clement of Alexandria (150?–215?) refer to efforts to preserve Dionysos's phallus.[32] The persistence of this motif resulted—as Károly Kerényi (1897–1973), a leading authority on ancient mythology, emphasized—from the occult tradition of the Dionysian mysteries, which not all scholars judged in the same way. Thus in his book on Dionysos (1933), Walter F. Otto (1874–1958), a classicist and great admirer of the Greek gods, tried to obscure the motif, conceding the existence of phallic symbolism in the Dionysos cult (though not as enthusiastically as Marcel Detienne) but refusing to connect it with the god's castration:

> The learned Varro was very well informed when he declared that the sovereignty of Dionysos was not only to be recognized in the juice of fruits whose crowning glory was wine but also in the sperms of living creatures. From this sphere of the god's activity he traced the origin of the custom in which a phallus was crowned with wreaths and carried around in the god's cult. We certainly know how great a role this symbol of procreative power played in his festivals. "A wine jar, a vine, a goat, a basket of figs, and then the phallus"—this is the description Plutarch gives us of the original simplicity of the Dionysiac celebration. A song was sung to the phallus. We have inscriptional evidence for the use of a large wooden phallus in the processions of the Dionysia in Delos. Each colony sent a phallus regularly to the Athenian Dionysia.
>
> There is no need to pile up more evidence. We see that the phallus enjoyed a high position as the attendant and announcer of the god. The phallus out of fig wood was called by the Rhodians *thionidas*, as was Dionysos himself, and in Methymna the god, whose statue was reputed to have been fished out of the sea, carried the epithet of *phallen*. Dionysos could even be identified with Priapus, who was otherwise considered to be his and Aphrodite's (or one of the nymphs') son. However, the phallus is, after all, only an attendant of Dionysos, a potency which looms absurdly large in his circle but betrays in the process how far it is separated from the majestic reality of the god.[33]

Taking into account everything we know about Dionysos (who is identified with Osiris), including even W. F. Otto's contributions to an understanding of the god, we can clearly see that the efforts to replicate Dionysos's phallus were a direct result of his emasculation. The mythological fact that his penis had to be fished out of the sea recalls the wickedness of Seth (Typhon) who tossed Osiris's severed phallus into a river. None of this necessarily leads to that curious explanation in which the phallus became an autonomous entity. Thus we can without hesitation accept the explanation presented by Kerényi, the Hungarian-born humanist who for years lived in exile in Switzerland and was an active member of the Eranos circle, a discussion group on religious history. Kerényi stressed the appropriateness of Clement of Alexandria's equation of Dionysos with Attis, "because [Attis] too was separated from his reproductive organ," and he noted that "[eunuchism] was one of the secret components of the Dionysian religion, but to the connoisseurs of the Dionysos cult cited by Clement it was an open secret."[34] In contrast to W. F. Otto, Kerényi understood that the Greek myth called for comparison with the Egyptian, which was at least as ancient as Plutarch's treatise *On Isis and Osiris*.

Dionysos—"he with two mothers" (Persephone and Semele) who was ultimately born from his father Zeus's thigh—was sometimes represented as a fat, bearded old man and sometimes as a youth. This probably reflects his essentially dual nature. One might even speak of the markedly "unphallic" iconography manifested in the many depictions of the Dionysian idol in Lenaion which are reminiscent of representations of Osiris. These show Dionysos as lord of the underworld. The mask over the idol has a beard and below the mask is a long garment, features that can also be found in the often-discussed murals in the Villa dei Misteri at Pompeii. Toward the end of the so-called hall of preparation murals we see the horror on a woman's face as she catches sight of the god's phallus lying in a basket (cf. Reinhold Merkelbach[35]).

This would not be a balanced study if we failed to mention the fact that a markedly "phallic" iconography was used to depict the other side of Dionysos's nature. Thus, Martin Nilsson writes in his history of Greek religion:

> The phallus is the constant companion of Dionysos. It seems to have been absent from scarcely any Dionysian procession; the participants tied it to themselves, so that it became an accessory of comic actors and was also set up as a choragic monument. The god never wears it, but his companions, the sileni and satyrs, are ithyphallic. Phallus processions and merry Dionysian festivals were held throughout the Greek countryside. As Plutarch describes them, "in the lead an amphora of wine and a vine branch were carried about; then came a man drawing behind him the sacrificial animal, a he-goat; another followed him with a basket of figs, and last a phallus was carried.[36]

The vegetative nature of the Dionysian cult is reflected in the cycle of Dionysian myths and their iconography which was influenced by the well-known tree cults of Asia Minor and thus shared a number of features with the later Roman mysteries of Cybele and Attis. The nearly universal "religion of Dionysos" encompassed yet another element of the sexual imagination which might be described as an expression of the invincible "power of the sexual drive, even when it leads to nothing," i.e., when there is no thought of procreation. This finding is supported by the fact that the myths that have come down to us do not specify what kind of emasculation was performed on Dionysos and that the iconography associated with the god—which shows mules copulating (in the original sense of linking the sexes together but not necessarily generating new life)—conveys this meaning and only this meaning. It is further reinforced by the portrayals of Dionysos riding on mules and of Dionysos's "ship car" being drawn by mules. It is precisely this factor that elucidates the ecstatic character of the Dionysia that have been described as orgies and regarded as secret rites of initiation in which "madness" was used to transcend the real world and penetrate the power that holds the universe together. Even Mozart (1756–1791) shows an understanding of the secret of the mysteries when in *The Magic Flute* he has the two "armed men" in Act II sing:

> Man that is born of woman, walks through life in shadow,
> Yet light and truth may pierce through pain and sorrow.
> Man must brave Death, the dread that haunts him
>   from his birth—
> Then he shall find his heaven here on earth.
> Enlightened Man will see truth pure and whole,
> And, finding truth, he shall find his immortal soul.

Given the varied forms assumed by the myth of Dionysos and its component parts, which have changed and expanded over time, there is a multiplicity of possible interpretations. What is certain, however, is that Dionysos's castration helped to give him the Bacchanalian image that survived antiquity and lived on into the Renaissance and Baroque.

Thus the story of Dionysos would not be complete if we failed to mention the story of Pentheus, whose image has been preserved in the splendid painting in the House of Vettii at Pompeii. Pentheus, whom Euripides (c 480–406 B.C.) immortalized in *The Bacchae,* was torn to pieces when Dionysos inspired his frenzied female worshipers to murder the Theban king:

> "Women, I bring you the man who has mocked
> at you and me and at our holy mysteries.
> Take vengeance upon him."[37]

Pentheus refused to recognize Dionysos's divinity and became the object of Dionysos's terrifying vengefulness:

> So,
> you *are* attractive, stranger, at least to women—
> which explains, I think, your presence here in Thebes.[38]

Pentheus even ordered Dionysos to be imprisoned. However, it did not take long for the god to react. He called out encouragement to his devotees who included the Bacchae, led by Pentheus's mother. The women became wild with fury:

> With that, thousands of hands
> tore the fir tree from the earth, and down, down
> from his perch fell Pentheus, tumbling
> to the ground, sobbing and screaming as he fell,
> for he knew his end was near.[39]

Before killing Pentheus, who was dressed in women's clothes, the Bacchae apparently castrated him. And the fir tree that the women felled—a symbol of fertility in Dionysos's (and Attis's) Phrygian homeland—also seems to point to emasculation. The myth's *Sitz im Leben* (situation in life) helps to elucidate not only the struggle of the Greeks with cults they deemed to be alien, but the ability of those cults to take root and endure:

> And if there is no god of wine,
> there is no love, no Aphrodite either,
> nor other pleasure left to men.[40]

Thus the eternal "Dionysian" entered philosophy through Friedrich Nietzsche's (1844–1900) unique portrayal of Greek tragedy:

> So what is Dionysian? . . . "one who knows" is speaking, the initiate and disciple of his god. Perhaps I would now be more discreet, less eloquent, in discussing such a difficult psychological question as the origin of tragedy among the Greeks. One fundamental question is the Greek relation to pain, their level of sensitivity—was that relation constant? Or did it radically change?—the question of whether their ever more intense *craving for beauty*, for festivals, entertainments, new cults, grew out of a lack, out of deprivation, melancholy, pain . . . And what, then, would be the meaning, physiologically speaking, of that madness out of which both tragic and comic art arose, the Dionysian madness?[41]

Nietzsche thus emphasized the sufferings of Dionysos. Although he never directly referred to castration in *The Birth of Tragedy* or any of his other works, it was Nietzsche who made Dionysian suffering into an issue that would engage the attention of the modern age.

We have only touched on a few examples of the practice of castration among the gods as reflected in oriental and Mediterranean cultures by presenting. Clearly it left its mark on cult practice. The result was that ritual castration was a widespread phenomenon and the terminology associated with it was much richer than is the case today, when we tend to speak only of transsexualism. One of the most important characteristics of cultic life was the rite of sacrifice. And the highest sacrifice a human being could conceivably make was self-sacrifice. However, this was feasible only in extreme situations, if at all, as the history of Christianity shows. In principle a substitute sacrifice was made. In the Old Testament, for example, Abraham offered up a ram in place of his son Isaac (Genesis 22:2–13). Eroticism and sexuality could doubtless switch from one extreme to the other, from devotion and ecstasy to self-denial, self-mortification, and self-mutilation. But here too substitutions were possible. An example is the practice of circumcision among the Jews as a sign of the covenant between God and the descendants of Abraham (Genesis 17:12f.; Joshua 5:2–9).

The Semitic fertility cults that extended to Carthage—as portrayed in Flaubert's *Salammbo*—and its western colonies as well as the Greek and Roman religions of classical antiquity celebrated sacrificial rites in which gifts such as pomegranates, fish, pigeons, mice, hares, bulls, and even human beings were offered up to the gods. These rites also involved the participation of self-castrated high priests such as the *megabysos* of the Ephesian Artemis and the *korybantes* of the Meter. These emasculated priests generally behaved like transvestites and wore female clothing. They served the cults of Hecate of Laginas in Caria (Karyai), who was regarded as a moon goddess. In addition, Hecate was associated with secret societies whose rituals became part of folk religions that would sometimes celebrate them as witches' sabbaths. Emasculated priests can also be found in the syncretic Greco-oriental cult of Aphrodite and Astarte. The best known of these priests were the *galloi* who, beginning in the 7th century B.C., were linked to the cult of Cybele that was well known to the Greeks. The *galloi* appeared throughout the Roman empire as itinerant and mendicant priests and therefore often became the butt of Martial's mordant wit: "Lest the cockerel grow thin by over-draining his loins, he lost his testicles. Now I shall consider him a—cockerel."[42]

CHAPTER 3

"Sacred Kingship" and Its Consequences

> "Twin-born with greatness, subject to the breath
> Of every fool, whose sense no more can feel
> But his own wringing! What infinite heartsease
> Must kings neglect that private men enjoy!
> And what have kings that privates have not too,
> Save ceremony, save general ceremony?
> And what art thou, thou idol ceremony?
> What kind of god art though, what suffer'st more
> Of mortal griefs than do thy worshipers."
> —Shakespeare, *Henry V*, act 4, scene 1

The mythical vision of a divine order and its relation to earthly events manifested itself, on the one hand, in cultic activities that followed a calendar-like (cyclical) sequence of events, events that in every culture and society are conditioned by this same cyclicity. And on the other it was reflected in the power structure of the state, which was regarded as a gift from the gods, the true rulers of mankind. The gods could act and produce results directly (theocracy) or through a representative, the anointed (messiah) or consecrated one. In the beginning, therefore, the gods asserted their right to decide how the world should be ordered as well as their right to castrate themselves and one another. This motif later developed into an archetype of cosmic events and became embedded in mythology, leading to the concept of emasculation as a divinely decreed act. In many of the myths that have come down to us from ancient Egypt, Mesopotamia, Asia Minor, the Mediterranean world, and China, the gods—or at least demi-gods (i.e., the children of a god and a mortal woman)—became founders of states that one can only describe as "sacred" monarchies.

It is virtually impossible to reduce the views of different scholars on the origin and nature of these archaic power structures to a common denominator, because their opinions were not always determined by the actual situation of these institutions. Rather, they were premised on ideology. An excellent illustration is the portrayal of the Roman Empire in *Bread and Circuses*, the monumental work by the French historian Paul Veyne. Veyne fashioned a questionable historical sociology that deals more in terms of dialectic than fact with issues that had a determining influence on the nature of sacred kingship from prehistory to the modern era. Veyne's argument reflects the spirit of the French Enlightenment. It neglects to take into account the fact that more than two centuries have elapsed since that time and that during that time we witnessed not only the emergence of Marxism but of new ways to approach spirituality and the mystical knowledge of phenomena that cannot be fitted into rational categories. Veyne writes: "The monarch is a god. Which means that he reigns by his own right and also, paradoxically, that he is less than a demi-god, a mere hero . . . The emperor was not deified because the gods were no longer easily distinguished from heroes and men (the emperor was very clearly distinguished from both), but because men no longer found it scandalous to deify other men, particularly dead people. That is why the Greco-Roman cult of the sovereigns has something about it that is anodyne, moderate and even sometimes Voltairean, with nothing of the 'oriental' ponderousness of the cult of the pharaohs. For the Egyptians continued to consider that a man is not a god, so that deifying pharaoh was an almost tyrannical act of violence, an assault by a potentate upon human modesty. A Hellenistic king, however, did little violence to people's consciences when he had himself, or let himself be, worshiped: it was just sentimental weakness."[43] We can understand these bygone times only if we suspend our rationalist skepticism and empathize with the logic of myths. "Mythical consciousness" (Cassirer)[44] is constant and continuous; whereas the critical rationalist, the representative of the Age of Enlightenment, takes delight in negating the idea of continuity and ends up searching, in the "spirit of utopia" (Ernst Bloch),[45] for some lost paradise, like those ascetics of old who withdrew to the desert to live.

These theoretical preconditions are key to understanding castration as a sacred obligation that is based on the existence of a divine, numinous power. This is why the question arises as to the nature of the "sacred" king in his capacity as representative of a charismatic power, an idea common to many peoples and cultures. Max Weber (1864–1920) described just such a king as a charismatic figure "with specific and supernatural (i.e., not available to everyone) endowments of body and soul."[46] Since it is impossible in the context of this study to treat the nature of "sacred" kingship on a comparative basis according to language, religion, and culture, we think it sufficient to limit ourselves to an investigation of the concept in Semitic culture. This will not only help us to understand the psychological basis of this kind of state institution but also familiarize us with one of the fundamental assumptions of biblical (i.e., western) thinking.

Let us start, as is traditional, with language. Look for a moment at some of the words derived from the tri-consonantal Semitic root *mlk* ("king"): *mla* ("fill," "be full"); *mlak* ("angel," "messenger"); and *mlh* ("salt"). Reflecting on them may reveal the nature and substance of this numinous power and its grandeur. I do not intend this to be an exhaustive analysis of the theological meaning of these terms.[47] I simply wish to bring out certain semantic field associations that help to characterize sacred kingship. In addition to terms such as "mission," "consecration," "anointing," "divine election," "divine worship," and "sacrifice," we find a hidden charismatic meaning in this God-given office, an office that God himself could very well fill. In this context, the identification of Jesus with the king as restoration of the original meaning of the office becomes clear. Thus sacred kingship becomes a real-life myth, for only God is capable of having a messenger do good and fight on behalf of righteousness as an intermediary between himself and humankind, as his representative. The king thus becomes the bringer of the time of salvation (redeemer), the dispenser of harvests, and the enhancer of the fruitfulness of nature. This is possible because only God himself and the king—the latter being a descendant of the gods specially chosen by them—possess the power to do these things. This is how the idea of theocracy emerged among the Egyptians, Jews, Christians, and Muslims and led to the concept of "the king's two bodies" (Ernst Kantorowicz),[48] which was based on certain facts that Veyne and a number of others fail to take into consideration.

Allowing for local variants, we find the idea of sacred kingship reflected in the founding legends of many ancient states. In their attempt to do justice to divine kingship, however, a number of studies have disregarded and in some cases completely suppressed the sexual aspect. The story in the Osiris and Isis cycle has shown us that a god had every right to occupy the throne of Upper and Lower Egypt by himself. This is the chief reason why the rulers of the Nile called themselves Horus and not pharaoh. As Horus, i.e., the descendant of a god, the king was the legitimate heir to the throne, to its power and majesty. The divine procreation and birth of the kings are represented by pictorial illustrations in their temples (Luxor, Deir el-Bahri, Karnak). The god Amon begets the future king with a specially selected mortal (usually the queen). The king is the first unambiguous paradigm of what Ernst Kantorowicz meant by the concept of "the king's two bodies." As an institution the Egyptian ruler is divine: he is Horus himself; he is the progeny of the god. After he dies he goes to the Netherworld to rule as the god Osiris. Otherwise the king is a human being, and in his human form he is both an intermediary and a high priest whose task is to ensure that the gods continue to make the land bountiful and look with favor upon it. So long as Egypt respected and carried out the laws of God (the sacred king), it would enjoy the blessings of the gods.

Akhenaton (c. 1340–1324 B.C.), also known as Amunhotep (Amenophis) IV, was a reformer and worshiper of the god Aton and described himself as "the mother and father (of mankind and the gods)." The extremism he fostered embraced the idea, rooted in primordial myth, of a god that had generated itself and had no need to appear as either wholly male or wholly female. This notion also gave rise to the authorized "unmanly" portrayal of Akhenaton, a portrayal that differed radically from that of all other kings in which their sexual arousal in the presence of the gods was suggested, in accordance with religious precepts, by the stiffened fabric of their kilts. Except for the hostile priests of Amon, hardly any ancient Egyptians grasped the significance of Akhenaton's androgyny, which almost made him appear like a castrato. Akhenaton's ideas died with him but left their mark on many of the monuments erected during the age of the Ramessides. To what degree his ideas affected the precepts of sacral purity and chastity is hard to tell. What is clear, however, is that they formed the basis of many cultic rites. Whether these rites were merely transient phenomena or permanent in nature cannot be determined. Later Hellenistic accounts indicate that the priests of the god of the Nile probably looked with favor upon castration as a necessary precondition for maintaining the uninterrupted flow of nature's bounty. This is attested by depictions of fertility goddesses that exhibit eunuch-like characteristics.

In both Egypt and the ancient Middle East, we find a good deal of evidence pointing to a type of sacred kingship that was often symbolized by the "sacral marriage" of a goddess to a man specially chosen by the gods (*lugal*, "great man"). Marriages such as these indicate how the tendency toward

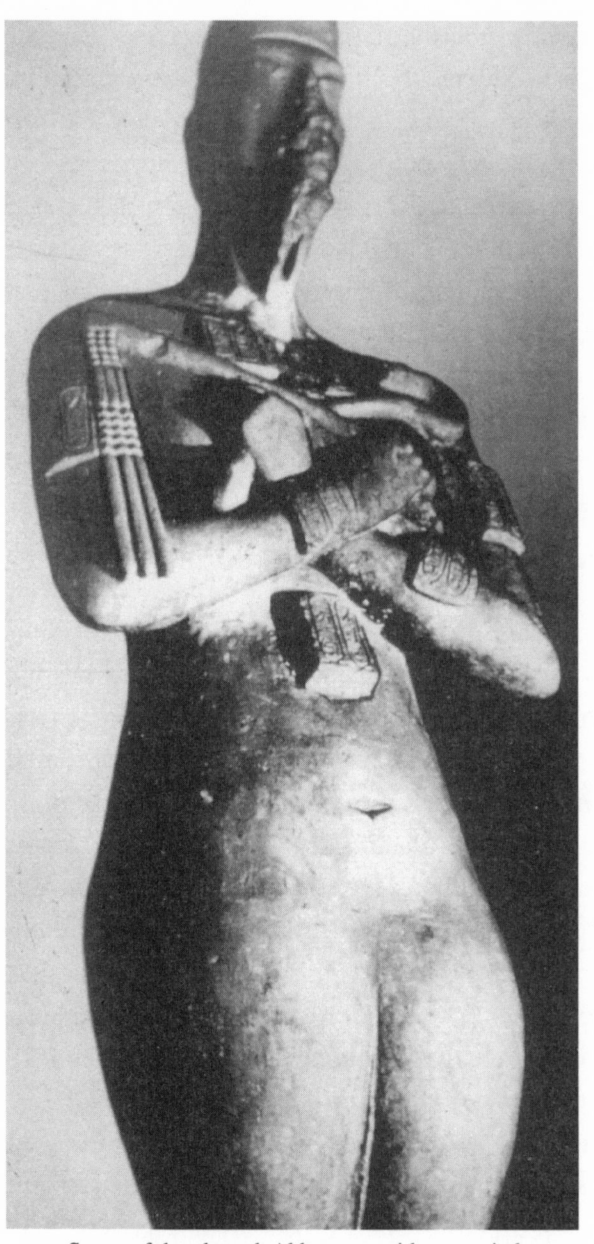

Statue of the pharaoh Akhenaton without genitals
(Museum of Cairo)

matriliny, if not matriarchy, increased the importance of eunuchism. Having been deprived of their masculinity and rendered sterile, eunuchs became the servants and confidants of the queen, who could consort with them without any fear of becoming pregnant. This was the situation that obtained, for example, at the court of the legendary Semiramis. This Assyrian queen, immortalized in history and myth, personally helped to promote the idea of eunuchism, surrounding herself with castrated catamites—in the sale of whom, by the way, she also did a brisk business. Beginning in antiquity Semiramis was often the subject of literature, painting, and music, e.g., the opera *Semiramide* by Gioacchino Rossini (1792–1868).

In 1989 the Italian Assyriologist Giovanni Pettinato completed a monumental study of the historical Semiramis, the wife of Shamshi-Adad V and the mother of Adadnirari III. However he did more than simply produce a history of the reign of Sammuramat (Semiramis being the Greek form of the name) and her life, which covered part of the 10th and 9th centuries B.C. He also described the historical and cultural context in which this peculiar monarch exercised power over the Middle East. His book is therefore much more than a biography; it is a history of Assyria that searches for Semiramis's *Sitz im Leben*.

Pettinato took a very critical view of eunuchism, maintaining that eunuchs were nothing more than beardless "butlers" and therefore had no claim to any influential offices in the administration of the state. Yet one need not even go as far back as the Byzantine Empire to show that eunuchs often held the highest offices of state, especially in sacred monarchies in which the institution of the "queen mother" was never in dispute, because it was an integral part of the religious view of matriliny's relation to the seat of power. The king's mother was called *ama-gal* (the Great Mother). She was comparable to the great goddesses and worshiped with the abject reverence that is characteristic of cults. Thus we read in a document from Ras Shamra (Ugarit): "Seven and seven times from afar I threw myself down before the feet of my mother. May my mother remain in good health. May the gods protect and preserve you."[49] The king's mother had the right to take her seat in the throne room at the right side of the monarch. The Bible speaks in the same vein with regard to Bathsheba, Solomon's mother: "So Bathsheba went to King Solomon, to speak on behalf of Adonijah. The king rose to meet her, and bowed down to her; then he sat on the throne, and had a throne brought for the king's mother; and she sat on his right" (I Kings 2:19).[50]

Throughout the Middle East, as far as Egypt and south of Egypt to Kush, sacred kingship was a recognized state institution. In Assyria it was introduced during the reign of Semiramis, owing to the influence of peoples who had been conquered by the Assyrians. To administer these state organizations sacred kings required the services of eunuchs. Therefore we cannot exclude the possibility that Shamshi-ilu—royal confidant, general (*turtanu*), and long the first man in the state—was in fact a eunuch. As Pettinato correctly points out, Shamshi-ilu was "a would-be Assyrian king." His unusually long life (typical of many eunuchs) and career recall the later Byzantine eunuchs, Narses and Basil. Long after Semiramis's death Shamshi-ilu ensured the continuity of Assyrian politics and the power of the state down to the time of the celebrated Tiglath-pileser III (745–727 B.C.). Shamshi-ilu's title—"general deputy, grand herald, keeper of the temple, supreme commander of many armies, he who governs the land of Hatte"[51] corroborate our assumption that he was in all likelihood a castrato.

It is no coincidence that the Assyrians used the well-known term harem (*harim*, *haram*) in this context, for the palace and in particular the royal chambers were virtually "sacred and therefore prohibited" areas. Ever under the Roman and Byzantine emperors they were called *sacri cubiculi*.

Concubinage, which resulted in part from the presence of the many so-called "ladies of the palace" and their children, posed an obvious and constant threat to any potential royal successor and his mother, the (possible) future queen mother, particularly as they became embroiled in dynastic intrigues and palace revolts. Semiramis, by the way, probably also started her career as a concubine. Later, such intrigues were common in the Byzantine Empire and especially in the harems of the Ottomon Empire. Thus it is reasonable to assume that those who did not wish to be constantly involved in fighting off various rivals turned to the more "humane" solution of castrating possible pretenders to the throne, after having assured them of a senior position at court. This is in fact how eunuchs came to be appointed high court officials, patriarchs, and statesmen. Their special background thus helps to explain the positions they occupied and the influence they had at court. True, their aspirations to become emperor had been frustrated. But at the same time their new status allowed them to participate directly in the exercise of power. It was probably the king's mother herself who made the final decision as to which pretenders to the throne would be castrated. Her power was unique. Since time immemorial no one has disputed the role of a powerful queen mother, which also helps to explain Semiramis's influential position as queen-regent during her son's minority.

Based on the sources, we can assume that Semiramis was a Syrian. In mythology she is depicted as the daughter of the Syrian goddess Derketo or even Atargatis. She is said to have been raised by doves, which is reflected in her name (dove) and places her in virtually the same category as the mother goddesses. Her association with Atargatis not only puts her in a league with the bloodthirsty love goddess Ishtar, queen of the heavens; it also helps to explain the idea of her numinous but paradoxical greatness, namely that she appears as both virgin and mother, male and female, queen and goddess. All this probably fueled the myths that grew up around Semiramis's various undertakings which included, among other things, sending 500 castrati to the Persians to serve as catamites. She is even said to have invented castration, a story passed on by the Roman historian Ammianus Marcellinus: "finally [came] the throng of eunuchs, beginning with the old men and ending with the boys, sallow and disfigured by the distorted form of their members; so that, wherever anyone goes, beholding the troops of mutilated men, he would curse the memory of that Queen Semiramis of old, who was the first of all to castrate young males . . . "[52]

From the ancient writers included in Diodorus's (1st century B.C.) *Bibliotheca Historica* we learn that after the death of Ninos, Semiramis's legendary consort, the Assyrian queen disguised herself in men's clothing in order to pass herself off as her young son. To this end she is said to have ordered all the manservants at court to be castrated lest her female characteristics startle anyone. Stories such as these reflect the patriarchal attitudes of those who refused to accept a woman as ruler. In the East, however, the situation was different. And in the course of time the eastern point of view prevailed in the West as well; one need only think of the powerful and increasingly legitimate position of the Byzantine empresses. The Hellenistic tradition, in which the figure of the Assyrian queen alternates between myth, history, and legend, lives on in the "hanging gardens of Semiramis" and in works of art rich in fantasy, many of which were produced by Mannerist and Baroque painters. All this goes to show the effect Semiramis had on generating an archetypal image.

Ancient chronicles and the oldest surviving examples of legislation, including the Code of Hammurabi (1728–1686 B.C.), all make reference to eunuchs and to castration as a form of punishment. The fact that Babylonian law recognized and dealt with eunuchism presupposes that it was a widespread phenomenon. Castration is thus a very ancient custom, deeply rooted in various cultures. Hundreds if not thousands of eunuchs could be found at the courts of Babylonia, Assyria, Egypt, Persia, and Kush. Some of them can be identified in the reliefs of rediscovered Mesopotamian palaces where they are portrayed—in contrast to normal men—without beards.

The absence of a beard was an iconographic symbol of the loss of virility, not just in the ancient Middle East and Egypt, where Osiris is a classic example of this phenomenon, but also in later Byzantine iconography in which beardlessness was used to identify this unique characteristic in certain saints.

Banquet scene with the Assyrian king Assurbanipal accompanied by the queen and the eunuchs, Niniveh, about 645 B.C. The king has a beard; the eunuchs are beardless. (British museum)

They were virginal and chaste and therefore holy. They had overcome their male sexuality—in the form of a dragon or a snake (Seth/Typhon)—as the image of St. George slaying the dragon indicated to the faithful. St. George is in fact the logical successor to his pagan predecessor Horus, who slew the villain Seth in the form of a dragon. Even today we can see an illustration of this on a Coptic window grate.

Everywhere we look we find evidence of the survival of these deeply-rooted motifs. They help to explain many things that have long disappeared from our consciousness. Even now, for example, the custom of wearing a beard or a moustache is widespread throughout the Muslim world as a visible and probably archetypal sign of virility, not to mention as an expression of the need to distinguish oneself from eunuchs who have lost their male growth of beard as a result of having been castrated. However the question whether eunuchs in the ancient Middle East were always castrated has never been resolved. There are many reasons for us to presume that at some of the courts where they held important positions as "confidants" or chief stewards, eunuchs were not castrati. The Bible contains indications to this effect when referring to Potiphar and other palace officials (Genesis 39:1; I Samuel 8:15; I Kings 22:9). In addition, there are references to the *saris* who have usually been translated by the Greek term *eunouchos*, though a correct rendering would be "he or she who has a leading position," without any reference to castration. Why in the course of time was the term eunuch equated with an emasculated or castrated man?

The history of the later Babylonian empire, in which the king has been known since time immemorial as the *sar*, provides us with examples of customs that date back to very ancient times. These are largely connected with the New Year festival (*akitu* festival), which may offer an interesting explanation of how eunuchism came to be identified with the practice of castration. Like comparable renewal festivals in other well-known cultures, this festival celebrated the mythical meaning of nature's cyclicity in which blossoming and withering form an integral and everlasting part of a god's death and rebirth.

"Living myths" were reenacted in ritual "games." The king, who was identified with the god, was obliged to devote his attention to the rites of renewal. We are reminded in this connection of creation myths in which the gods were castrated in order to ensure the fertility of nature. The king was expected to go through a similar ritual. The Babylonian sources thus suddenly tell us of the appointment of a temporary substitute king who was to assume power for the duration of the festival in order to devote himself to the rituals in lieu of the monarch and thereby ensure the resurrection and regeneration of the real king. Not only did this create an institution that to this day lives on—in a somewhat corrupted form—in customs associated with carnivals (carnival kings, princes and courtiers); it also gave rise to an institution that provides us with a basis for understanding the origins of castration, a practice that was originally connected to religion and life at court.

The results of research covering the Greco-Roman period indicate that even though this explanation seems plausible, it is not necessarily valid in every case. One can safely assume that not all recruits for high office in Egypt, Kush, or Israel were castrati, a fact that is reflected in, among other things, the varying views of sacred kingship. In Egypt the future monarch was legitimized by the king's mother who, having been chosen by the god, rose to become the "mother of god" (*mwt ntr*) after the birth of her divine child, which helped to give credence to the idea of theogamy. The situation was not much different in Kush, although this state in what is now the lower Sudan filled the office of king in a different way, namely through the oracle (college of priests) at Napata (now Jebel Barkal) which was responsible for selecting the god-king from among a number of candidates. In Kush this meant that the *kandake* (king's mother) would receive her title and office only after her son had been elected king and had actually ascended the throne. This is corroborated by the story of the mother of Taharqa (690–664 B.C.), the best-known king of the 25th Ethiopian

(Kushite) dynasty. Alhough it is possible, even in these states, to conceive of the emasculation of courtiers as a way of ensuring the sacred inviolability of Amon's "divine consort," it was probably part of a later development that did not necessarily encompass all aspects of life at court. Here we see the difficulty of drawing a line between what constituted the province of the temple and that of the palace, since there was no sharp dividing line between the two in antiquity.

The kingdom of Israel occupies a unique position in the ancient Middle East. It was a decidedly theocratic state, and the prevailing customs reflected such archaic traditions that we must briefly touch on them here. The ideas and traditions of this period characterized the ancient Middle East as a whole as well as the early stages of Judaism. As we examine these ideas and customs it becomes increasingly clear that the male sexual organ was associated with a number of fundamental concepts whose origins are no longer transparent to us, even though they continue to be part of our everyday vocabulary. In the Old Testament, when a man took an oath, he normally put his hand on another man's testicles to emphasize the solemnity of the act. Thus we read in Genesis 24:9 (see also 47:29): "So the servant put his hand under the thigh of Abraham his master, and swore to him concerning this matter." A person therefore swore an oath, as it were, to divine fecundity, to the seed of Horus.

This custom, which constituted part of the process of taking a legally binding oath, may have been practiced in antiquity by peoples other than the Jews. Traces of the tradition can even be found in various precursors of the western legal system, the terminology of which still reflects the origins of the custom.

Following Roman law we still speak, for example, of a "testament" as a formal declaration of a person's wishes as to the disposal of his or her property after death. Yet we never think of the term as being based on the Latin word *testis* (meaning "witness," but basically "testicles"). In German the terms *Zeug* ("material" or "stuff"), *zeugen* ("to beget"), and *Zeuge* ("witness") have a similar etymology. The Latin word *testa*, pl. *testae* ("earthenware," "potsherd"), for example, was a synonym for "instrument," namely the potsherd that was originally used—even before the stone knife—to perform castrations (of the *galloi*, the priests of Cybele, for instance). Thus the *galloi* used objects derived from the earth (Gk *gea*, L *terra*), the very symbol of fertility.

According to biblical law, a stone knife also had to be used to perform circumcision, an essential part of the Jewish religion. Exodus, the Second Book of Moses (4:25), and in particular Joshua 5:2 ff., stress the importance of the ritual and how it is to be performed: "At that time the Lord said to Joshua, 'Make flint knives and circumcise the Israelites a second time.'" This is confirmed in Genesis 17:9 ff.: "God said to Abraham, 'As for you, you shall keep my covenant, you and your offspring after you throughout their generations. This is my covenant, which you shall keep, between me and you and your offspring after you: Every male among you shall be circumcised. You shall circumcise the flesh of your foreskins; and it shall be a sign of the covenant between me and you. Throughout your generations every male among you shall be circumcised when he is eight days old, including the slave born in your house and the one bought with your money from any foreigner who is not of your offspring. Both the slave born in your house and the one bought with your money must be circumcised. So shall my covenant be in your flesh an everlasting covenant. Any uncircumcised male who is not circumcised in the flesh of his foreskin shall be cut off from his people; he has broken my covenant.'"

Jews regard circumcision strictly as a religious rite representing the fulfillment of the covenant between God and Abraham. On the one hand, this sheds light on the genital origins of all ancient practices that involve entering into an agreement or administering an oath. On the other hand, though, it does not take into consideration a possible connection to the cultic practice of castration, even though we know that Hellenized Jews discussed the Roman emperors' decrees prohibiting circumcision. What they omitted to mention, however, was that these prohibitions were part of a general ban on the practice of castration. We have already seen how cults justified castration as an offering to the divine So it is clearly within the realm of possibility that emasculation was also known and practiced among the Semites, including the *habiru* (Hebrews). Over time the cultic ritual of castration, which was meant to curtail procreative activity, was "humanized" through the introduction of circumcision and a strict ban on the practice of emasculation (Deuteronomy 23:1): "No one whose testicles are crushed or whose penis is cut off shall be admitted to the assembly of the Lord." This prohibition plus the fact that the same instruments that were used to perform castration were also used in circumcision indicate that the Hebrews may very well have been familiar with the practice of emasculation. Otherwise there would have been no need to outlaw it. Judging by the etymology of certain words we have good reason to assume that the office of king (Heb *mlk*) was related to both the term used for a circumcised individual (Heb *ml/h*) and that used for a messenger (Heb *mlak*). With that the convenant was sealed between god and a king who had been circumcised as his envoy.

The ideas, laws and myths of the ancient Middle East lived on and influenced Hellenistic culture, which merged with Roman civilization in the West and was "orientalized" in the East. In this so-called Age of Hellenism, castrated eunuchs became increasingly important in religion, cults, and life at court, as was particularly evident in late antiquity and then in Byzantium. According to Hellenistic and various other literary sources, there were myriad figures, from Egypt to India, who were referred to by the Greek term *eunouchos* and often by the term *spado* as well. Arguably these words were used to make a sexual distinction. In spite of the fact that individuals referred to as eunuchs may have been high officials, generals, advisors, or priests, their real names remain unknown, for the names that have come down to us are those that were given to them by their masters.

The Hellenistic world followed the tradition of the Persian court which had virtually become a paradigm for the treatment of eunuchs in the East and in antiquity. Because of the close ties between Persia and Greece and the later campaigns of Alexander the Great (336–323 B.C.), detailed information has come down to us regarding the eunuchs who lived during the Achaemenid dynasty. There were said to have been more than 3,000 eunuchs at the Persian court. Beginning with the reign of Cyrus II (559–529 B.C.) we have nearly a complete list of the chief eunuchs at the court of the Persian "kings of kings."

Many were extremely important factors in the organization of the state and exercised enormous influence. Not only did they accompany the king wherever he went; they carried out diplomatic assignments abroad, took part in making important decisions, and were even involved in political intrigue and murder. In fact, they became so powerful that Artoxares, the favorite court eunuch of Artaxerxes I (464–424 B.C.) and his successor Darius II (424–404), decided to make himself king. In order to be accepted as a man, he had an artificial beard made for himself. However his plot was betrayed, whereupon Parysatis, the wife of Darius II, ordered him to be seized and executed.

Court eunuchs bore the title "friend of the king." This was the case, for example, with Bagoas, the chief steward of Artaxerxes III (358–338 B.C.) who eventually became commander-in-chief of the Persian army. The Great King made no decisions without consulting his trusted eunuch. It is said that Bogoas ordered the murder of Hermeias, the gifted Greek ruler of Assos, even though the latter was a favorite of the Persian king. Hermeias was presumably a eunuch too.

Once again the question arises whether court eunuchs were always castrati. There are many indications that in antiquity the word eunuch may have been a purely courtly title. Although it was perfectly proper to apply the term to a castrato, it was not limited to castrated men. We infer this from the other term we encounter in the sources—*spado*. There was, for instance, another person by the name of Bagoas who was described as both an *eunouchos* and a *spados*. He was the catamite of Darius III (336–330 B.C.) and was later presented as a gift to Alexander the Great. He was said to have been particularly beautiful and youthful-looking. According to Curtius, a Roman writer who lived during the 2nd and 1st centuries B.C., this catamite exercised an inordinate influence over the Macedonian king who was said to have been extremely fond of him. As Ferdinand Justi's (1834–1907) research at the end of the 19th century showed, there were an enormous number of eunuchs in Persia.

Eunuchism developed into an institution that influenced the state organizations of neighboring areas, especially Armenia and the Mediterranean world. Even the lesser courts of the Persian aristocracy employed eunuchs and castrati. The custom continued well into the Islamic period, despite the fact that eunuchs seem to have lost some of their importance in certain areas. In Persia, in fact, there was scarcely a single sphere of public life in the post-Achaemenid period, under the Parthians and Sassanians, where one could not find eunuchs employed as governors (satraps), commanders-in-chief, emissaries of the Great King, administrators, or servants at court. Even the Diadochi, the Macedonian generals among whom the empire of Alexander the Great was divided after his death, adopted this well-established institution.

Some examples from the Ptolemaic period indicate the historical continuity of eunuchism, which reached its zenith during the Age of Hellenism. Even in Judaea, where the practice of castration was frowned upon and outlawed, Herod the Great (37 B.C.–A.D. 4) found it impossible, as Josephus Flavius (A.D. 37–95) relates, to manage his affairs without eunuchs. Eunuchs held high office under the Ptolemies. Thus Eulaeus, originally an attendant to the royal wives of Ptolemy V Epiphanes (205/4–180 B.C.), was appointed tutor to the king's son, the future Ptolemy VI Philometer (180–145 B.C.), who supposedly sought to prevent Cleopatra I (176 B.C.), Ptolemy VI's mother, from becoming the true ruler of Egypt as regent for her young son. As specified in the will of Ptolemy VI's father, Eulaeus took over the guardianship of the young monarch after Ptolemy V's death and even served as regent. Legally, of course, Ptolemy remained king; however, coins struck during his reign, between 176–170/169 B.C., carried the name of Eulaeus in abbreviated form. Little is known about the background of this influential eunuch, but we cannot rule out the possibility that he was originally a slave. Owing to his education and the wisdom of his counsel he was held in high esteem. In accordance with ancient Egyptian tradition he saw to it that Ptolemy was married to his sister Cleopatra II and then declared of age.

In an effort to disparage eunuchs in general and their achievements in particular, Eulaeus was wrongly accused of responsibility for many of the negative political and economic developments that took place during this period.

We encounter a similar story in ancient literature dealing with Potheinus, "friend of the king" Ptolemy XIII, the official husband of Cleopatra VII, the Egyptian queen famous in history and drama. As guardian of the minor king he fought against Cleopatra and helped to expel her from Egypt. He negotiated with the Romans and presumably ordered the murder of Pompey on 28 September 48 B.C. This part of the story seems to reflect more the usual attempt to belittle eunuchs than it does the actual facts. Eulaeus attempted to maneuver as deftly as possible between Caesar, the royal family, and the eunuch Ganymede, who served Arsinoe. However, he ended up on the losing side and Caesar, Cleopatra's defender, ordered him to be executed.

These examples should suffice to illustrate the function and role of these "confidants" within the governing institutions of ancient states—states that existed by the grace of God whether he was called Aton, Marduk, Ahura Mazda, or even YHWH.

In the sacred chambers of the palace there was no room for normal human activity or relationships. This remained true whether these chambers were found in the ancient Middle East, China, Byzantium, the Islamic caliphates, or, later, behind the walls of medieval castles. The constant interaction between the human and the extra-human sphere, between the monarch and the gods or those who were identified with the gods, called for a measure of chastity and purity that we can even now observe in the practices of archaic cultures that have survived into the modern era. One example is that of Ethiopia, where the idea of the divine right of kings evolved gradually out of a long historical tradition that had its roots in the ancient Middle East and survived intact well into modern times. In countries such as Ethiopia we are able even today to study customs and traditions that serve as a key to a general understanding of sacred kingship as the pivot of power in the state along with the eunuchism associated with that power.

The history and traditions of this nation situated in the northeasternmost part of the Horn of Africa touch on those of the ancient Middle East as well as on the civilizations of the Nile Valley and black Africa to the south. These influences merged to produce an odd picture that has been reconstructed on the basis of ancient accounts and ethnographic observations collected and collated by Eike Haberland (1924–1992), a scholar of Ethiopian history. Thus we find in Ethiopia the formative idea of a virginal boy as the only person allowed to remain overnight in the palace with the king (or other ruler, the title being of secondary importance) and his wives. The boy's sexual immaturity and natural chastity allowed him to be associated with sacred persons and remain with them in their chambers. Arguably what we see expressed here is the archetypal desire of a man or a ruler to be alone with his wife or wives while at the same time showing off his virility and potency. These ideas constitute the theoretical underpinnings of the oriental harem, for the "virginal boy" could continue to keep his job only if he were to have himself castrated.

Ethiopians continued to observe pre-Christian customs even after the highland regions once known as Abyssinia had been Christianized. Now, as in the kingdoms of medieval Europe, only monks had ready access to the king and the royal palace. The French traveler and explorer J. Perruchon has left us some interesting accounts and observations in this regard, which Eike Haberland has included in his *Untersuchungen zum äthiopischen Königtum.* There we read about one of the Ethiopian church's dignitaries: the aged keeper of the watch,[53] the third person in importance at the time in the hierarchy of the Ethiopian Church, whose office one may identify with that of a eunuch:

> Nobody could see him entering or leaving his house. Two or three children alone had access to his residence, which was connected to the king's palisade [i.e., a strong fence for defense surrounding the palace]. If the king needed anything, he [the keeper of the watch] would call one of his loyal monks and send him [to fetch it] regardless of whether it was close by or far away. All this [he

> did] for the glory of the monarchy, for he alone had access to the king. His "virginal boys" never came in contact with any other people and had no home to call their own and always remained inside [the palace]. And when they went out, they did so only in the company of their handlers. They knew no women, never cut their hair without the king's permission and always wore clean [clothing]. If they went to other people's houses to eat, drink or amuse themselves, they would be prosecuted and sentenced to death as would those who had entertained them.[54]

These "chaste boys" and superannuated monks were the only persons permitted to be with the king when he performed ritual acts. They prepared his food, put it in his mouth, and handed him his cup, for neither the king nor his wives was allowed to touch their food or drink. On the other hand, accounts concerning the Christian period reflect a negative attitude toward castrati in spite of the fact that emasculated men could still be found in many places throughout the country.

A different situation obtained in the Islamic kingdoms in the eastern and southern parts of Ethiopia. The customs practiced there seem to have been the same as those observed throughout the rest of the Muslim world. Consequently it is difficult to speculate on the prevailing customs in the kingdom of Axum's pagan past. All the same, the law requiring celibacy was faithfully observed by employing "virginal boys" and old men (who were deemed to be neuters). Ethiopia represents yet another example of the fact that the title "eunuch" could be conferred on a palace official who was not necessarily a castrato.

In the kingdoms of western Christendom, by contrast, eunuchs who were unquestionably castrati had long been employed in a number of official capacities, not only in late antiquity and in the Byzantine Empire, but under the Carolingians, the Hohenstaufen emperors, and the Ottonians as well. Despite the great differences in space and time with regard to our data, we see the emergence of a general picture, the outlines of which allow us to make certain assumptions about the origins of castration-based eunuchism. To the "mythical consciousness" sacred kingship was an essential and charismatic institution established by God or the gods, an institution that necessarily differed from the so-called "normal" world. We see evidence of this even in the Ethiopian dynasties of the 19th and early 20th centuries.

As God's envoy and intermediary and, in some cases, even as the god himself, the king was endowed with certain magical, healing, and supernatural powers. Given his unique status, he would make offerings to the gods so as to maintain the cycle of life. Sometimes he would even sacrifice himself (the ritual killing of the king) or, as a substitute, his virility and sexual potency by re-enacting the cultic rite of emasculation. And since the act had a mythic significance, the king probably did not suffer the same consequences as other men who underwent the operation. One need only think of the divine monarch Osiris, whose fertility was restored by Isis, or of the later idea—espoused in particular by the Chinese—that castrati would eventually regain their procreative power after a certain period of time had elapsed. It was because of notions such as these that the Muslims made it a practice to remove both the testicles and the penis and to inspect court eunuchs, especially harem attendants, on a regular basis.

Since it was impossible in reality to restore the capability to procreate, substitute rituals were instituted. For example, a temporary "substitute" king would be elected who could then be castrated in lieu of the actual ruler. This helps to explain not only the special nature of the king's office; it also suggests why castrati were able on occasion to occupy such high positions at court, only to end up—in place of the king again—as a scapegoat for malcontents.

What we observe in history is a constant struggle between the idea of a chosen ruler (elected by God, an oracle, a council of elders, etc.) and that of a ruler who has come to power because of his lineage. Whereas the former could manage without castrated eunuchs, the latter appointed them to positions at court in order to ensure that their dynasty would continue. Naturally this presupposed that only a man capable of reproducing could become the king or ruler. The birth of a royal child was considered proof that the monarchy would be extended into the future.

This archaic notion of the importance of "one's issue" has survived, in rudimentary form, into the modern era, so that even now some Christian cultures regard infertility as grounds for divorce, for dissolving the "indissoluble bonds of holy matrimony." This brings to light a more recent phenomenon, namely patriliny. Together with the idea that the divine right of kings was hereditary, the practice of patriliny was used to pave the way for dynasticism. The result of all this was that usurpers would try to eliminate legitimate pretenders to the throne and, failing that, have them castrated and thereby rendered sterile and incapable of producing royal progeny. Later developments may have obscured the archaic beginnings of eunuchism, making it impossible to clarify the origin of the court eunuch. Consequently scholars resorted to their ideological preconceptions, trying to explain the phenomenon by usng popular socioeconomic theories and labeling eunuchs slaves. As a result of their asexuality, castrati had a unique status, possibly in a religious sense as well. On the one hand they were no longer part of this world. And on the other they were not yet part of another. Whether they also represented a permament warning sign as to the future of the dominions of this earth or symbolized various apocalyptic fears and hopes is another question, one that would thrust itself on people's consciousness whenever sacred kingship was in danger of collapse. On one side there were emasculated priests and on the other castrated slaves, useful creatures who posed no danger of polluting the blood line or, if you will, of overwhelming the victor by infiltrating their blood—the blood of the vanquished—into that of his progeny. It was between these two poles that institutions developed and took root that increasingly shaped the image of states. And even though various *éminences grises* and other confidential advisors of the sovereign often made the real decisions in these states, their renown paled so in comparison to the brillliant light of the king's glory that posterity did not even deem them worth mentioning.

Nature provided the model for the usefulness of castrating the creatures of this earth. Thus Hesiod wrote:

> Nor is the early sixth either suitable
> for a girl-child
> to be born, but for gelding kids, and lambs,

and for putting
an enclosure around the sheeppen
it is a day kind and propitious.[55]

Still, castration was not always a necessary precondition for being a dignitary at the king's court. Eunuchs doubtless continued to function as "bedchamber attendants," as the Greek term suggests. They were specially entrusted to make sure that the occupants of the bedchamber had a good night's sleep, and they were also privy to many of the sleepers' secrets. It is impossible to determine with any precision the social classes from which eunuchs were recruited, especially if one considers the different cultures, societies, and periods in which they are encountered. On the one hand they could be relatives, even one's own children. And on the other they might be especially talented and trustworthy longtime companions, priests or advisors (or all in one), or finally catamites for either sex. History is replete with stories, reports, and graphic portrayals of eunuchs that come to us from the spheres of religion, government, culture, and personal life. And since these various areas are inextricably intertwined, it is impossible to tell where one ends and another begins.

The West's earliest glimpses into the ancient past came from the picture of the world presented in the Old Testament. Later, other historical sources and the accelerating pace of archeological research expanded our knowledge of that bygone world. Eunuchism and the practice of castration grew out of ancient fertility cults. These same cults also gave rise to castration rituals that were modeled on the activities of the gods and ultimately provided a rationale for emasculation as a means for providing protection to the king's wives. Since goddesses were surrounded by self-emasculated men, their earthly counterparts demanded no less for themselves. And human beings, steeped in mythology, had no scruples when it came to mindlessly imitating the gods.

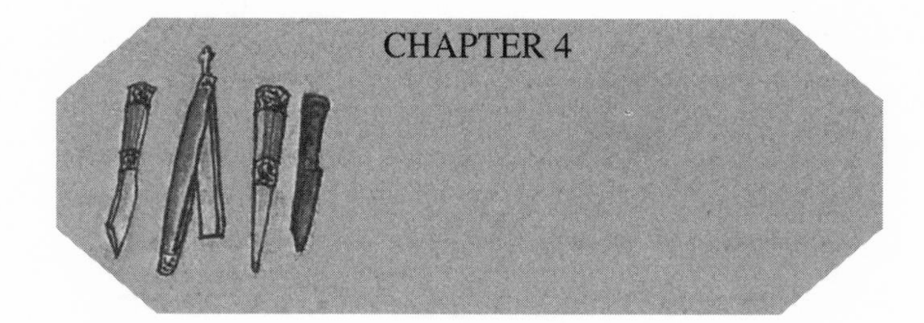

Eunuchs in the Hellenistic and Roman Worlds

> "What morals! What times!" said Tully long ago, when Catiline was plotting impious villainy, when daughter's spouse and father[56] were clashing in murderous combat and the sad soil was doused with civil slaughter. But why do you now say 'What morals!' why now 'What times!' What is there to displease you, Maecilianus? No brutality of war lords, madness of the sword is here. We can enjoy assured peace and happiness. It's not *our* morals that make you despise your times, Maecilianus, it's your own."
>
> —Martial, *Epigrams* 9.70

Orgiastic religions made their way from the Orient to the cultures and peoples of the western Mediterranean at a very early period in history. The process was facilitated by the influence of Semitic colonies of Phoenicians in Carthage, Sicily, and the Iberian peninsula as well as by the adoption of foreign gods and cultures, which the Greeks and Romans generally felt were alien to their way of life. Among these imports were Dionysos and his retinue of maenads and satyrs and the later cult of Cybele and Attis with its eunuch priests, the emasculated *galloi* or *galli*. Both cults—they have even been called religions—were associated with popular ideas and myths about vegetable life that dated back to the prehistoric past. The archeological evidence for the Asian origin of these cults can be found in the shrine of the Great Mother at Çatak Hüyük (Anatolia) that dates from the 7th century B.C. Here in Phrygia in west central Asia Minor, where many religious and cultural currents intersected, these cults flourished. It was also here that syncretic forms of these cults developed with great rapidity, making their influence felt into late antiquity and in some instances even into the Middle Ages. Various external circumstances and the course of history in general favored the spread of these cults, thereby laying the foundations for the future great religions of the world that are so intimately connected to the rise and fall of ancient Mediterranean civilizations.

The cult of Cybele and Attis arrived in Rome in 204 B.C. at the time of the Punic Wars and later, under the empire, spread throughout the Roman state, where it reached its zenith. In the second millennium B.C. Cybele was known to the Hittites and Hurrians as Kubaba. Later she was worshiped as the "mother with the mural crown" at a shrine erected in her honor at Pessinus by King Midas in the 8th century B.C. With the approval of Apollo's oracle at Delphi, the cult was imported to Rome toward the end of the second Punic War (218–201 B.C.), where Cybele became known as the *Magna Mater*, great mother [of the gods]. The Romans called her *Mater deorum Magna Idaea*.

The Romans acted instinctively to make Cybele part of their

The fertility goddess Cybele with Attis in a heavenly vehicle (ca. 400 A.D.).
Attis castrated himself out of love for Cybele;
many priests of this cult followed his example.
(Milan Soprintenza Archaeol. della Lombardia)

ancient heritage and link the cult to Vergil's epic of the Trojan Aeneas, the traditional founder of Rome. Aeneas's home was therefore identified with that of Cybele and the kingdom of Pergamum, which had entered into friendship with Rome. From the beginning the cult of the Mater Magna was celebrated as a national festival from which slaves and foreigners were excluded, a practice that was problematical given the oriental nature of the cult. Therefore the city fathers tried, though without success, to banish and suppress the oriental cult of Attis that was inextricably linked to Cybele. The introduction of the cult to the "Seven Hills of Rome" began when its symbol, a sacred black meteorite, was taken by ship from Pessinus (where a temple, the Megalesion [Megalesia = Cybele], had been built in honor of the goddess) to Pergamum. From Pergamum it was transported on a magnificent vessel to the gates of Rome, whence it was brought into the city in a ceremonial procession. This is how Livy (59 B.C.–A.D. 17) described the event:

> This young Scipio, then was ordered to meet the Goddess at Ostia, accompanied by the married women of Rome; he was to receive her out of the ship, carry her ashore, and deliver her into the matrons' hands. When his ship, according to instructions, reached the mouth of the Tiber, he sailed on out to sea, received the Goddess from the priests, and took her ashore. The leading women of Rome, of whom one distinguished name is that of Claudia Quinta, then took her from him—Claudia, whose previously dubious reputation, the story goes, has made her virtue all the more famous in after times as a result of this solemn service in the cause of religion. The women then passed the Goddess from hand to hand, one

> to another in succession, while all the population came thronging to meet her; censers were placed before the doorways on her route with burning incense, and many prayers were offered that she might enter the city of Rome with kindly purpose and benignant thoughts. So the procession moved on, till they brought her to the temple of Victory on the Palatine. It was the day before the Ides of April, and that day was held sacred. People crowded to the Palatine with gifts to the Goddess, and there was a Strewing of Couches and Games, called the Megalesia.[57]

The sacred stone, which was said to have magical properties, was first housed temporarily in the temple of Victory on the Palatine. That same year the construction of a temple in honor of the goddess was begun. The anniversary of the inauguration of this temple was celebrated annually on 4 April. The temple was completed ten years later, in 191 B.C., and dedicated to Cybele. From 4–10 April, public games, the Megalensia (*Ludi Megalenses*), were held to commemorate her arrival in Rome. During the festival animals were sacrificed, plays staged, games put on in the Circus Maximus, and banquets held. Ovid (43 B.C.–A.D. 17) has given us a memorable description of the festivities:

> Let the heavens revolve three times on their eternal axis,
> let the Sun hitch and unhitch his horses three times,
> and at once the curved Bercyntian flute will blow and
>   the festival
> of the Great Mother of Ida will commence.
> The eunuchs will parade and strike their hollow tambourines,
> and cymbal clashing on cymbal will jingle.

"They beat cymbals instead of helmets, tambourines
instead of shields:
as before, the flute produces Phrygian tunes."
She was finished. I began. "Why does the fierce lion species
serve the goddess as unusual beasts of burden?"
I was finished. She began. "People believe their ferocity
is gentled by her, as her chariot attests."
"But why is her head loaded down with a crown
bearing towers?
Because she gave towers to the earliest cities?"
She nodded. "Where," I asked, "does the impulse for
self-castration
come from?" When I was silent, she began to speak:
"In the woods, a remarkably handsome Phrygian boy, Attis,
held the tower-bearing goddess in chains of pure love.
She wanted to keep him for herself, to safeguard her temple,
and said,
'Make sure that you want to be a boy forever.'
He gave his word at her behest and said, 'If I am untrue,
let the love I cheat you with be my last.'
He cheated her with the nymph Sagaritis, and ceased to be
what he'd been.
The goddess' wrath exacted a price from the girl:
she cut down the Naiad with blows inflicted on a tree,
and that one
was done for; the tree was the Naiad's talisman.
Attis went mad, and believing his bedroom ceiling
was collapsing,
he took off and headed for the heights of Dindymus.
Now he shouted, 'Take away the torches,' now, 'Take away
the whips,' often swearing the Furies were after him.
He even hacked at his body with a sharp rock,

> and dragged his long hair in the filthy dust.
> He cried, 'I deserved it, I'll pay the deserved price in blood.
> I wish that these parts which harmed me were done for.
> I wish they were done for,' he repeated: he removed the
> burden of his groin,
> and suddenly there wasn't a trace of his manhood left.
> This madness set an example and the soft acolytes toss
> their hair and cut off their worthless organs."[58]

In detailing the exotic aspects of the festivities Ovid also suggested why the Roman state wanted to separate the cult of Cybele and Attis from the worship of the *Mater Magna*, which, by the way, it never succeeded in doing. As early as 102 B.C., Roman authorities expelled a slave who had emasculated himself during a service in honor of Cybele. In 77 B.C., however, the *galli*, being freedmen, were granted full civil rights. The picture painted by Ovid reflects the ascendency and spread of the cult whose temple was situated near the emperor's residence. During classical antiquity there was no single explanation for the cultic castrations described by Ovid; they were interpreted as representing everything from a sign of mourning for a "suffering god" to an expression of joyfulness at his victory and salvation. Nevertheless, the essence of the Cybele and Attis legend, which spanned nearly two millennia, remained unchanged. The themes that recur are the love between Cybele and Attis, leading to the death of Attis following his remorse at his unfaithfulness to Cybele, and culminating in his resurrection in the fruitful womb of the *Mater Magna*. The ceremonies associated with the myth developed into remarkable displays of religious emotion that were heightened by the annual lamentations for Attis as his "pine tree" was carried in procession into the temple of Cybele. Clearly the myth made a lasting impression on Catullus in the first century A.D.:

> Rapidly carried over the towering seas in his vessel,
> when speed & desire led his feet to the Phrygian woodlands
> Attis rushed into that forest-encircled place of the Goddess,
> and there, stung by the fury of madness to utter distraction
> he took a piece of sharp flint & hacked off the weight
> of his manhood.
> Then, just as soon as she felt that her limbs were no
> longer virile,
> while her fresh blood was still staining the soil of the earth
> beneath her,
> she quickly seized in her snow white hands the tambour
> you love so,
> that tambour whose rhythms summon men to your mysteries,
> Mother;
> and as her delicate fingers rattled that shell of taut oxhide,
> she sang these words in a high-pitched, quavering voice to
> her comrades:
> "Go up to her mountain forests together, O Gallae, get going,
> go on together, wandering sheep of the Lady Cybele!
> —you who have chosen to live as exiles in hostile
> surroundings,
> obedient to my orders, going wherever I led you,
> bravely enduring the truculent waters of a salt crossing;
> you who've emasculated yourselves out of hatred for Venus,
> now gladden the heart of your own mistress by rushing
> in mazes!
> Empty your minds of delay & go on together, go ranging
> the Phrygian home of Cybele, Phrygian woods of the
> Goddess,

where the cymbals clash together & where the tambour
re-echoes,
where the Phrygian flutist hurls out the clear note from
his curved reed,
where the frenzied Maenads toss their passionate heads
crowned with ivy,
where wild ululations announce the form of their worship,
where the mad horde of the Goddess Cybele goes to be
aimless,
where it is right that we meet together for intricate dancing."
As soon as Attis, that counterfeit woman, finished her
singing,
her band of orgiasts flutter their tongues & cry out insanely:
their beaten tambours bellow, their cymbals clatter in answer
as the swift dancers go on their sinuous way to Mount Ida.
—With Attis leading them rushing to wander breathless
in frenzy
the rest of them plunge into the dark forest, strung out
behind one
who bolts like an unbroken ox, shy of the yoke's heavy
burden:
racing, the Gallae surge in the path of their turbulent leader.
Reaching the shrine of Cybele at last, they drop in
exhaustion,
too tired from their exertions even to bother with eating.
A leaden drowsiness seals the eyes they can scarcely
keep open
and the great fury of madness leaves them to lie there
in quiet.
But when the golden-faced Sun arose & with radiant vision
surveyed the clarified air, the firm earth & the formless
waters,

while his fresh horses were busy scattering Night's tattered
shadows,
Attis woke up abruptly as Slumber rushed off from
beside him,
anxious to lie down in love once more with divine Pasithea.
—No longer sleeping, no longer held by his turbulent
madness,
Attis turned his mind to those things which he had done
to himself and
calmly now, clearly, he saw where he was & what he
was lacking:
struck with horror, he ran back to the windblown fringe
of the ocean
and stood there in tears, staring out over that desolate
vastness,
wretchedly mourning his loss in these words, addressed
to his homeland

. . . .

"Is there a single form which my body hasn't already taken?
A woman now, once a young man, an adolescent, a boychild,
and in those days a brilliant athlete, the pride of the
gamefield:
lovers thronged at my doorway, they crowded hotly on
my threshold,
leaving the front of my house strewn with their colorful
garlands
before I rose from my bed & went out each morning at
daybreak.
Must I now be called a priestess? Must I be Cybele's
handmaid?
A Maenad—a broken part of what I was—a barren creature?
Must I be forced to remain here on the snow heights of

Mount Ida?
Must I spend my life under the towering Phrygian summits
with the deer that haunts the woods & the boar that
wanders the forests?"

. . . .

Mighty Goddess, Goddess Cybele, sacred Mistress of
Dindymus,
grant that my house may be kept safe from all your furor,
my Lady:
drive others off into frenzy, drive others off into madness.[59]

Catullus's poetry had a long-lasting impact over the centuries. It stimulated the imagination of painters such as Andrea Mantegna (1431–1506), Pietro Perugino (1448–1523), and Arnold Böcklin (1827–1901), and it inspired modern librettists and composers to take the material that formed the basis of the strange love of Attis for Cybele and transform it into great works of art. Thus we find two operas bearing the name *Atys*—one composed by Jean-Baptiste Lully (1632–1687), a naturalized Frenchman attached to the court of Louis XIV, and the other by Niccolò Piccini (1827–1900), the last great representative of the Neapolitan school.

Despite the fact that there were celebrations of the myth in which different traditions confronted one another, the festival featuring Attis's castration ultimately became the most important. Known as *Sanguem*, the Day of Blood, it was celebrated, as Catullus tells us, by novice *galli* on 24 March. Though it seems that the festivals in honor of Attis were originally put on the March calendar in order to separate them from the April festivals, one cannot rule out the possibility that, in accordance with oriental custom, they were movable holidays corresponding to the phases of the moon.

Accounts of the emasculation of the priests of Attis have come down to us even from the Greeks, in particular Pausanias[60] and Arnobius.[61] With only a few discrepancies, they recounted the same legendary Phrygian myth, a myth they had hellenized and that therefore called for some amplification. And since we can now draw more easily than before upon the wealth of resources offered by the vanished local religions of Asia Minor, we can supplement their version of the myth. Newly discovered monuments and texts now enable us to understand the origin, development and spread of the myth in all its various forms.

Thus—according to the mythological narratives—the Olympian god Zeus engendered the hermaphrodite Agdistis/Cybele by spilling his sperm over a mountain. In other traditions the bisexual Cybele grew out of the earth, a story which finds expression in the name of the mountain near Pessinus whence the meteorite came—Mount Agdus. The sacred stone was later transported to the temple of Cybele in Rome. The close connection to mountains and rocks is also reflected in the archaic traditions of castration and circumcision, operations that in cultic practice were to be performed only with knives made of stone.

Taken together with the Hittite sources that Volkert Haas has collected and partly translated in his book *Hethitische Berggötter*, all these myths can logically be viewed as variants of a single archetype. According to the Hittite sources the legend originated in events that took place after the Flood. As in all other stories of the Flood that derive from Asia Minor, the supreme god was angry at mankind and decided to destroy it.

Only one god-fearing couple escaped after having spent nine days and nine nights in their ark. The couple was saved. As a sign of their gratitude they offered sacrifices and received instructions from god to create a new race of human beings "by covering their heads and unfastening their girdles and casting the 'bones of the Mother,' that is, stones, 'behind them.'"[62] From the stones thrown by the man, men were created, and from those thrown by the woman, women emerged. This also explains the special significance accorded to stones as living things.

Let us once again give the ancient authors a chance to speak. Since the gods feared the power of the hermaphrodite Agdistis/Cybele, they ordered Dionysos to castrate him. According to Arnobius, Dionysos added wine to the spring from which Agdistis/Cybele drank, causing the hermaphrodite to become intoxicated. Dionysos was thus able to subdue him and tie his genitals to a tree. On waking, Agdistis leapt to his feet with such force that he inadvertently emasculated himself. From the remnants of his genitals a magnificent almond tree shot up. Nana, the beautiful daughter of the River Sangarios, then picked a blossom off the tree and put it into her bosom. The bosom can be equated with the womb, similar to the way in which female deities are depicted with a so-called belly altar in ancient Semitic monuments.

Suddenly the blossom vanished, and Nana found herself pregnant. She subsequently gave birth to a boy, Attis, whom she abandoned but who was kept alive by a nanny-goat. Then Agdistis/Cybele fell in love with Attis. However, the king of Pessinus wanted Attis to marry his daughter. In his jealousy Agdistis/Cybele drove Attis mad. Attis then emasculated himself under a pine tree and died. Seeing Attis dying, the bereaved Agdistis/Cybele regretted his behavior and beseeched Zeus to raise Attis from the dead and resuscitate him. The god, however, refused his request and only allowed Attis's body to remain uncorrupted, his hair to grow, and his little finger to stay alive and move.

This myth, which has a number of features in common with Semitic (Adonis) and Egyptian (Isis and Osiris) vegetation myths, formed the basis of the self-emasculation practiced by the priests of Cybele and Attis, the *galli*. The process of syncretism made the Cybele and Attis cycle of myths increasingly opaque, mingling the cults of Dionysos and Cybele/*Mater Magna* in a number of strange ways. One example is the story of the music-obsessed Silenus Marsyas, which reflects the struggle among different religious traditions within Greece. The castration of the mythical pipe-player, which is only hinted at and never made explicit, does not hide the fact of his ultimate triumph over native Greek traditions. His instrument, the panpipe or syrinx, was a regular feature in many rituals and festivals associated with vegetation gods and represented an important element in oriental art. The literature of antiquity has presented us with a vivid picture of colorful processions that began when the sun reached the vernal equinox, the celebrants ululating loudly and dancing wildly to the accompaniment of shrill and orgiastic music—a sight that surely bewildered the Romans. After certain introductory rites, such as the carrying of reeds in procession to commemorate the first days of Attis's life, the celebrations of the cult continued with the cutting down of a pine tree which was decked with violets and carried in procession into the temple where it was laid in state.

This was followed by several days of mourning and abstinence until 24 March, the *dies sanguinis*. On this day the *galli*, whipped into a state of religious ecstasy by music and dancing, flagellated themselves until the blood came and with it they sprinkled the effigy of the goddess Cybele, her altar, and various cult objects. Novices who were about to enter the priesthood emasculated themselves—according to an archaic custom—with a sharp stone or potsherd. This was followed by the day of joy and relaxation (*hilaria* and *requietio*) and finally the day of bathing (*lavatio*) at the little Almo river, where cult objects and effigies of the goddess were also cleansed.

The priests regarded emasculation as an expiatory sacrifice. They considered themselves Cybele's slaves. This is attested by their tattoos which were covered by gold leaf after they died. In their ecstasy they tried to use pain and suffering to free themselves from sensual lusts in the hope of overcoming the materialism of life and saving their souls. This idea lived on for quite some time, not only in the gnosticism that flourished in the early centuries of the Christian church, but also in some Russian Orthodox sects such as the *skoptsi*.

As the cult developed in Rome, especially during the imperial period, its goddess coalesced in a general syncretism with other, mostly oriental, deities. In fact, the same priests often participated in the rituals of many different cults. Substitute castrations were performed in the cult of Cybele. The Roman emperor Elagabulus (whose real name was Varius Avitus, his imperial name being M. Aurelius Antoninus, 218–222) subjected himself to just such an act and also took part in the so-called *taurobolium* (the capture or killing of the bull). He later assumed the office of *archigallos*, high priest. In the *Historia*

Augusta we read:

> He also adopted the worship of the Great Mother and celebrated the rite of the taurobolium; and he carried off her image and the sacred objects which are kept hidden in a secret place. He would toss his head to and fro among the castrated devotees of the goddess, and he infibulated himself, and did all that the eunuch-priests are wont to do; and the image of the goddess which he carried off he placed in the sanctuary of his god [the sun god]. He also celebrated the rite of Salambo [Tanit, Mater Magna] with all the wailing and the frenzy of the Syrian cult . . . [63]

The ritual of sacrificing the bull was initially performed in connection with the cult of Cybele/*Mater Magna* in the 2nd century B.C. It seems to have been a substitute for castration. The initiates who took part in the sacrifice would descend into a pit covered with boards in which holes had been drilled. On the wooden platform over the pit a bull would be killed and its blood would drip down through the holes onto the heads of the initiates. As it was being slaughtered the bull was also castrated and thereby served as a substitute for emasculating the initiates.

This gruesome ritual was also practiced in other oriental cults of Mithras, for example in the Phrygian and Thracian cult of the god Sabazios which in late antiquity had spread as far as ancient Germany. Ecstatic, orgiastic cults embraced all social classes and characterized many syncretic Hellenistic religions, with all their well-known deities—Bellona, Isis, Dionysos/Bacchus, and Jupiter Dolichenus. The devotees of these gods were called *fanatici*, "those who are attached to a temple (*fanum*)." Mysteries were special initiation ceremonies that were esoteric in character and encompassed a variety of rites. At the heart of these mysteries were phenomena that we would now describe, along with Arnold van Gennep, as rites of passage, and esoteric practices that covered the various stages of initiation into hermetic knowledge. The obligation to strict secrecy is one of the reasons that our picture of the mysteries is sketchy. Here is how Apuleius (123–c. 170), who was himself an initiate into the mysteries of Isis, reveals some of its secrets:

> Perhaps, my zealous reader, you are eager to learn what was said and done next. I would tell if it were permitted to tell; you would learn if it were permitted to hear. But both ears and tongue would incur equal guilt, the latter from its unholy talkativeness, the former from their unbridled curiosity. Since your suspense, however, is perhaps a matter of religious longing, I will not continue to torture you and keep you in anguish. Therefore listen, but believe: these things are true. I came to the boundary of death and, having trodden the threshold of Proserpina, I travelled through all the elements and returned. In the middle of the night I saw the sun flashing with bright light. I came face to face with the gods below and the gods above and paid reverence to them from close at hand. Behold, I have told you things which perforce you may not know, although you have heard them. . . .[64]

The origin of the mysteries can be traced back to the archaic period of chthonic cults, fertility rites, and the doctrine of the four elements. The mysteries took their character from their own gods and local sanctuaries. Thus the mysteries of Demeter, for instance, were celebrated at Eleusis. Only the *mustai* (initiates) were initiated into all the rituals and secrets of the mysteries; they alone were vouchsafed direct knowledge of the existence of God and could rest assured that their souls would enter the next world. The later development of the mysteries in the Hellenistic and Roman worlds only reinforced and confirmed these ideas. The gradual decline of the ancient pagan mysteries took place in tandem with the rise of Christianity. As a result the last temples to fight steadfastly against the new doctrine of salvation—the temple of Serapis in Alexandria (389) and that of Isis on Philae (535)—were shut down.

Nonetheless, certain practices became part of the cultic area of the Church's life and were thus preserved, albeit with new meanings attached to them. Other aspects of the mysteries fueled superstitions and popular religion and were revived during the Renaissance.

Ecstasy played a central role in the Dionysian, oriental, and Hellenistic mysteries. By ecstasy we mean a physical and psychological state of exaltation in which one stands outside or transcends oneself, a state induced by enthusiasm verging on frenzy or "ritual madness." Today, however, the term enthusiasm has lost its original concrete religious referent. If we accept the definition of ecstasy offered by Wunibald Müller as representative of modern psychology, the word means a deeply felt life-sustaining experience. Ecstasy has also been viewed as an escape from our mundane existence, as a state of intoxication, and even as madness.

Cultic castration was not the only form of emasculation in antiquity that the Greeks and Romans had long barred their citizens from practicing. It is unlikely therefore that the *archi-*

Gallos, the chief priest of the Magna Mater. In this relief, which emphasizes his feminized appearance, he is surrounded by all the characteristic symbols of the Cybele cult. (Museum of the Capitol, Rome)

galli referred to in imperial decrees dealing with cults in the Roman empire were castrati, for they were usually recruited from among the Roman populace and their duties were apt to be more of an administrative than a religious nature. Thus it is probable that castration was performed mainly on foreigners and slaves. From the seven Greek terms for emasculation—*spadon* ("tear off"), *ektomias* ("cut out"), *tomias* ("castrate an animal"), *apokopos* ("cut off"), *thlibias* ("squeeze" or "crush"), *thladias* ("crush the testicles"), and *ithris* ("eunuch")—and the roughly ten Latin terms—which include the word *castrare*, of course ("castration")—we can infer that castration was a widespread practice, which, as we have already noted, served a variety of purposes. It was not only an essential part of cultic activities; it fulfilled the hopes of homosexuals who felt they could thereby preserve their youthfulness and live as catamites (*pathici*), male prostitutes. Finally, we should mention the medical, moral, transsexual, and "sexually aesthetic" reasons for castration that run like an invisible thread through many spheres of culture and life.

The numbers and value of castrati increased markedly during the Age of Hellenism, in late antiquity and in the periods immediately following antiquity. The oriental institution of the court eunuch became synonymous with extravagance and wastefulness. The slave trade flourished and catamites became "products" that were in great demand, even among the Romans who had enacted strict laws forbidding the practice—and yet continually amended them to suit the whims of individual emperors. Finally, even though castration was prohibited in the empire, Roman law permitted traffic in non-Roman eunuchs up to the time of Justinian I, as we gather from reading the *Codex Justinianus* : "We ordain that Romans who have been castrated abroad or on Roman soil should not become the property of another person. The harshest penalty shall be imposed on those who have dared to perpetrate such acts . . . However we grant permission to all merchants and all others engaged in commerce to buy and sell, wherever they wish, castrati of foreign extraction who have been emasculated in territories outside our dominions."[65]

Castrati were considered luxury items and were rarely used for slave labor. The prices paid for them reflect the so-called "economic factor." A slave laborer in Rome in the second to first centuries B.C. cost 500 denars, whereas a castrato commanded 2000 denars, which corresponds to the figures cited by Terence in his comedy *The Eunuch*. There is evidence, however, that these numbers may actually be underestimates, because we know that ordinary slaves sometimes commanded as much as 250 times the figures cited above. Thus Pliny the Elder (23–79) reports in his *Natural History* on the excessive price paid for the catamite Pæzon:

> The highest price ever given for a man born in slavery, so far as I am able to discover, was that paid for Daphnus, the grammarian, who was sold by Natius of Pisaurum to M. Scaurus, the first man in the state, for seven hundred thousand sesterces. In our day, no doubt, comic actors have fetched a higher price, but then they were purchasing their own freedom. In the time of our ancestors, Roscius, the actor, gained five hundred thousand sesterces annually. Perhaps, too, a person might in the present instance refer to the case of the army commissary in the Armenian war, which was of late years undertaken in

> favour of Tiridates; which officer, in our own time, received his manumission from Nero for the sum of thirteen million sesterces; but, in this case, the consideration was the profit to be derived from the war, and it was not the value of the man that was paid for. And so, too, when Lutorius Priscus bought of Sejanus, the eunuch, Pæzon, for fifty million sesterces, the price was given, by Hercules! rather to gratify the passion of the purchaser, than in commendation of the beauty of the slave. Universal sorrow and consternation then reigning, the public were too much pre-occupied with it to put a stop to a bargain of so scandalous a nature.[66]

The values reflected in this account reveal certain trends in imperial Rome, the tendency toward excess, for example, which permeated society, particularly the imperial court. Why were eunuchs held in such high esteem that people would pay any price to acquire them, and why had they become such status symbols? Effeminacy and impotence were triumphant. Although effeminate men were in great demand during antiquity, they were also derided in the comedies of the time in which their distinguishing characteristics—pale skin, beardlessness, soprano voice, and certain physical features peculiar to hermaphrodites—were the object of satire. There was a wealth of terms to describe these characteristics: "half-man" (*semivir*); "gelding" (*eviratus*); "womanish man" (*mollis*); "castrated catamite"; a "man who dances like a woman" (*malakos*). Together they suggest the range of archetypal images produced by the cast of mind representative of antiquity, images that continued to have an impact long after the ancient world had vanished from the stage of history. The word *effeminatus* ("womanish") became a term of abuse that lived on in European proverbs, fables, and folktales. Examples of this use of the word, including those taken from the realm of dreams, can be found in the works of authors ranging from Aesop (6th century B.C.) to Artemidorus (2nd century A.D.). Thus the appearance of eunuchs in a dream indicated false expectations: "Castrated men and eunuchs . . . these men, even if they say nothing, indicate false expectations, since they cannot be numbered among men or among women due to their physical condition."[67]

These motifs of classical antiquity, as we shall see, resonated throughout the Middle Ages, in the Renaissance, and down to the modern era. Castrati were not only objects of ridicule; they also had an aura of the exotic. As the "third sex" they created quite a stir, especially as the influence of the Orient began to make itself felt on Roman fashions and ideas. Nevertheless castrated men remained isolated and alienated in a society that ultimately held them in contempt. Ironically, it was for this very reason that they became such loyal and trustworthy servants of their masters.

Castrati, who more often than not came from outside the empire, were commonly bought or presented as gifts when they were just young boys and so came into the possession of private households or the courts of the nobility at a very early age. The fact that they were acquired when they were so young plus the fact that eunuchs had a relatively long life span served only to strengthen the bonds that developed between them and their masters, especially if they were also employed as teachers or tutors. Since they were often recruited from the priesthood, eunuchs were frequently masters of many disciplines, including medicine and astrology. Their abilities in these fields enabled them to exercise a considerable influence not only on the private lives of rulers but on their political decision-making as well, an influence that Franz Cumont (1868–1947) documented in his study on astrology in Ptolemaic Egypt. Ancient sources attest to the fact that eunuchs were well educated. Josephus Flavius (37–95), for instance, in discussing his son's education reported that even Jews—who strictly forbade the practice of castration—would have their sons instructed by emasculated slaves.[68] Part of the reason was doubtless the fact that slaves from the Hellenized Orient tended to have a broader educational background than Romans, who were schooled mainly in the art of warfare. Nevertheless the Romans still felt quite drawn to the Orient and its customs, as the history of the early empire shows. Castrated slaves and servants were part of daily life in both pagan and later Christian antiquity. They accompanied their masters and mistresses on the street, on trips, and in both their public and private lives. Whether it was in the bathroom or the bedroom, while their masters or mistresses were doing their toilet, or in their capacity as tasters and cupbearers—eunuchs were to be found throughout the household. In short, they made themselves indispensable. They carried their master's umbrella and fan. They were the most respected barbers. And they composed the troupe of variety artists who entertained their master's guests at banquets with their musical performancs and singing. Thus it was said that Sporus, Nero's catamite, delighted listeners with the beauty of his voice. Even though the practice of castrating boys for sexual reasons had been outlawed in Rome, the frequent reference to this phenomenon confirms the extent to which the custom had actually spread. There was a feeling that one could preserve the beauty of ephebes—which was more highly esteemed in antiquity than that of women—and their youthful appearance if they were castrated in their prime. Petronius gives a striking description of the practice:

> It shames me to speak out, detail our fate
> of ruin—the way they seize, emasculate
> young men half-grown (if that), break them to lust
> *à la Persane*, and by forestalling, trust
> to halt the hastening years and manhood's flight
> while nature lacks itself . . . [69]

Specifically, these ideals of beauty derived from the exaltation of the androgyne and the hermaphrodite. We can trace them back to the influence of the oriental aesthetic, which also helped to shape the Hellenistic idea of the beautiful.

A few catamites are known by their real names, even though their lovers often gave them different ones. The best known is probably Sporus, a freedman whom we have already mentioned. Nero fell in love with him because he looked so much like the Emperor's second wife, Poppaea Sabina, who had died in 65. Cassius Dio (c. 155–after 229) recounts the story of Sporus's castration:

> Nero missed her [Poppaea Sabina] so greatly after her death that on learning of a woman who resembled her he at first sent for her and kept her; but later he caused a boy of the freedmen, whom he used to call Sporus, to be castrated, since he, too, resembled Sabina, and he used him in every way like a wife. In due time, though already "married" to Pythagoras, a freedman, he formally "married" Sporus, and assigned the boy a regular dowry

> according to contract; and the Romans as well as others publicly celebrated their wedding.[70]

Nero in fact went on a honeymoon to Greece with his catamite, about which Suetonius (70–120) writes:

> . . . he [Nero] took him [Sporus] to his palace with a great crowd in attendance, and treated him as a wife. A rather amusing joke is still going the rounds: the world would have been a happier place had Nero's father Domitius married that sort of wife. He dressed Sporus in the fine clothes normally worn by an Empress and took him in his own litter not only to every Greek assize and fair, but actually through the Street of the Sigillaria at Rome, kissing him amorously now and then.[71]

Sporus was Nero's paramour until the Emperor committed suicide (68). He then "married" Nymphidius Sabinus, who had entertained hopes of becoming emperor, and was called Poppaea. Nymphidius Sabinus's death drove Sporus into the arms of Emperor Otho (30–69) and Vitellius (15–69), Nero's former friends, who had hoped thereby to legitimize their claim to power. However Sporus chose the same fate that had befallen his emperors. Here is Cassius Dio's account:

> Vitellius, when he heard about it, remained where he was and even then went on with his luxurious living, among other things arranging gladitorial combats. In the course of these it was proposed that Sporus should be brought on to the stage in the role of a maiden being ravished, but he would not endure the shame and committed suicide beforehand.[72]

There were of course court eunuchs before the reign of

Nero, as Peter Guyot has discussed in some detail. Their increased prominence was doubtless connected to the spread of the Cybele and Attis cult. The first well-known eunuchs at the court of Claudius represented the first class of influential bureaucrats. They had been appointed by the Emperor to counterbalance the power of the knights and senators. In 202, C. Fulvius Plautianus, prefect of the guards to Septimus Severus (193–211), ordered a hundred castrations to be performed so that he could bequeath a powerful household to his daughter, Fulvia Plautilla, the wife of Antoninus Caracalla (198–217). According to the *Historia Augusta,* eunuchs were the real rulers of the empire. Court eunuchs rose to positions of great power under Elagabulus, for instance, and many bizarre stories were told about the Emperor:

> He would likewise model the expression of his face on that with which Venus is usually painted, and he had his whole body depilated, deeming it the chief enjoyment of life to appear fit and worthy to arouse the lusts of the greatest number. He took money for honours and distinctions and positions of power, selling them in person or through his slaves to those who served his lusts.[73]

Under Severus Alexander (222–235), Elagabulus's successor, conditions at court changed for a while, though under Gordian III (238–244) eunuchs once again rose to positions of power. The *Historia Augusta* has the following to say about Alexander's reign:

> He removed all eunuchs from his service and gave orders that they should serve his wife as slaves. And whereas Elagabulus had been the slave of his eunuchs, Alexander

> reduced them to a limited number and removed them from all duties in the Palace except the care of the women's baths; and whereas Elagabulus had also placed many over the administration of the finances and in procuratorships, Alexander took away from them even their previous positions. For he used to say that eunuchs were a third sex of the human race, one not to be seen or employed by men and scarcely even by women of noble birth.[74]

Castrati could thus be found not only in the emperor's suite but also in close proximity to the ladies-in-waiting. In the second century their number included Hyacinthus, the confidant of Marcia, Emperor Commodus's paramour. Commodus was likely a Christian who used his influence to help free many of his co-religionists, including entire communities of Christians in Sardinia (c. between 189 and 192). Beyond the confines of the court it had also become customary for women to employ castrated men as catamites. Thus Theophrastus tells us that women would have their slaves castrated so as to satisfy their sexual desires without having to fear the possibility of becoming pregnant. Martial corroborates the practice: "Do you ask why your Caelia has only eunuchs, Panychus? Caelia wants to be fucked, but not to have children."[75]

As a result of changes in the law, castrated men and Roman women even got married to ensure that their relationship would be morally sanctioned. Women who wished to achieve sexual gratification but avoid pregnancy found a "simple" solution to their dilemma. They had their slaves' testicles removed only during the later stages of puberty so that, as Juvenal (c. 67–140) indicates, they would still be able to engage in sexual intercourse:

> Some there are whom unwarlike eunuchs and their soft
> Kisses enrapture, and their despair of any beard,
> And the fact that no abortive's needed. Greatest joy
> However, is this, when now in its fiery youth a mature
> Groin is delivered to the doctors, quill now swart.
> So the awaited testicles are ordered first
> To grow and, after they've begun to weigh two pounds [*sic*],
> To the loss of just the barber grabbed by Heliodorus.[76]

We should not assume, however, that these radical practices were very widespread. Often just talking about the procedure was enough to satisfy the desire for sensation. Under the emperors' protection castrati—*spadi*—exercised their influence as both catamites and tasters. The duty of the latter was to taste food and drink about to be served to their master in order to detect poison. This assumes of course that the tasters themselves were not part of a conspiracy to kill the master, as happened for instance in the case of Lygdus who poisoned Drusus and Halotus, who allegedly murdered Claudius. Thus it was vitally important for any ruler to have absolute confidence in the castrated officers who served him in the palace, especially as their areas of responsibility increased over time. Many eunuchs assumed the office of procurator, military commander, or, in Anicentus's case, "prefect of the fleet." The eunuch Anicentus quickly rose to become one of Nero's closest confidants and the instrument of his master's deeds of terror and of vengeance, as Tacitus relates in the *Annals*: "Mother wit came to the rescue in the person of Anicentus the freedman, preceptor of Nero's boyish years, and detested by Agrippina with a vigour which was reciprocated. Accordingly, he pointed out that it was possible to construct a ship, part of which could be artificially detached, well out at sea, and throw the unsuspecting passengers overboard:—'Nowhere had accident such scope as on salt water . . .'"[77]

Financial and administrative officials were also recruited from the ranks of the court eunuchs, a practice that continued well into the Byzantine period. This system clearly illustrates the way in which the emperors used eunuchs, most of whom came from the lower classes, to help counterbalance the power of their aristocratic rivals.

Like punitive laws in the Orient, the Roman penal codes permitted the use of castration as a form of criminal justice. Tarquinius Superbus (534–510 B.C.) was the first Roman king to sentence rebellious citizens to this pernicious punishment. When Christians were subjected to persecution, castration was also used as a means of torture. In cases of adultery an aggrieved husband was granted the right to have the adulterer castrated as punishment and as revenge for having committed the act, a custom that survived into the Middle Ages. It was not until the reign of Domitian that this odious practice was outlawed for a time. In the words of Martial:

> It used to be a game to betray the sacred marriage torch and a game to castrate innocent males. You forbid both, Caesar, and come to the aid of future generations; for by your order their birth is made safe. Under your rule no man shall be either eunuch or adulterer. Formerly (alas for our morals!) even a eunuch was an adulterer.[78]

Castration that seemed to bear absolutely no relation to religious ideas was in fact rooted in the religiosity that helped to shape the habits of mind characteristic of ancient cultures.

Hence for much of history it was castrated men who had a determining influence on the way one served one's gods and one's divine rulers.

The Emperor of China and His Eunuchs

"A body like dry bone,
A heart like dead ash.
True in the realness of his knowledge.
Not one to go searching for reasons.
Dim, dim, drowsy, drowsy,
Mindless, you'll get no advice from him.
What kind of man is this?"
—*Chuang-Tzu*, XXII, 2

When Bernardo Bertolucci's film *The Last Emperor* was first shown in movie theaters in 1987, audiences got a chance to look through the gates of the Forbidden City in Beijing. Their view was enhanced by the filmmaker's extraordinary ability to exploit the visual grandeur of the site. The terracotta armies of the first Chinese emperor seemed to come alive before our very eyes. Shots filled with thousands of eunuchs, who not so long ago actually peopled the imperial palaces of the Chinese capital, appeared eerily archaic. What kind of civilization produced and sustained all this? How was it able for so long to adhere to customs that to us seem so cruel and inhumane?

In the conservative culture of China, so strongly bound to tradition, the institution of the court eunuch survived into the 20th century. Sun Yao-ting (1902–1996), "the last eunuch of the Emperor Pu-I," wrote a lengthy book detailing the institution's most recent manifestation in Chinese history.[79] Sun's work, as the Sinologist Wolfgang Bauer has pointed out, is in the finest tradition of the autobiographical self-testimony which has been cultivated in China since the 7th century B.C. This is the same genre in which the famous castrato and celebrated historian Ssu-ma Ch'ien (Sima Qian, 145–90 B.C.), following the Confucian tradition, composed a shocking self-analysis that has become a monument of Chinese historiography.

> When I look at myself I am forced to realize that my mutiliated body and I are vegetating in filth and at every turn I can see my crimes in my mind's eye. If I tried to be of use to anyone, it would only be to that person's detriment . . . I once heard someone say that to devote oneself to moral self-improvement was to be a treasure-house of wisdom; that to give something to someone else joyfully was the beginning of humanitarianism; that genuine giving and taking were the signs of a dutiful man; that it was only in times of humiliation and defeat that courage was truly in evidence; and that ultimately the aim of all one's actions should be to acquire a reputation as a good person. Only when someone has proven that he possesses these five qualities can he truly take his place in the world and be accepted into the ranks of outstand-

ing men. No worse misfortune can befall him than to be driven by base desires, no greater anguish than to grieve over the state of one's spirit. No act is more reprehensible than bringing shame on one's ancestors, and no insult greater than the "punishment of the palace" [castration] . . . How, when even then I was not in a position to make any important suggestions or ventilate any of my ideas, how can I now, being scarcely better than a slave who sweeps the streets, being mutilated and having been degraded to a level far below that of the lowliest and most common palace servant, how can I possibly lift up my head, look around proudly and discuss justice and injustice? . . . It is not easy to discern the beginning and the end of things. When I was a boy I had an irrepressible nature, and as I grew older I felt I was not accomplishing anything worthwhile in my native land. Nevertheless our lord, in gracious memory of my father, permitted me to devote my meager talents to the court and to have free access to the inner recesses of the palace. Thus I severed my relations to my friends and acquaintances and neglected my family obligations. I focused all my thoughts on the duties of my office and sought to attain only one thing: the favor and love of our lord. However things turned out to be quite the opposite of what I had hoped for; I became the victim of a terrible misunderstanding . . . I was thrown into prison and deprived of the chance to prove the depth of my loyalty. Since people believed that I had defamed the Emperor, I was turned over to a court for sentencing. My family's means were insufficient to have the sentence commuted by paying a sum of money. And no friends and acquaintances came forth to speak a single word on my behalf.

> Even of those who had the Emperor's ear, none put in a good word for me. I am not made of wood or stone, and yet I was obliged to face the court all alone. And who was there to turn to in the depths of that dungeon? . . . I now have the courage no longer to remain unassuming, but rather to devote myself entirely to this perhaps useless screed. And so I have collected ancient sources that are scattered around the world and woven them into a single narrative . . . It is not easy to go on vegetating here at the bottom while camarillas at the top continue their intrigues. Because of my candor, misfortune has befallen me with all its force, so that even in my native village I am condemned and ridiculed and my ancestors are dragged through the dirt. How can I possibly face my parents' grave? Even a hundred generations from now my shame will only become greater. These are the thoughts that trouble me nine times a day. When I sit at home I feel anxious, as though I had lost something, and when I go out I do not really know where I am headed. I constantly think about how I was violated; my back frequently becomes wet with perspiration making my clothes moist. I am not much better than a slave in the women's chambers . . . Normal people would never back me; they would simply humiliate me. What I hope for is that after my death the question of what is just and what is unjust will finally be resolved.[80]

The institution of the palace eunuch (*huanguan*) had a long tradition in the history of the Middle Kingdom, dating back to the third millennium B.C. Evidence pointing in this direction comes from some of the oldest anthropomorphic statues (c. 3000 B.C.) excavated in Lingjiatan/Lingchiatan (Anhwei province), statues that show no distinct sexual characteristics. Later finds from the period of the legendary Shang dynasty (c. 1300–1030 or 1765–1222 B.C.) corroborate this hypothesis. In 1976 little figurines of servants (c. 9 cm in height) were discovered in the grave of Fu Hao, wife of the Emperor Wu-ting (Wu-ding); they are considered the oldest known representations of palace eunuchs. Although written historical records date from a later time, they clearly indicate the existence of institutions that were so highly developed—institutions in which palace eunuchs already played an important role—that we have to assume that castrati had already firmly established their situation during that earlier period.

While the ancient Middle East and the world of classical antiquity did not clearly delineate between eunuchs and castrati, in China so-called "eunuchs" were invariably castrati and served at the court of the king or emperor. At times their numbers increased so dramatically that at the end of the Ming dynasty (1368–1644), for example, there were more than 70,000 eunuchs, whereas at the beginning there were only several hundred. Eunuchs were described variously according to the type of castration performed on them. The Chinese language apparently has only one word for eunuch or castrato, although terms such as "servant," "prisoner," and "Director of Ceremonial" (*silijian*) are used synonymously. Eunuchs directed a number of official service agencies responsible for carrying out various assignments throughout the Forbidden City and were a central constituent element of the imperial apparatus that had developed over the centuries. The palace personnel and bureaucracy consisted exclusively of eunuchs; under the last emperors they are said to have numbered more

Photograph of Chinese palace eunuchs. (Museum of the Forbidden City, Beijing)

than 100,000. And this figure does not include eunuchs living in households belonging to the Chinese aristocracy! The aggregate number employed there was probably not any lower. We must not overlook the fact that this practice had consequences for the demography of the country as well.

Originally most castrati were recruited from the lower classes, probably to counteract the influence of the various aristocratic clans (some Sinologists speak of cliques) at court. This was also true, by the way, of the last dynasty, the Ch'ing (1644–1911, also called the Qing), which saw a return to Confucian principles. However the example of Ssu-ma Ch'ien clearly speaks against the attempt by modern Chinese historiography to generalize this pattern. In the course of Chinese history many extraordinary personalities emerged from the ranks of the so-called "third sex" in spite of the fact that Chinese historians frequently tried to portray eunuchs in the worst possible light and blame them for all the evils in society. Thus Sun Yao-ting tells how he was even reproached by a police offical in Republican China: "Since time immemorial you eunuchs have been the ruin of China! No sooner does the sacred and enlightened Sun of Heaven vanish from the scene when you gang of wily, dissembling eunuchs come along. You've hatched plots and slandered people, heaped charges on the loyal and the good, and done the dirty work for criminals . . . Fortunately Mr. Sun Yat-sen abolished the imperial régime and saved our Chinese people from droughts and disastrous fires."[81]

This opinion—which has parallels, by the way, in accusations leveled against eunuchs during classical antiquity—cannot obscure the fact that these are complex issues in which specific acts of castration can be linked to various different motivations and causes. Castration was used very early as a form of punishment both for criminals among one's own population and for prisoners taken in war. Judging by the example of Ssu-ma Ch'ien we may assume that castration was used

Painted statue of a Chinese court eunuch, beardless and dressed in the blue cloth that was typical for court officers. (Beijing, Palace Museum)

early on as a substitute for the death penalty in cases involving political crimes. This allows us to assume further that eunuchs represented a potential intelligentsia that did not conform to the notions of the dominant Confucian bureaucracy which was constantly trying to shape the empire in its own image and suppress or persecute non-Confucian points of view (Taoism, Buddhism, Christianity). The origins of the Chinese Empire, which lasted until 1911, had a mythic character that was reflected in the cosmic order or wisdom that existed at the beginning of time. The celestial and sage foundational figures of Chinese culture—the "five model emperors"—set the stage for the subsequent thousands of years of China's civilizational development. It is nearly impossible to use the periodization applicable to Western history—antiquity, the Middle Ages, the early modern period, and the modern era—as a basis for comparison because these chronological divisions are totally foreign to Confucian thinking. The governing maxim in Confucianism reads as follows: "What Heaven has conferred [on humankind] is called the Nature. An accordance with this nature is called the Path of Duty . . . This Equilibrium is the great root (from which grow all the human actings) in the world; and this Harmony is the universal path (in which they should all proceed). Let the State of Equilibrium and harmony exist in perfection, and heaven and earth would have their (right) places, (and do their proper work), and all things would be nourished (and flourish) . . . 'the superior man (exhibits) the state of equilibrium and harmony; the small man presents the opposite of these states, the superior man exhibits them, because he is the superior man, and maintains himself in them . . . '"[82]

The mythic beginnings of the empire can be traced back in historical time to the third millennium B.C. This period was idealized as a time of equilibrium and harmony between heaven and earth. The early part of the empire's history, called its golden age, was said to have been an era of peace and happiness. This state of affairs gradually changed, however, with the advent of the Yao and Shun dynasties, both of which have their roots in history. As a result of archeological research, our knowledge of their place in Chinese history is being continually expanded. It was during this period, characterized by totemism, that the first clans emerged. They promoted their representatives to positions of power only to manipulate and exploit them later on. Over time court institutions became increasingly complex and the circle of those who exerted influence on them grew steadily. These circles of influence included the emperor's family, in particular the emperor's mother, the imperial concubines, the military, the highly developed Confucian bureaucracy, and finally the eunuchs, who in some cases managed to have their own candidates enthroned in defiance of the previous emperor's will and thereby rose to the highest positions and occupied the most important offices in the state.

It was hoped that by strengthening eunuchism the emperor would achieve a certain degree of independence from his clients. However, this proved to be the case for only a short period of time. It became clear that the court eunuchs too found themselves in various dependent relationships. On the one hand they were beholden to the clans that had introduced them at court and then exploited them, and on the other to the castrati cliques that had formed as a result of having been granted permission to adopt sons. High dignitaries would emasculate themselves so they could become the emperor's confidants within the bounds of the palace—an act fraught with dire consequences if one considers that the continunity of ancestor worship was put in jeopardy as a result.

However, fate was not always kind to the court eunuchs. At the end of the Han dynasty (206 B.C.–220 A.D.), for example, thousands of them were slaughtered during the reign of the "Son of Heaven" Yuan Shao (189 A.D.) in an attempt to curtail their influence. The attempt failed, however. The usurpers who followed one another in rapid succession felt obliged for reasons of tradition and religion to maintain the various rites, customs, and ceremonies. Hence they found it imperative to give one party at court preference over another: either the scholar-bureaucrats or the eunuchs that were an essential part of the rites at court (with reference to the sacred character of the empire). Thus when one of the parties felt strong it tended to suppress the other.

In contrast to other areas of cultural history, Sinology has made the "court eunuch" a major topic of study. Two recently published works warrant our special attention. The first, a study of the political function and social status of the eunuchs in the later Han period (25–220 A.D.) by Ulrike Jugel,[83] covers only a relatively short period of time; however, since it has some of the features of a conceptual model, parts of it could serve as a basis for a general discussion of eunuchism in the Middle Kingdom. The second, *Eunuchs in the Ming Dynasty* by Shih-shan H. Tsai,[84] is limited to the approximately 250 years of the next-to-last imperial dynasty. However, it offers comprehensive coverage of the relevant Chinese literature on a period during which the number of eunuchs had grown inordinately large and in which there was not a single area of politics or culture in which eunuchs were not represented.

Primary sources and cultural histories confirm the fact that the methods of castration employed in China remained unchanged for literally thousands of years. There were even certain facilities in the Forbidden City that specialized in performing castration in order to meet the court's demand for eunuchs. If one multiplies x number of eunuchs times the 2000 concubines that an emperor would normally keep, one gets an idea of the enormous number of castrati needed to operate the women's palaces in the imperial capital, assuming of course that almost every kind of job in the palace was done by a specially assigned eunuch.

Despite a certain tendency to embellish, the account given by Sun Yao-ting, the "Emperor's last eunuch," is of interest as an example of cultural history. Even though one may question the authenticity of his description of a boy's castration, it nevertheless conveys the drama of the event and its various implications:

> On the fifteenth day of the eighth month in the year 1912 according to the farmer's almanac (the father said to his son): "I understand you have to urinate immediately after the operation or your urethra will become blocked and you'll die."
>
> Lujin immediately drank every last drop of water. Sun Huaibao checked the latch on the door again and had Lujin, who was naked below the waist, lie down on a wooden shutter that served as an operating table. Lujin was shaking so much that the shutter rattled. Sun

Huaibao got a piece of coarse rope and bound Lujin up in such a way that he was unable to move his hands or feet. Then he tied a thin piece of hemp cord around the boy's penis fastening the other end to the window frame. Thus the little penis was stretched out lengthwise. He then picked up a razor sharp butcher's knife . . . Sun Huaibao put the knife between his teeth and lighted some candles and incense. Striking his forehead three times he paid homage to the spirits of the bodhisattvas and the Buddha. He prayed silently: "You spirits and Buddhas in heaven, please give me a sign as to whether all will go well. And if it will, let this incense form three smoke rings . . . "

With his head turned to the side Lujin watched everything that was happening. His pale face was expressionless. He recalled the words he had spoken two days earlier: "I hereby renounce my right to beget offspring! . . . "

He picked up the knife, put it in the oven, turned it around a few times, rubbed it with a rag, and moved toward Lujin. Again the knife stopped at the base of his thigh . . . He gripped the handle of the knife firmly and plunged it in the direction of Lujin's testicles. There was blood everywhere. Fountains of red, white and yellow liquid spouted from the wound. Sun Huaibao felt dizzy and sick; his body was bathed in cold sweat. Without aiming he kept slicing away with the knife . . . He then held something soft and bloody in his hand; his knees felt as though they were going to buckle. He tried to draw himself up but was unable to do so.

Both of Lujin's eyes were shut and he lay unconscious and motionless on the wooden shutter. His thin face was as white as snow. His teeth had left deep bite marks on his lower lip…

After the castration has been performed, a goose quill is inserted into the urethra to prevent it from closing. Sun Huaibao had prepared for this in advance, but in his haste and the confusion he had forgotten to place the quill where he would have easy access to it. Tian Fu assumed the role of expert and poked around Lujin's lower abdomen with a quill until he found the boy's urethra. By this time Sun Huaibao had pulled himself together and plugged the wound with tampons that he had dipped in wax, sesame oil and pepper . . .

Lujin slept for three days and three nights. His whole body was as hot as fire and his fever would not subside. His mother never left his side and changed his bandages regularly. Only when his urine finally began to flow again—while he was still unconscious—did everyone breathe a sigh of relief . . .

"The wound healed in a few days. I instructed some people to go to Beijing and seek out Zhang the steward. If the news is positive, you can start packing and leave for your job in the palace!" he said and took out a little package wrapped in oil paper: "This is for you. When you're in the palace, put it in a bushel of grain, hang the bushel on the beam supporting the ceiling of your room and raise it a little higher each year. Then it will protect you and ensure that you will grow every year. And remember one more thing: when you are near death, it must be with you in the grave or the six lines of your ancestors will be incomplete. Those who are neither man nor woman cannot be reborn! Your father will precede you and will no longer be able to worry about these

> things; you will have to remember them yourself!" Lujin had no idea what the package contained, so he opened it and looked in. There it was, the member of which he had been "cleansed." It had already turned black. He quickly repacked it and kept it safe in his little wardrobe.[85]

In comparison the account by Ce Shaozhen (Tsedan Dorji) seems more down-to-earth but not any the less gruesome:

> A Chinese who was originally destined to become a eunuch described for me how one entered their ranks. One was chosen when one was a child. Most of these future eunuchs came from Hejianfu in the province of Hebei. The children were between the ages of eight and ten—to have performed the operation later would have been too risky—and were taken to an old eunuch who acted as their master. Until the operation was performed a boy was obliged to work for the master. Meanwhile the master instructed the boy in the manners and customs of noble families. At night he would regularly come to the boy's bed and massage his genitals, sometimes for a half hour or even longer. Did the boy sense what what he was being prepared for? Naturally it hurt when the old man pulled his penis, which he did frequently. And when was the child ready for the operation? The massages lasted for at least a year . . .
>
> After the boy disrobed the master grabbed his penis and scrotum and pulled hard. Then with his other hand he took a sharp knife and in one swift motion chopped his genitals off. Did it cause terrible pain? Did it bleed profusely? Well of course it hurt horribly. But then again it was not that bad because the knife was sharp and the master skillful. Drugs were used to stop the bleeding, the

> wound was bandaged and the newly minted eunuch was allowed to rest until his wound healed.[86]

These modern accounts do not begin to cover the gamut of gruesome procedures used to perform castration, which since ancient times was carried out using three main methods: crushing the testicles; cutting off the penis; or complete resection. Since Confucianism called for a person's body to be preserved in its entirety after death, eunuchs saved the severed portions of their anatomy so that they could later be buried together with them. As a result of this custom Chinese castrati made it a practice to carry with them a small case or bag in which to keep their severed genitals, just as the "Emperor's last eunuch" described in his autobiography.

Since the history of Chinese eunuchism is at the same time the history of the Chinese Empire, there are only a few special instances in which court eunuchs participated in such a way as to make them stand out. Not always were they anonymous. Some can be identified in scroll paintings, book illustrations and on murals, and others in early examples of the photographic art. As in the ancient Middle East, eunuchs can be recognized by certain characteristics. In countless paintings depicting court life, for instance, they are invariably portrayed as beardless, in contrast to the Emperor who can be identified by the fact that he wears a beard.

Court eunuchs preferred Buddhism to Confucianism, a fact that is reflected in the Buddhist iconography of the 12th to the 15th centuries. Introduced from India, the Buddhist religion was deeply colored with practices and ideas that were alien to the Chinese, such as monastic asceticism, celibacy, and renunciation—ideas that only helped to make court eunuchs more socially acceptable. The ability to reproduce and the necessity of begetting progeny lost significance. Crucial to this new doctrine was the idea of "transcending the material world." Consequently painting flourished as never before. And in Chinese Buddhist paintings almost all the individual portraits seem to be of eunuchs. The Chinese-oriented bodhisatvvas with their feminine features and their aura of self-enlightenment are at a far remove from anything to do with sexuality. The characteristics that typify the male of the species have vanished. The message conveyed by images of the Buddha seemed to be that gender was irrelevant or non-existent. Sexuality had lost its significance; the new maxim of the Middle Kingdom was to transcend and triumph over sexuality. One of many recorded self-testimonies, the revelations of the philosopher and historian Shen Yo (441–513), a political advisor to the Emperor Wu Ti during the Liang dynasty (502–550), should be understood in this context:

> Back when I was still young and ignorant and my mind had barely developed, I gave free rein to my desires in wild antics and caused a lot of damage as a result of my brutal behavior. I would put on my trencher any creature that roamed the earth or flew in the air or swam in the water. And if any of them crossed my path, I would attack them with knife and club . . . For while I committed all these outrageous acts I was always with a group of friends and never alone. Acting like a gang of foreign thieves we would attack and harrass people in the surrounding area. Once we stole fruit from their gardens, and another time we made off with their domestic animals. Being immature and naive we took an impish delight in our deeds and were amused to no end . . .

> When I examine the years of my youth I realize that, since I was at the peak of my strength while embroiled in affairs that stemmed from these depraved relationships, my blood and my juices were as hard to control as a mountain stream. I truly had countless affairs with women, and I also had frequent relationships with young men. It is not easy to erase these facts in this cage between life and death . . . Now however shame and remorse have accumulated in my heart but I don't know how to straighten out my sinful life . . . I want to dissociate myself from the mistakes of the past and rid myself of my carnal appetite. I want to correct the error of my ways and devote myself to the Enlightened One . . . If one doesn't take truth as the basis for cleansing and negating one's being, one cannot remove the chains encumbering a tainted heart . . . I bare my crown and bow my head now that I have revealed the secret of my sins and have shown my resolve to better myself. May this desire to improve myself, having once begun, continue without interruption, just as the days and the years go by, and may it never come to rest as we pass from life to life. I pray that I shall not relapse into my old ways before attaining redemption.[87]

When the writing of history began in China during the Han dynasty, this "pivotal period" (Karl Jaspers) developed not only into a time in which the central government consolidated its power and expanded its territory; it also became the stage for a series of sensational politically motivated crimes in which a number of influential court eunuchs were involved. The Dutch Sinologist and diplomat Robert van Gulik (1910–1967) drew heavily on this world of crime, violence and lust in writing his much-praised detective stories. Favoritism, corruption, murder, intrigues, betrayal, palace revolts, and treachery are part of the eternal power game, bolstering the thesis that these and similar phenomena had a determining influence on Chinese politics well into the 19th century.

Whether in the alcoves of the Empress Dowager or in the private chambers of the Emperor—everywhere eunuchs exercised enormous influence. They reached the apogee of their power when the Emperor Shun (126–144) issued a decree allowing them to adopt sons, thereby eliminating all obstacles to their advancement. They even became personal secretaries (*shang-shu*) to the emperors. Eunuchs were granted administrative and aristocratic titles, and their "sons" and heirs even tried to seize the dragon throne. The grandson of the eunuch Ts'ao T'eng, the grand counselor and victorious general Ts'ao Ts'ao (Cao Cao, 144–220), is a prime example. Tsao Tsao's grandfather had been ennobled, given a large fief (a county), served four emperors, and adopted Ts'ao Ts'ao's father, Ts'ao Sung. He was a member of the circle that helped the Emperor Huan-ti (r. 146–167) to ascend the throne following the murder of Huan's predecessor Liang Chi. Starting with the reign of the child emperor An-ti (b. 97, r. 107–125) and his regent, the Empress Teng, he was involved in every conceivable kind of intrigue at court. Court eunuchs, by the way, owed an especially large debt of gratitude to the Empress Teng who, after the death of the Emperor Ho (b. 79, r. 90–105), enthroned the 100-day-old minor Shang-ti (A.D. 106). Together with other like-minded eunuchs, Tsao T'eng acted as a mediator between the Empress Dowager and the Emperor. In doing so he gained a great deal of influence over the Prince and future Emperor Shun and played a leading role in drafting the edict that ultimately gave preferential treatment to eunuchs. His tightly-knit network of relationships makes it almost impossible to distinguish him from among his associates and understand his character. In listening to his power-crazed grandson, though, we hear echoes of his grandfather's intentions that seem to corroborate the negative opinions people had of him. In giving his speech Ts'ao Ts'ao used the first person, a form of address reserved for monarchs, even though he was only granted the imperial title (Wu-ti) posthumously by his son, the Emperor Ts'ao P'ei (188–227):

> I shall become the Chief Counselor, the highest-ranking subject [of the Emperor], which is more than I had ever hoped for. As I say this now, it must seem as though I am trying to make myself out to be someone great. In truth I merely want people to stop telling falsehoods about me; this is the only reason that I cannot keep silent. If I had not existed, I would not care to imagine the number of people who would now call themselves emperor or king! Yet there are many who, because they see my power and by nature do not believe in the truth of the Heavenly Mandate, are afraid that deep down I have somethng against them. They maintain that I am hatching evil plots against them. This pains me in the extreme . . . What I am saying now, I am not just telling you gentlemen; I also constantly admonish my wives to mark my words . . . However if someone asks me to disband my army and send it home and return to my dukedom in Wup'ing—that I cannot do. And why not? Likely because I fear that

> the moment I part with my army, others will emerge to send me to my doom. Apart from the fact that I have to think of my sons and grandsons, my ruin would also signal the collapse of the state. This is why I do not seek certain death by striving to attain an uncertain name . . . I have received power and charisma from the state, led military expeditions with battle axe in hand, helped the weak and defied the strong, remained a modest person and taken leave of glory. What I had planned in my mind was to let things take their course; why shouldn't I save the world when it was that which my heart commanded me to do! So after I have pacified the Empire and when I harbor no shame for having fulfilled my destiny to rule, then one may say: Heaven helped the house of Han; this was no human power . . . The untamed territories along the rivers and lakes have not yet been cleared of rebels, and therefore I still cannot leave my post![88]

Particularly ironic in this story is the fact that just when the eunuchs' "progeny" were aspiring to the highest offices in the state, the eunuchs themselves were being slaughtered wholesale (A.D. 189). In Chang Jang's biography we read the following:

> In the sixth year (A.D. 189) the Emperor died. Yüan Shao, Commander of the Middle Army, persuaded General-in-Chief Ho Chan to order the killing of the eunuchs so as to fill the Empire with joy. When his plan became known to Chang Jang, Chao Chung and others followed Ho Chan to his office where they murdered him. However Yüan Shao managed to persuade some soldiers to decapitate Chao Chung, seize the eunuchs (*huan-kuan*) and

> behead them all, regardless of age. (Jang and several dozen other people kidnapped the Emperor, held him hostage and escaped up the Huang-Ho in the direction of Ch'ang-an.) When their pursuers caught up with them, Jang and the others spoke amid tears of sorrow: "We shall all be annihilated, and the Empire is in chaos. Please take care of yourself, Your Majesty." Then they threw themselves into the Huang-Ho and died.[89]

Factional intrigues such as these signaled the end of the Han dynasty, one of the most splendid periods of Chinese history in terms of its cultural achievements. It is doubtful, however, whether one can describe the political strife between the Confucian aristocracy and the eunuchs during this period as a struggle between litterateur-officials or intellectuals on the one hand and "corrupt, uneducated eunuchs" on the other. Although the eunuchs' influence in politics became significantly weaker as a result of persecution and decimation, they managed to regain their standing as the central government consolidated its authority. The personal and at times even intimate contacts between the Emperor and his servants gave rise to a new series of dependent relationships that made it nearly impossible to separate the official from the private sphere.

By 800, the situation had reached a point where eunuchs had become a determining factor in choosing who was to accede to the imperial throne. Their rise to power coincided with the introduction into China of new religious forces (beginning in the 5th century), especially Buddhism, which they found particularly congenial to their way of life. For example, when they were old, eunuchs generally wished to retire to a monastery and were generous in their support of monastic establishments. They continued to practice the custom long after Buddhism had lost much of its strength and support in China. In fact, the "Emperor's last eunuch" seems to have been a product of Buddhist groups that looked upon castration as a means of purification with as much fervor as other ascetic religious movements, such as Gnosticism and Manichaeanism, which had also gained a foothold in China. Ce Shaozhen (Tsedan Dorji, b. 1914) reported as follows on a monastic community of former imperial eunuchs:

> To the west of Peking, at the foot of the Fragrant Hills (*Xiangshan*), stands the temple where the eunuchs spent the autumn of their lives. It was also a popular destination for foreigners going on an outing. In my day it took an hour and a half to bicycle the distance. In 1946 or 1947 I traveled there with an Austrian journalist by the name of Tichy. The "abbot" (also a eunuch) received us in his study. He was quite portly and well dressed but unfortunately not very communicative. Nevertheless we learned from him that there were forty "brothers" living in his monastery. They worked on the surrounding estates as farmhands. Most, he told us, had been eunuchs at the Emperor's court and came from what had once been princely palaces. They had no families of their own to look after them. The temple itself had been built in honor of a Ming dynasty commander who had also been a eunuch. The abbot then took us to the altar of the eunuchs' god in the main building. It was located in a large room in the middle of which stood a statue of the commander facing a long narrow table with candles and incense holders. The walls were hung with scrolls decorated with calligraphy. Just as we went out into the gar-

> den, the brothers returned from their farm work. What a contrast to the obese abbot! Pathetic-looking creatures in tattered clothes—ragged, undernourished old men.
>
> The abbot left us alone to talk undisturbed to the eunuchs. They were timid and taciturn and responded mostly in monosyllables. Yes, I was in the imperial palace. I saw the "old Buddha" (the Empress Dowager Tz'u Hsi/Cixi). No, I just worked in the imperial kitchen, and so forth. We asked them how they were faring. They said that they had enough to eat but that their work was very demanding. Many were so senile that they did not understand our questions.
>
> My companion was enough of a gentleman not to ask any untoward questions, something which one cannot say of all journalists. My sister, for instance, once visisted the same temple with a woman journalist from Germany who was doing a photo essay on China. The woman asked one of the eunuchs to pull down his trousers so she chould take a picture of him without his pants on. This created quite an awkward situation.
>
> In the meantime the eunuchs are almost an extinct species. I recall a few years ago, probably in 1983, seeing a picture of China's last eunuch in the newspaper. Perhaps he still lives somewhere in the environs of Peking.[90]

But back to Chinese history! As old values and customs were revived in the 9th century, Buddhist doctrine and practice were decried as un-Chinese. "Cultural nationalists" (Old Style Movement, *ku-wen*) stepped onto the stage and sought to eliminate anything they deemed at odds with the evolved national character of the Chinese. Buddhist, Nestorian, and Manichaean monasteries and places of worship were systematically destroyed. Thousands upon thousands of monks (c. 260,000 Buddhist monks and nuns) were returned to the laity and their religion proscribed. These persecutions were followed by a spate of uprisings. As the Würzburg Sinologist Dieter Kuhn has pointed out, these rebellions were not peasant uprisings, but rather campaigns of pillage under the principal leadership of the notorious Huang Ch'ao (killed in 884). Their victims included foreigners (according to Arab sources, 120,000 foreigners were "eliminated" in Canton alone) as well as Tang dynasty government troops, not to mention members of the general populace who were forced to endure the worst reprisals—murder, looting, pillage, rape, and cannibalism. Finally, in 903, eunuchs who had accompanied the Emperor to their last day were killed in a bloody massacre led by Chu Ch'üan-chung (Zhu Wen, 907–923), the founder of the later Liang dynasty.

A new era ensued in which the court no longer regarded the aristocratic ideas of status and ritual, espoused by many eunuchs, as vital to maintaining the interests of the state. These ideas, in fact, degenerated into a seemingly ineffectual courtly etiquette. However, to maintain the etiquette of court functions, eunuchs continued to be in demand. Their services had once again become indispensable, especially to usurpers and new emperors. Thus one cannot rule out the possibility that even under foreign rulers, especially the Mongols (1279–1368), eunuchs were employed other than as court functionaries, a role that in any event did not come into full flower until the rise of the Ming dynasty. We know, for example, that under Kublai Khan's rule (1216–1294) a eunuch named Guo Shoujing helped to build part of the Grand Canal near Beijing and that another eunuch, Taijian, was responsible for China's irrigation system.

In the late 14th and early 15th centuries, the nomadic invaders of the so-called Yüan or Mongol dynasty were driven out of China and, after being defeated by Ming forces, retreated into the steppes of Central Asia. The Ming policy of expansion bore fruit; Chinese forces, led mostly by eunuchs, conquered neighboring territories and expanded Chinese influence into Southeast Asia. We know a number of these eunuchs by name, many of whom were Muslims—Ma Bin, for example, who worked directly for the Emperor. Because of their religious affiliation, Muslims always used the name Ma so as to honor the prophet Muhammad. Under the Emperor Yung-lo (Yongle/Ch'eng-tsu, 1403–1424) eunuchs even led expeditions to China's western regions. One of them, Cheng Ho (Zheng He, c. 1371–1434), is regarded as one of the world's most famous navigators. He was a Muslim from China's Yunnan province, the son of a respected Muslim (probably Mongolian) of Central Asian origin. His father had even made a pilgrimage to Mecca, which indicates his elevated status and his ancestor's connections to the rulers of the Yüan dynasty. When Yunnan fell to Ming forces, Cheng Ho and his family, together with the Mongol aristocracy, were captured and sent into captivity. It was probably in prison that he, like many other captives, was castrated. Beginning in 1382 he entered the service of Prince Yan, the future Emperor Yung-lo. Yung-lo sinicized his surname from Ma to Cheng/Zheng. He held a number of important positions in the military, built a navy to stop the menace of the Japanese pirates, and undertook seven maritime expeditions under the Emperor Yung-lo and his successor Xuande (1425–1435). In so doing he carried on a time-honored tradition begun by his predecessors. As early as A.D. 987, eight court eunuchs had been commissioned by the Sung Emperor to sail their fleet to the East African and Western Asian coasts in order to obtain spices, rhinoceros horn, and other exotic goods for China.

Cheng Ho's maritime explorations for the Emperor during the years 1404–1433 took him to Southeast Asia, Indonesia, India, Ceylon, the Persian Gulf, Aden, the east coast of Africa, and Arabia. According to the sources that have come down to us, he is said to have visited more than 30 states. The Chinese fleet was 90 times bigger than that of the Portuguese under Vasco da Gama (1469–1524). Besides Cheng Ho the fleet's principal officers were all court eunuchs, for example, Wang Jinghong, Hou Xian, Li Xin, Zhou Liang, Zhou Man, Hong Bao, Yang Zhen, Zhang Da, and Wu Zhong. Together they commanded around 30,000 people. In the course of his expeditions Cheng Ho made important political contacts with, among others, the Mamluks in Egypt, who then sent their missions to Nanking. Unfortunately Cheng Ho's voyages of exploration did not have an enduring impact on China, even though the admiral left posterity several important geographic surveys which his companion, the Muslim eunuch Ma Huan, published in 1451. His first work, *Notes on the Barbarian Countries of the Western Seas*, came out in 1434, the year of his death.

In East Asia he was revered as a god, and even now his temples bear the name Sanbao miao to honor him. Unfortunately the high point of his expeditions, which he carried out using a compass (already long familiar to the Chinese), coincided with the end of China's maritime expansion. We cannot exclude the possibility, as W. Bauer correctly suggests, that Cheng Ho's voyages of discovery were not given proper recognition because he was an outsider, a naturalized Chinese and a Muslim. The fact that he was a eunuch was of only secondary importance. Still we should bear in mind that Neo-Confucians at the Ming court were inclined not only to prohibit court eunuchs from any involvement in political activities but even to prevent them from learning how to read and write. Neverthless, just fifty years later, palace servants were once again the most powerful people at court, in part because they were responsible for organizing and administering the feared secret police.

Eunuchs, who had a longer than average life span, strengthened the central government, controlled the administration, and formed a "kitchen cabinet" that represented the real power in the state, especially during the reign of short-lived emperors. They frightened and terrorized the "scholar-officials" and bureaucrats who had earlier sought ways of countering the influence of the court eunuchs, most of whom came from the north. But for quite some time they had nothing to show for their efforts. Liu Chin (Liu Jin) is a prime example of the power exercised by eunuchs during this period. He exploited the inexperience of the young Emperor Wu-tsung, who had ascended the throne in 1505 at the age of fifteen and was uninterested in governmental affairs. During his reign of terror, Liu ordered the beheading of 300 of the most prominent bureaucrats and put his own people in charge of all important government posts. As a result he became immensely wealthy. A search of his house revealed 240,000 bars and 57,800 pieces of gold, 1,593,000 taels and 5 million bars of silver, two bushels of precious stones, two suits of armor in solid gold, 3000 gold rings, and much else besides. The total value exceeded the annual budget of the entire state! Under the leadership of the moral philosopher Wang Yangming (Wang Shoujen, 1472–1528) the Neo-Confucians managed to thwart Liu Chin's attempted coup and had him arrested in 1510. His cohorts were exposed and eliminated, and he himself suffered the fate of his power-hungry predecessors.

The Emperors' Neo-Confucian advisors came from one of the finest group of intellectuals ever to govern China; even now their achievements are reflected in Chinese political literature. So long as men like Chang Chü-cheng (1525–1582) were in power, the eunuchs were in a difficult position. Thus the year 1582 represented a unique opportunity of which the eunuchs took full advantage. First under the Emperor Wan-li (Shen-tsung, 1573–1619) and then under the Emperor Hsi-tsung (Tianqi, 1621–1627), they again began to manipulate power as they saw fit. Wei Chung-hsien (Wei Zhongxian, 1568–1627) became head of the eunuch party. He sought an open confrontation with the scholars of the "Eastern Depot" (secret police apparatus), critics who regarded themselves as "men of integrity." To pay his gambling debts Wei had had himself castrated and with the support of the Mistress Ke, the wet nurse of the future Emperor Hsi-tsung, gained access to the court. Even though he was largely illiterate, he was made a knight. With utter ruthlessness he sought to repress all intellectuals who served the state loyally; he shut down their academies and had 700 alleged conspirators executed. In heaping curses on himself, the Confucian scholar Huang Tao-chou (1585–1646) illuminates the brutality of the time:

> Therefore cut your heart into small pieces, tear out your eyes, chop off your legs and have yourself and your body parts hung on the gate to the capital so you can be massacred in front of everybody. Then throw your eyes as far away as you can, separate yourself from your heart, smash your legs, scatter your fingers and commit your body to chaos as a mark of the infamy of these times! Let yourself be trampled by cattle and sheep, inundated by icy waters, seized by mountain demons and torn to shreds by tigers and jackals! May you be subjected to every kind of gall and poison in the world! You sent for all five spirits as witnesses to your curse—what could you have been thinking of?! O heaven divine, behold these three sacrificial animals so that I may undo this curse![91]

The contrast between the uneducated, mutilated castrati from the lower classes of North China and the highly cultured philosophers and scholars from the south was never greater than during the Ming dynasty. The contrasts were in fact so stark that they became a metaphor for the way in which eunuchism would later be regarded in China. The brutal eunuch Wei Chung-hsien was murdered under the last Ming emperor (1628–1644), but the dynasty that had promoted him also came to an inglorious end.

Thanks to the Confucian academies Ming scholarship flourished. With the help of a eunuch named Pan Tian-shou, the Jesuit Matteo Ricci (1552–1610) gained access to the imperial court and was granted permission to remain in Beijing. A few influential eunuchs became Christians, and even several members of the imperial family (mostly women) converted to Christianity.

The following period was marked both by popular uprisings and by the rise of the Manchu dynasty, the last to occupy the dragon throne but not the last in which court eunuchs played a part. This time, however, the positions they held were in no way as influential as they had been in the past. The Manchus spoke of eunuchs as *oboi* or "retainers," and they were not always castrati. Their influence was severely restricted by the Emperor K'ang-hsi (1654–1722). New popular uprisings and riots cast a cloud over the country. Interestingly, this unrest almost coincided with the French Revolution and other revolutionary movements in Europe.

Under the Emperor Ch'ien-lung (1735–1795/1799) and his successor Jen-tsung (Chia ch'ing/Shih-tsung, 1796–1821), eunuchs attempted once again, in 1813, to insinuate themselves into political life by helping members of the Celestial Law Sect (T'ien Li Chao), a secret religious organization, to enter the palace defenses and attack the emperor. Quick action on the part of the imperial family, however, resulted in the suppression of the revolt, which was a harbinger of the later Opium War.

The political history of eunuchism in the Middle Kingdom was rooted in the tradition-bound organization of the imperial palace. Both the Emperor and his innumerable concubines had made themselves reliant on castrated male servants who, as a result of their condition, were precluded from encroaching upon the patriarchal duties of the Son of Heaven. Since ordinarily no outsiders, i.e., uncastrated males, were ever permitted inside the residential quarters of a Chinese palace, close personal relationships developed between the ruler and his eunuchs. From the outside these relationships were difficult to understand, since from the beginning of the eunuch system they were basically taboo. In accordance with a nearly 5,000-year-old tradition, these quarters were considered "sacred." In fact, we still do not know everything about them. "Secret" reports and chronicles were produced at various times and recorded events inside the palace sometimes contained suggestive stories about "illicit" homosexual relations between the Emperors and their eunuchs as well as about imperial concubines who treated themselves to the pleasure of "hidden" eunuchs, i.e., eunuchs whose genitals had "miraculously" grown back. There were also candid accounts of eunuchs involved in sadistic practices:

> Many wealthy eunuchs got married, by the way, and a number had women on the side or regularly visited a brothel. How come? Old women have told me that the worst fate that could befall a young girl was to spend the night with a eunuch. Eunuchs beat and pinched them so much that their bodies were covered with black and blue marks. And they bit them so hard that their wounds would still be bleeding the next day. "May you sleep with a eunuch" was one of the worst things one prostitute could wish on another.[92]

The eunuch system in China, where it was especially well developed, had an influence on other civilizations with which the Chinese maintained economic and cultural relations, especially Persia, Byzantium, the Arab caliphates, and India. The growing trade and cultural ties between the Yellow Sea and the

Mediterranean furthered the spread of foreign customs and practices that live on to this day in many fables and folktales.

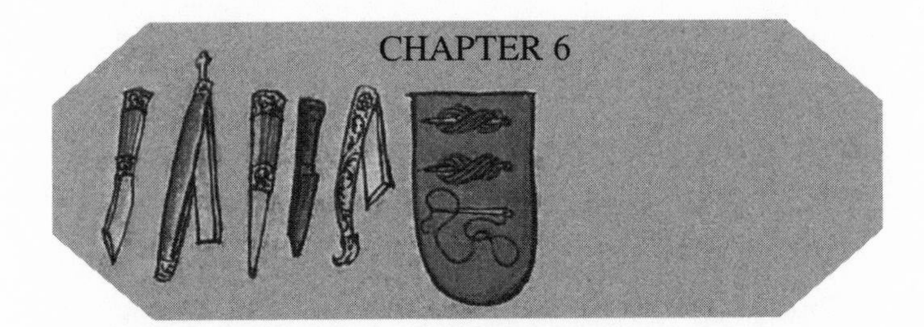

"Chastity of the Angels": Sexuality in Early Christianity

"For there are some eunuchs who have been so from birth, and there are eunuchs who have been made eunuchs by others, and there are eunuchs who have made themselves eunuchs for the sake of the kingdom of heaven. Let anyone accept this who can."

—Matthew 19:12

"So [Philip] got up and went. Now there was an Ethiopian eunuch, a court official of the Candace, queen of the Ethiopians, in charge of her entire treasury. He had come to Jerusalem to worship and was returning home . . . the eunuch said, 'Look, here is water! What is to prevent me from being baptized?' He commanded the chariot to stop, and both of them, Philip and the eunuch, went down into the water, and Philip baptized him. When they came out of the water, the Spirit of the Lord snatched Philip away; the eunuch saw him no more, and went on his way rejoicing."

—Acts 8:27–39

Conversion to Christianity of a eunuch (whose name we do not learn) during the reign of the queen of the Ethiopians, as related in Acts 8, seemed so unusual that some exegetes have dismissed it as a legend. In so doing, they reveal their inadequate knowledge of the "cultures on the margins" of antiquity, such as the culture of the Ethiopians. These exegetes also incorrectly equated eunuchs and castrated men.

The empire of Candace was no imaginary land, but an actual country south of Egypt, which the ancient Greeks associated with the Ethiopians ("people with burnt faces"). Its history paralleled that of Egypt to some extent, but was essentially independent. The peoples of the ancient Near East called their inhabitants Kushites (this name also appears in the Bible), in the country later known as Ethiopia; in the 7th century B.C. they even ruled over Egypt as the "Ethiopian dynasty." The cultural artifacts of this empire, taken from the sand of Nubia (now called Northern Sudan), have both revived and revised our understanding of one of the oldest civilizations of Africa.

The report of the conversion of the Ethiopian court official in Acts accords with our knowledge of this period and would appear to be a reliable account. Even before Paul's conversion, the dark-skinned official representative of a now-forgotten empire embraced the new belief, which he then disseminated in his own land. The Ethiopian, the *eunuchos dynastes*, became the first, albeit anonymous apostle on African soil; to stretch a point, one could claim that Meroë, the land south of Egypt, was a primary center of Christianity in the ancient world, even earlier than Rome. Luke, the author of Acts, provided no names in his account. He used only titles, in this case the Meroitic title "Candace" for the ruling woman, because he

Baptism of the eunuch of Candace: painting by Salomon Koninck (1609–1656).
This motif was a popular theme among Dutch Protestant painters of the day.
(Basel, Public Art Collection)

found no equivalent term in Greek. For her chamberlain, Luke could consult the Septuagint, which designated the high officers at the court of the Egyptian as eunuchs (Genesis 37:36). The apostle Luke, the first Christian historian, was thus primarily interested in highlighting the social and political status of new converts, irrespective of gender. In Meroë, the structures of the sacral kingdom offered fertile ground for the adoption of Christian doctrine, but there was no compelling reason to emasculate court officials. We may therefore safely assume that in the Hellenistic period, the term *eunuchos* was used other than as a synonym for castrati.

The conversion of African eunuchs became a popular iconographic motif in Netherlandish painting of the 16th and 17th centuries in the paintings of Rembrandt (1606–1669), Pieter Lastman (1583–1633), Leonaert Bramer (1596–1674), Salomon de Braij (1597–1664), and Cornelis Moeyaert (1590–1655). Of special significance is *Conversion and Baptism of the Eunuch of Candace*, a painting by Salomon Koninck (1609–1656), which depicts the convert as an aristocratic Ethiopian (in conformity with those who were encountered in Europe after the 16th century). Modern painters have continued to portray this conversion, notably Herbert Boeckel (1894–1966) in the Seckauer Chapel.

In yet another respect, Luke's account speaks against the notion that the Meroite official was emasculated. Had the act of voluntary emasculation been theologically grounded, the scriptures of the first churchmen who opted for voluntary emasculation (based on their conviction that it was imperative to lead a chaste life) would have cited this episode as a theological precedent. However, the episode goes unmentioned.

Christianization took place in a time and world that knew not only pagan cults and mysteries with emasculation rites, but also widespread celibacy motivated by religion. In many ways, the new doctrine carried forth existing practices, as is evident in the figure of John the Baptist. He became the model of Christian asceticism, which was grounded primarily in these words of Jesus: "For there are some eunuchs who have been so from birth, and there are eunuchs who have been made eunuchs by others, and there are eunuchs who have made themselves eunuchs for the sake of the kingdom of heaven. Let anyone accept this who can." (Matthew 19:12)

These words have been taken to mean many different things; however, they must be interpreted in the context of early Christian reception, such as the following statement by Clement of Alexandria: "There are scores of eunuchs, who are little more than panderers; because of the trust they inspire, since they are incapable of sexual pleasure, they can minister to those wanting to carry on some love affair and not incur suspicion. The true eunuch, however, is not he who is unable, but he who is unwilling to gratify his passions."[93] Clement of Alexandria is speaking here not only of physical castration, but of a voluntary decision to forgo marriage in order to enter the "kingdom of heaven." The image of emasculated men was used in antiquity as a synonym for those who renounced sexuality freely without physical castration, especially among the Jews, for whom castration was prohibited. Requisite chastity (in the cultic sense) has been a basic tenet of nearly all known religions since time immemorial, as Eugen Fehrle has shown.[94] Chastity in the sense of moral and cultic purity requires sexual abstinence; compliance was facilitated by fasting and refraining from indulgence in practices that were held to be evil, such as incest and bodily contact with corpses.

This ascetic attitude was not restricted to Christianity. Asceticism was also widespread in India. During the period of Hellenism and early Christianity, Indian monks came to Alexandria and Syria to meet with Christian theologians, especially Clement of Alexandria. The doctrine of the Upanishads is just one example among many, as evidenced in this passage from the Brihadaranyaka Upanishad: "When all the desires that dwell in his heart are got rid of, then does the mortal [man] become immortal and attain Brahman in this very body."[95] Men who lived secluded in chastity, as anchorites and later as monks, considered the sexual act a spiritual loss of power that blinds a person to the essence of life. This conviction explains the requirement for temporary chastity in the general population as well, when preparing for initiation, battle (for instance, during the Islamic *jihad*), weddings, and most religious ceremonies and celebrations. Thus chastity underlies all true piety and ushers in the state of grace that brings about mystical and spiritual union with the godhead.

The priesthood strove to achieve this ideal. Even in ancient Egypt, priests on the grounds of the temple were required to maintain absolute chastity. This obligation stemmed from the notion that self-sacrifice was surrender and a path to redemption. In order to embark on this path, many founders of religions, notably Buddha and Mahavira (Jainism) in the 6th century B.C., demanded celibacy and renunciation of all physical desires. For this reason, these holy men were portrayed without sexual characteristics, a sign that they had risen above their gendered identity. Transcendence of the sexual sphere is also reflected in Christian iconography, both in imagery of Christ and in depictions of the redeemed on Judgment Day. In the earliest stages of Christianity, absolute chastity (and I here take exception to the view of Uta Ranke-Heinemann[96]) seems to have been advocated by leading theologians and bishops.

An extreme position was adopted in the theology of the Encratites. This form of gnosticism elevated sexual continence, following the model of Christ, to the very essence of Christianity. Their writings, which include the so-called Gospel of the Egyptians (mentioned by Origen in his homily to Luke [1:1]), the *Gospel According to Thomas*, the *Odes of Solomon*, the writings on abstinence and castration by Julius Cassianus (ca. 170), and Tatian's *On Perfection According to the Doctrine of the Savior*, provide a theological foundation for this outlook, which is based on the view that Christ did not consider it possible to conquer death as long as women gave birth. In this way, abstinence in its extreme form of *enkrateia* became the absolute requirement for liberation from death. On the subject of renunciation of desire, Julius Cassianus, a gnostic who probably lived in Egypt, disputed the view that the differing physiology of men and women indicated God's approval of sexual intercourse: "if this disposition was from the God towards whom we are eagerly pressing, he would not have blessed the eunuchs [Matthew 19:12], and the prophet would not have said that they are 'not an unfruitful tree [Isaiah 56:3]". He went on to assert that the Lord had told Salome that the victory over death would be at hand "when you trample underfoot the integument of shame, and when the two become one and the male is one with the female, and there is no more male and female."[97]

In the years 1945 to 1946, a fourth-century Coptic library was discovered near the Middle Egyptian village of Nag Hammadi. This discovery provided access to new sources and parallels to the encratite evidence that reaches back into the second century A.D. The words of Jesus in the gnostic *Gospel According to Thomas* are revealing: "When you make the two one and make the inside like the outside and the outside like the inside and the above like the below, and that you might make the male and the female be one and the same, so that the male might not be male nor the female be female, when you make eyes in place of an eye and a hand in place of a hand and a foot in place of a foot, an image in place of an image—then you will enter [the kingdom]."[98] In another passage, Jesus is quoted as saying: "When you strip naked without being ashamed, and take your garments and put them under your feet like little children and tread upon them, then [you] will see the child of the living. And you will not be afraid."[99]

These statements, which cite Jesus as their authority, reveal that for Gnosticism, absolute renunciation of the world and the desire to redeem one's soul were paramount. The practical consequences of this attitude were evident in the numerous gnostic currents in the Christian world. Retreat from the world and absolute chastity, even castration, were the order of the day. Marcion, the founder of a gnostic community from the early Christian period (ca. 85–160), forbade his followers marriage and all sexual activity. Adolf von Harnack, the leading Church historian of the German Weimar Republic, describes Marcion's reasoning as follows: "[Marcion] staked the life and growth of his community exclusively on the winning of new members, for the believers were not permitted to reproduce.

Medieval miniature with figures depicted as sexless being redeemed by Jesus (Stuttgart State Library)

Procession of the Dea Syria (Syrian goddess)
with the attributes of the Cybele festival

Marriage not only is filthy and shameful, but it also brings forth death . . . . Thus the determined rejection of sexuality on Marcion's part is not only a protest against matter and the flesh but also a protest against the God of the world and the law . . . . This is the "more complete rule of discipline" which Marcion prescribed, desecularizing and disembodying of life carried to extreme."[100]

Marcion's doctrines became quite popular, but were far too radical for many Christians. The result was devastating conflicts between the various gnostic tendencies. Followers of this heresy embraced martyrdom as a liberation from the earthly prison in which the soul striving for light was trapped: "For the defilement of the Law is manifest; but undefilement belongs to the light. The Law commands [one] to take a husband [or] to

take a wife, and to beget, to multiply like the sand of the sea. But passion which is a delight to them constrains the souls of those who are begotten in this place, those who defile and those who are defiled, in order that the Law might be fulfilled through them. And they show that they are assisting the world; and they [turn] away from the light, who are unable [to pass by] the archon of [darkness] . . . "[101]

This theology, which saw a new beginning in Christ and called for nullification of the laws of the Old Testament, was closely allied with the Church Fathers as well. Jerome (350–420) wrote that while marriage fulfills the earth, virginity fulfills paradise.[102] It is therefore difficult to draw a sharp distinction between heretical and orthodox concepts in the first few centuries of the spread of Christianity. Asceticism triggered the rise of monachism, first in Egypt (Pachomius, fourth century), then throughout the West. Asceticism was used to abolish evil. It became the cornerstone of Manichaeism and of Augustine's polemics.

Evil in general and the devil in particular were invariably associated with sexuality. In contrast to the angels, the devil was considered to embody sexual carnality, with women as his vehicles. Benjamin Walker summarized the gnostic view, which is also found in the texts from Nag Hammadi, as follows:

> Woman, it was held, is dangerous because of her beauty, which creates in man a raging torment of brutish passion. Her eyes are meant to entice, her feet swift to go wrong, her soft words to deceive. Her enchanting face, her soft breasts, her rounded buttocks, her seductive movements, are an invitation to voluptuous delights. She is the embodiment of temptation, leading men to their doom. The pathway to hell lies through the vagina, for the abyss of hell is the womb. Woman is inherently impure, a snare of nature, a tool of the devil, used by Satan to possess the souls of men. It is best to stay away from them, but where their company is unavoidable they should be kept in subjection. The devil has given women so much power that it is right that men should give them little, so as to redress the balance.[103]

These views provided the impulse for many self-emasculations and castrations, which were not forbidden until the year 325 at the Council of Nicaea. Its first Canon stated:

> If anyone has been castrated by surgeons operating on him during an illness, or by barbarians, he is to remain in

> the clerical estate; but if someone enjoying good health has castrated himself, this matter is to be investigated, and his belonging to the clerical estate is to be at an end, and in the future such persons must never be brought forward (1). But since it is clear that this applies to those who do such a thing intentionally and who dare to castrate themselves, it follows, then in regard to those who have been made eunuchs by barbarians or by their masters, that the canon (2) admits such men as these, be they found worthy, into the clerical estate.[104]

Up until the time of this injunction, the doctrine of chastity was spreading in heretic-gnostic and orthodox-ecclesiastical circles. Both literature and early Christian painting portrayed the devil as the symbol of evil, the master of desire and sensuality, culminating in the monumental artistic visions of the *Temptations of St. Anthony*. The *Isenheim Altarpiece* of Matthias Grünewald (1460/70–1528) reveals the power of this motif, which was immortalized by Hieronymus Bosch (ca. 1450–1516), Pieter Bruegel (ca. 1520–1569), Jan Mandyn (1502–1549), D. Teniers (1660–1690), and others. Gnostic imagery provided the foundation for a visual gnostic dimension, which opened the way for later Christian art. From the start, the Church was hostile to images. Heretical and gnostic circles were the first to create a theology of images as a visual accompaniment to texts, notably the Persian Gnostic Mani (216–276), whose picture book *Ardahang* is unfortunately no longer extant. This theology of images used biblical and early mythological motifs (serpents, flower symbolism, etc.), providing a repertoire of syncretic, apocalyptic, and gnostic images as difficult to decipher as the metaphoric and symbolic texts of what Hans Jonas has called a "cosmo-soteriological system."[105] This system also demanded the most rigorous asceticism, including vegetarianism and abstention from marriage. Only suicide was considered too radical a method for retaining one's purity.

This outlook provided ample justification for the strict gnostics in many lands, from Egypt to China (Manichaeans in the Turfan oasis). Moreover, the words of Jesus seemed to endorse castration (Matthew 19:12). The most prominent man to have chosen the path of castration was Origen (ca. 185–254), about whom Eusebius (ca. 260–339) wrote:

> [W]hile responsible for the instruction at Alexandria, Origen did a thing that provided the fullest proof of a mind youthful and immature, but at the same time of faith and self-mastery. The saying 'there are eunuchs who made themselves eunuchs for the kingdom of heaven's sake' he took in an absurdly literal sense, and he was eager both to fulfil the Saviour's words and at the same time to rule out any suspicion of vile imputations on the part of unbelievers. For in spite of his youth he discussed religious problems before a mixed audience. So he lost no time in carrying out the Saviour's words, endeavouring to do it unnoticed by the bulk of his pupils. But however much he might wish it, he could not possibly conceal such an act, and it was not long before it came to the knowledge of Demetrius, as head of the diocese. He was amazed at Origen's headstrong act, but approving his enthusiasm and the genuineness of his faith he told him not to worry, and urged him to devote himself more keenly than ever to the work of instruction.[106]

His influence was so great that many freely followed his example. Valerius (ca. 250), an Arab, founded a castration sect, which was later prohibited and persecuted. Other notable figures were Leontius of Antioch (d. 257), who became the Bishop of Jerusalem, and St. Hilary of Poitiers (d. 350), who lived in the desert (*enkrateia*) like many other anchorites and ascetics. The desert was a symbolic locus of renunciation and mortification of the flesh. It was also where the so-called Encratites settled. In Syria and Egypt, the centers of Christian monasticism, castration became the preferred means on the path to salvation. The prominent figures of this time included Macarius "the Egyptian" (330–390; his actual name was Symeon). The writings of Macarius are crucial for our understanding of gnostic doctrine. He provided a theological foundation for emasculations and adapted his doctrine to the teachings of the Desert Fathers.[107] The Coptic monasteries remained centers of castration of Asian slaves for a long time, even into the Islamic period.

Certain older formulations have become obscure or even incomprehensible to modern readers. The doctrine that man is created in God's image was predicated on the notion that humans first learned their sexual roles from the animals after their expulsion from paradise, hence the negative import of many animal metaphors. The following declaration in the *Hymns on Faith* of Ephrem the Syrian (306–373), one of the leading ascetics and teachers of the eastern Church, typified this attitude in depicting fallen man as a mirror of the repulsiveness of the animals: "For like unto beasts and brutes he made himself, as is written [Psalm 49; 12,20]. By them He shadowed forth man's own hideousness, that he might see how foul he had made himself; that when he saw his hideousness, he might be disgusted thereat; and when he saw the great blot upon him, he might feel ashamed; and when he saw whereto he was like, he might weep, and seek the brightness which he had lost."[108]

Our knowledge of this period has greatly expanded, but Gnosticism and the various heresies that accompanied the rise of Christianity have yet to be fully evaluated. This epoch, which marks a crossroads, merits the special interest of scholars, especially because its processes and structures are still in evidence today.

Although studies on the foundations of the "theology of renunciation" have focused on pre-Christian accounts, this theology was most clearly articulated by the Montanists. The Montanists came from Phrygia, the homeland of Cybele. Montanus, the founder of this movement, was active in the mid-first century A.D. Eusebius reports on his trance-like, ecstatic state, while overcome with spiritual excitement: "He raved, and began to chatter and talk nonsense, prophesying in a way that conflicted with the practice of the Church handed down generation by generation from the beginning."[109] This report recalls the narratives of the mystery cults of late antiquity. Montanus was formerly a priest of the Cybele who converted to Christianity after his castration. It is altogether possible that he had been drawn to several ecstatic-prophetic cults in the past. He now identified with the Paraclete, as typified the cults of both Cybele-Attis and Dionysus. Montanism spread quickly as a prophetic-ecstatic sect. Its adherents were intent on becoming "Phrygian" martyrs.

The central significance of the virginal prophetesses

Priscilla and Maximilla again points up a parallel to the Cybele tradition and stresses the apocalyptic character of this tightly organized movement, which survived continual persecution well into the fifth century in Asia Minor, Syria, and Northern Africa (Carthage). Its rituals closely resemble those of the Cybele-Attis cult, and it is possible that certain rites of that cult found their way into Christian liturgy by means of Montanism, especially the passion play about Attis. The movement was characterized by a strictly hierarchical priesthood, which was by no means the norm in Christian communities in the second century. The Phrygian ecstatic aspect reinforced the special character of this sect, which demanded an ascetic life of renunciation. This renunciation did not exclude emasculation, since it drew on the same enthusiasm as the pagan cults.

The Montanists are said to have mixed the blood of children with the Eucharist, although this claim cannot be substantiated. To whatever extent this contention has any basis in fact, the custom would most likely have stemmed from the pagan sacrifice of the initiates of the mystery cults, as was common during Cybele-Attis festivals. The emasculations practiced by the Montanists probably also took place in this context.

The special status of women in the sect developed from the same tradition. Their vow of chastity was on a par with that of the chaste (possibly emasculated) priests. It seems apparent, the current prevailing view notwithstanding, that the hierarchy of the Montanists was based not on gender, but on the precept of absolute sexual purity, that is, on a quasi-angelic existence. Up until the fourth to the fifth centuries and even beyond, ascetic convictions determined the path to salvation of the new Christian religion, which had spread to the East as far as China with the Manichaeans and the Nestorians. Sexual abstinence, which Marcion and Tatian demanded of baptized Christians, made them "angels" who were guaranteed resurrection. They observed stringent dictates even in their diet. They did not eat meat or drink wine, nor did they wed or engage in sexual intercourse. At the same time, however, there is mention of brides and bridegrooms, which makes sense because in Syrian, the language of most oriental Gnostics, the "Holy Ghost" is feminine. These terms therefore signify the mystical union of the soul striving for redemption with the Holy Ghost, which finds lyrical expression in the *Odes of Solomon*:

> Like the arm of the bridegroom over the bride,
> So is my yoke over those who know me.
>
> And as the bridal feast is spread out by the bridal
> pair's home,
> So is my love by those who believe in me.[110]

The Manichaeans, to whom even Augustine belonged for a brief period, held a similar view. They delineated multiple stages of renunciation, which were reflected in the organization of their communities into Archegos, the highest class; Electi, the chosen priesthood (teachers, bishops, priests); and Auditores, the hearers. Gnostic doctrines of the West thereby blended with Buddhist teachings. In the early part of this century, German discoveries of richly appointed libraries and paintings at the Silk Road, in the Turfan oasis, have provided new sources to reconstruct a "Jesus movement," which remained the state religion among the Uighurs in Kan-Chou well into the ninth century and, in some areas, as late as the thirteenth century. (Mani called himself an "Apostle of Jesus

Christ.") The Manichaean movement continued to flourish in parts of Central Asia and China, where it was then prohibited by legislation of the Ming emperors.

The demise of the Manichaeans was inevitable, both there and in the West, where they had a marked influence in Southern France as Cathari until their expulsion by Innocent III (1198–1216). These doctrines shared an abhorrence of sexuality, which was held to be the source of death. To break out of the cycle of worldly and secular society, marriage and procreation had to be dispensed with. Communities without marriage, as required by the gnostic-ascetic movements, probably resorted to radical methods more often than they admitted to remain true to their precepts. Consequently, the scholarly literature tends to ignore this aspect of the period. Peter Brown, author of *The Body and Society*[111] and numerous other books on this subject, rarely broaches this topic. Radicalism of this sort, which anticipated the later practices of the Central Russian *skoptsi*, resulted in emasculations. Had these not been practiced regularly, the Council of Nicaea (325) would not have needed to prohibit them. In all likelihood the formulation "becoming an angel" was a circumlocution for the practice that in the 16th and 17th centuries resulted in the "angelic voices" of the castrati. Clearly such radical views were unacceptable for a state church in the making during the Constantine era.

The introduction of Christianity as a state religion (313) did nothing to alter the deep-rooted Roman (secular) system of availing oneself of the services of eunuchs at the courts. If anything, the office of the attendant of the holy bedchamber of the Emperor or Empress (*praepositus sacri cubiculi*) only secured their status. This office, which was established in the time of Constantine, had its origin in official structures designed for emancipated castrati. It gained increasing significance because castrati, in contrast to other officials, served their emperors for life, unencumbered by sexual passions. Under Constantine's rule, court eunuchism was established definitively. In the eastern part of the Roman Empire, court eunuchism was adapted to oriental state structures, possibly the models of the Sasanid or even the Chinese Empire. It is no simple matter to figure out which head chamberlains were important at the time. In addition to many whose names are listed, there are also anonymous chamberlains in the catalogued registers of officials; the identities of these chamberlains remains elusive.

Late antiquity featured two parallel phenomena: the rise of Christianity with its ideology of chastity, and the continuity of customs of the Roman Empire with courtly structures in which eunuchs as well as emasculated Christians, such as Dorotheus and Georgonius, who were active at the court of Diocletian in Nicomedia (now called Izmir Körfezi), had a leading role in both Church and State.

Eusebius of Caesarea depicts eunuchs as not only important and influential dignitaries, but also martyrs of the Great Persecution of 303. The influence of the Church at the court was so pervasive that it was not even possible for the unbelieving Emperor Julian the Apostate (b. 331, r. 355–363) to enforce his court reforms against it. Ammianus Marcellinus (after 350), a Latinized Greek from Antioch on the Orontes, relates the following story:

> A barber who had been sent for to trim the emperor's hair presented himself splendidly dressed. Julian was aston-

> ished at his appearance and said: "I sent for a barber, not a treasury official." Then he asked what the man earned by his trade, and was told that it brought him in every day twenty men's allowance of bread and a proportionate amount of fodder for his beasts . . . . Julian's reaction was to dismiss the whole category of these people, together with cooks and the like, who were in the habit of receiving about the same amount. He declared that he had no use for their services and told them to take themselves off where they pleased.[112]

This anecdote clearly shows that there were attempts to shrink the retinue. These attempts were doomed to failure, however, because they met with neither understanding nor support. Even Julian was ultimately incapable of managing without eunuchs, as Ammianus Marcellinus emphasizes when reporting on the noble Eutherius:

> It may perhaps sound incredible, because if even Numa Pompilius or Socrates were to speak well of a eunuch and back their statements with an oath they would be accused of departing from the truth. But roses grow in the midst of thorns, and among wild beasts there are some that grow tame; so I will run over briefly the principal facts that are established about him. He was born in Armenia. His parents were free, but at an early age he was captured by members of a neighboring hostile tribe, who castrated him and sold him to some Roman merchants, by whom he was brought to Constantine's palace. There, as he grew up, he displayed rectitude and intelligence. He received an education suitable to his condition, and showed outstanding acuteness in the study and solution of abstruse and thorny prob-

> lems; he had a prodigious memory, and was so eager to be of service and so full of sound judgment that if the emperor Constantine had followed the honorable and upright course which Eutherius, who was then of mature age, urged upon him, he would have committed no faults, or at the worst only such as were venial. In his position as chamberlain he sometimes rebuked even Julian for being wedded to Asiatic manners and in consequence frivolous.
>
> Soon after withdrawing into retirement he was again summoned to the palace. He was calm and unusually consistent, and he cultivated the virtues of loyalty and moderation to such a degree that he was never charged with the betrayal of a confidence, unless it were to save another's life, or with the passion for gain which the rest of the courtiers exhibited.[113]

This passage conveys the impression that the court was stable and resistant to any change regarding the emperor. Its bureaucratic structures, which were strongly influenced by eunuchs, were decisive for late antiquity as a whole. Peter Brown correctly reminds us not to place undue emphasis on the exclusive power of the emperor, while ignoring the significant contributions of others: "Studies of late Roman law and political theory have tended to concentrate almost exclusively on the role of the emperor. By so doing, such studies run the risk of taking at its face value the vast 'institutionalized egotism'—the conviction that all power and all political initiative should reside in the person of the emperor—which characterized the imperial office in the fourth century in much the same way as it characterized the claims to absolute sovereignty made by Louis XIV. Yet in neither case did the ruler truly stand alone."[114]

The tradition of late antiquity specifies many court eunuchs by name, from which we can infer there must have been a large complement of emasculated men whose duty was to see to the interests of the Emperor, from attending to his personal needs to insuring his peace and quiet. There was also an increasing number of masters of ceremony and servants, most of whom were emasculated. They constituted a virtually homogeneous group that often embraced common religious tendencies, which proved problematic later on. For example, at the court of Constantine II, nearly everyone became Arians at the order of the influential *praepositus* Eusebius. He took their side when addressing the Emperor. Observers claimed that the ruler was completely dependent on the "almighty eunuch Eusebius." These religious and political power plays continued throughout Roman-Byzantine history. Court eunuchs became decision makers; traces of their power still determine the contours of Christianity between East and West.

A story from the year 431, which we learn from a chronicle by the Alexandrine patriarch Cyril (412–444), highlights the vital role of the *praepositi sacri cubiculi* (chiefs of the sacred household who were of great importance in Constantinople and ultimately wielded decisive power). This story offers us a glimpse into the tightly interwoven politics of Church and Empire on the eve of the Council of Ephesus in 431, at which the Virgin Mary was declared to be *Theotokos*, "she who gave birth to God." Oriental Christology, according to which the human and divine natures of Christ were inextricably and directly linked to Mary's conception, was thus reinforced.

According to Cyril's order, anyone who contradicted this doctrine was to be banned from the orthodoxy, naturally with the aid of imperial power. One of Cyril's adversaries was Nestorius (381–451), the patriarch of Constantinople, who later suffered precisely this fate.

In the interim, however, other events unfolded, initially in connection with the Council, which was conducted in the absence of important combatants, who were purposely excluded. Later, all possible means were employed to win over Emperor Theodosius II (408–450) to Cyril's side. This latter goal was pursued via his wife, Empress Pulcheria, with the aid of the court eunuch Chryseros. Chryseros used his well-established influence on the Empress, toward which end he was bribed with the so-called blessings of Cyril. The "secret" instructions contain a detailed list of gifts and gold presented to the retinue as a whole and the eunuch Chryseros in particular:

> That he might cease from opposing us, we have been forced to send him double amounts: that is, six large woolen tapestries, and four medium-sized, four large carpets, eight cushions, six table-cloths, six large woven hangings, six small hangings, six stools, twelve throne covers, four large curtains, four thrones of ivory, four stools of ivory, six Persian drapes, six large ivory plaques, six ostrich-eggs, and . . . if he helps us, he will receive, by the hand of the Lord Claudianus, two hundred pounds of gold.[115]

Bribery and corruption were the order of the day, but in this case the extent of the payments was outrageous. The court eunuchs usually left their fabulous wealth to the Emperors or the Church. This wealth thus wound up exactly where it had originated.

Every imperial court had a *praepositus sacri cubiculi*. However, it was not only the courts who placed castrated men in influential key positions. The Church also numbered castrati among its dignitaries; some even held the office of patriarch. In addition to those who had emasculated themselves for religious-ascetic reasons, there were also eunuchs, especially among the patriarchs, who had attained this honor for political reasons, owing to their descent from royal families. There were instances in which royal children were emasculated to prevent them from posing a threat to the ruler as pretender to the throne. In such cases, they were given the office of patriarch as a "consolation prize."

This fate probably befell Ignatius (847–858; 867–877), the son of Emperor Michael I (811–813, d. 844). Of course, the source material is not terribly clear on this point. The writers of church documents had two motives for censoring the subject. For one, there were the rulings of the Council of Nicaea; for another, they hoped to spare the prelate in question from the widely-held negative view of emasculated men.

A list of the names and achievements of the large number of men who belonged to this "unworthy" group and who steered the destiny of the empire since the time of Emperor Diocletian could fill volumes. Hundreds or even thousands of eunuchs were in the service of the Emperor, as was also the case in China. Only a few of this large group can be mentioned here as evidence of the omnipresence of eunuchs in Church and State. Office holders were expected not to mention their castration, which is why castration was seldom referred to overt-

Mosaic showing Emperor Justinian and his court.
The beardless figure can be identified as a *praepositus sacri cubiculi*. (Ravenna, Italy)

ly in the sources. This is even true of the *praepositi sacri cubiculi* and the *silentiari* and *cubiculari* who were their subordinates. The decision to conceal castration had legal as well as social ramifications. In the Christian era, acts of castration were punishable by law after the Council of Nicaea (325), which was explicitly restated in the West (400), and at the time of the Codex Justinianus (528–534). The illegality of castration notwithstanding, legislators continued punishing male homosexuality by having offenders castrated.

The most prominent example of the chamberlain's standing in the Byzantine empire was Emperor Anastasius (491–518). Under his predecessor, Emperor Zeno (474–491), Anastasius was commander of the silentiaries. With the aid of Zeno's widow, the Empress Ariadne, in whose favor he stood, he was able to rise to the highest office. Ariadne married him to legitimate him as Emperor. Before the Empress elevated him to the throne, he became Bishop of Antioch. Anastasius sympathized with the Monophysites, which made the patriarch of Constantinople, Euphenius, demand from him an oath of orthodoxy.

Anastasius was clearly influenced by the Manichaeans, since his mother had belonged to this gnostic group with its strict ordinances requiring chastity. He left a treasury of 320,000 pounds of gold to the Justinians, whom he especially favored. The fact that he had followed the strict ascetic rules of the best-organized Manichaean communities had enabled him to amass this sum of gold. It is reasonable to assume that Anastasius, who lived a life of celibacy, had emasculated himself as a young man. Owing to the unique degree of solidarity among the eunuchs and with their support, he attained a position at the court of the emperor that brought him into the immediate proximity of the rulers and gained the favor of the later widow of the Emperor. On the strength of his tax and monetary reform as well as his extraordinarily clever strategies, his reign was judged a success. His wife Ariadne died in 515, three years before his own death. They appear to have led a Josephite marriage.

The way was thus paved for Justinian, the next emperor. Justinian's rule is relatively easy to reconstruct. There are many extant sources, especially the writings of Procopius. In connection with him, mention must be made of the strategist Narses, who is called a eunuch in all accounts of him. Narses was an Armenian eunuch who began as an imperial *cubicularius*, and rose to *praepositus sacri cubiculi* and *protospatharius*. These positions gave him the right and privilege to supervise the imperial household and retinue, thus allowing him to wield a high degree of influence in court life. His clever strategies, vision, and pacifist stance distinguished his longstanding service of the throne. Narses had a pivotal role in Justinian's first Persian War, and in the Nika revolt he succeeded in breaking up the alliance of the Blues and Greens and leading the Veneti back to the side of the emperor. There are many monographs about Justinian and his wife Theodora, yet little scholarship focuses exclusively on Narses, although Justinian's ability to maintain power on the Bosporus was largely attributable to the energy and resourcefulness of Narses.[116] In *Justinian und Theodora* (1943), Wilhelm Schubart described Narses as "small, lanky, but virile, although a eunuch; energetic and clever, but lacking a fine education and awkward in speech . . . he loyally served the royal couple through thick and

used by the departure of the irate governor for Naples,
l Pope John was immediately despatched to try to pre-
l on him to return . . . The pope soothed the aged gov-
nor and brought him back to Rome.[118]

es is said to have died at the age of 95 in Rome (573),
h his age at death is the subject of some debate. He is
n a Bithynian monastery.

Byzantine Empire, Persia, India, China, and later the
n Empire were shaped to a significant degree by
s who had risen to positions of power despite their per-
reatment as outsiders. The figure of Basil, the illegiti-
on of emperor Romanus Lecapenus (r. 920–944, d.
one example among many. Constantine VII Porphy-
us (b. 905, r. 945–959), first co-regent and then emper-
had Basil castrated in order to eliminate him from con-
on as the heir apparent. Basil was the last of the line of
nanus I. By descent and birth, he was hardly an "out-
t the court. If anyone should have been regarded as an
', it should have been Basil's father, who had risen from
a peasant to emperor. As for Basil himself, his sister
was the wife of Constantine VII and thus the empress.
gh Basil set the policies of the Byzantine empire for
four decades, even under four successors of
ntine VII, and was also involved in arranging the mar-
f Princess Theophano to Otto II (b. 955, r. 973–983),
or of the Holy Roman Empire, his historical recognition
n slow in coming.

s own time, however, he was anything but a *persona*
ata. Under Emperor Nicephorus Phocas (r. 963–969),
ook over the post of the eunuch Joseph Bringas, the

thin over the course of decades and
mettle time and again."[117]

The exploits of the reign of Just
those of Narses. He became guarantor
or and also enjoyed the favor of the e
she died, Justinian followed her wis
over Belisarius. Narses spent the last
dwelling in the Palace of the Caesars
Ostrogoths and longstanding regent of
in his declining years and roused th
according to Ferdinand Gregoroviu
classic history of Rome in the Middle

> Narses . . . buried treasures so vast i
> town in Italy, that after his death it
> bring them to light. . . . Incapable of
> of Narses so long as Justinian lived,
> to overthrow the favorite as soon as J
> ceeded to the throne (565) . . . In 56
> rector of Italy for sixteen years,
> recall from the Emperor Justin . . . H
> ture to return to Constantinople, or
> mand on being informed of the thr
> Sophia that she "would make the eun
> the women." Legend relates that Na
> "would weave her such a web as wo
> time to unravel," and that forthwith
> from Naples summoning the Lombard
> Italy, sending, as evidences of the we
> choice fruits as well as other valuab
> fear of the Romans, who dreaded

thin over the course of decades and proved his extraordinary mettle time and again."[117]

The exploits of the reign of Justinian were in great part those of Narses. He became guarantor of the rule of the emperor and also enjoyed the favor of the empress Theodora. When she died, Justinian followed her wishes by choosing Narses over Belisarius. Narses spent the last years of his life in Rome, dwelling in the Palace of the Caesars. This conqueror of the Ostrogoths and longstanding regent of Italy fell prey to avarice in his declining years and roused the envy of the Romans, according to Ferdinand Gregorovius (1821–1891), whose classic history of Rome in the Middle Ages reports:

> Narses . . . buried treasures so vast in a fountain in some town in Italy, that after his death it took several days to bring them to light. . . . Incapable of shaking the position of Narses so long as Justinian lived, the Romans sought to overthrow the favorite as soon as Justin the Young succeeded to the throne (565) . . . In 567, after having been rector of Italy for sixteen years, Narses received his recall from the Emperor Justin . . . He either did not venture to return to Constantinople, or he defied the command on being informed of the threat of the Empress Sophia that she "would make the eunuch spin wool with the women." Legend relates that Narses replied that he "would weave her such a web as would take all her lifetime to unravel," and that forthwith he sent messengers from Naples summoning the Lombards from Pannonia to Italy, sending, as evidences of the wealth of the country, choice fruits as well as other valuable things . . . . The fear of the Romans, who dreaded his revenge, was

> aroused by the departure of the irate governor for Naples, and Pope John was immediately despatched to try to prevail on him to return . . . The pope soothed the aged governor and brought him back to Rome.[118]

Narses is said to have died at the age of 95 in Rome (573), although his age at death is the subject of some debate. He is buried in a Bithynian monastery.

The Byzantine Empire, Persia, India, China, and later the Ottoman Empire were shaped to a significant degree by eunuchs who had risen to positions of power despite their perpetual treatment as outsiders. The figure of Basil, the illegitimate son of emperor Romanus Lecapenus (r. 920–944, d. 948), is one example among many. Constantine VII Porphyrogenitus (b. 905, r. 945–959), first co-regent and then emperor, had had Basil castrated in order to eliminate him from consideration as the heir apparent. Basil was the last of the line of the Romanus I. By descent and birth, he was hardly an "outsider" at the court. If anyone should have been regarded as an intruder, it should have been Basil's father, who had risen from son of a peasant to emperor. As for Basil himself, his sister Helena was the wife of Constantine VII and thus the empress. Although Basil set the policies of the Byzantine empire for nearly four decades, even under four successors of Constantine VII, and was also involved in arranging the marriage of Princess Theophano to Otto II (b. 955, r. 973–983), Emperor of the Holy Roman Empire, his historical recognition has been slow in coming.

In his own time, however, he was anything but a *persona non grata*. Under Emperor Nicephorus Phocas (r. 963–969), Basil took over the post of the eunuch Joseph Bringas, the chief adviser of Emperor Romanus II (r. 959–963). As a *parakoimomenos* (manager of the Sacred Palace, the top office eunuchs could hold), he was appointed *proedros* and thereby became the new emperor's right hand. John Tzimisces (r. 969–976), the lover of the empress and murderer of Romanus II, succeeded the latter as emperor. As a consequence, the empress, under the pressure of the Church, was no longer able to share the throne with him and was banished. The eunuch Basil assumed the same influential role under the new emperor, which he retained even after his great-nephew Basil II (r. 976–1025) officially assumed power. It can even be claimed that the reign of Basil II, which was so successful for the Byzantine Empire, owed its success solely to the influence of his great-uncle, who not only introduced Basil II to political affairs, but also saved him from the propitious revolt of Bardas Sclerus with clever political and military schemes (979). Nonetheless, these two strong personalities could not work together over an extended period.

The elderly court eunuch owed his influence to his familial connections and to the trust the empresses placed in him. The first empress was his biological sister, and the second, a daughter of a tavern owner, the beautiful but unscrupulous Anastaso. Anastaso, whose royal name was Theophano, was the mother of the future emperors Basil II and Constantine VIII. After the premature death of her husband Romanus II, she found a suitable confidant in the mighty and experienced eunuch Basil. The third empress to confide in Basil was Theodora. Theodora was the daughter of Constantine VII and and the wife of John Tzimisces. She was also Basil's niece and the aunt of Basil II. The elderly eunuch, however, was embroiled in a conflict with the young ruler, when the latter began to exercise his power independently after 985. This may have been the year in which his mother died; she had been brought back from exile to Constantinople, most likely on the advice of his great-uncle, the eunuch Basil I. Neither could hold his own ground any longer; the queen died, and the eunuch had to go. Although Basil attempted to plot a conspiracy with Phocas against his ungrateful pupil, his plot was discovered, and the chamberlain was dispossessed like a rebel and sent into exile, where he soon died.

Bertha Eckstein-Diener's novel on the decline of Byzantium is a paean to court eunuchs.[119] However, its depiction of the Byzantine castrati, like other literary and historical works on the subject, overlooks the many outstanding contributions eunuchs made as monks, scholars, artists, and musicians. Even less is known about them than about the *praepositi sacri cubiculi*.

Unfortunately, little iconographic evidence remains from the early Byzantine period; most was destroyed in the course of iconoclastic conflicts. Only on the periphery of Byzantium, on the Sinai (Convent of St. Catherine), and in the earlier Christian Nubian empires that maintained their independence from Islam until the 16th century, do extant pictures bear witness to this cultural and historical phenomenon. The walls of the churches were populated with angels portrayed as beardless and genderless. These characteristics were unambiguous canonical symbols of chastity. There can be no doubt that later pictures of angels and saints, from Byzantium to Moscow, displaying these features should be interpreted as images of chastity. Other popular portrayals of saints also featured this symbolism, for example St. George as dragon-slayer, whose iconic rendering has its origin in the ancient Egyptian motif of the victorious Horus as Seth-the-dragon-slayer, and the Apostle Thomas, whose apocryphal gospel leaves no doubt that redemption can only be achieved by means of absolute chastity. Even John the Evangelist, who lived to a ripe old age, is portrayed as chaste. He is considered the symbol of unerotic love. We should also mention Pantaleon who, according to legend, was the personal physician of Emperor Maximian. Pantaleon died a martyr in 304. There is ample evidence to suggest that he was emasculated as punishment, as was common at the time. Byzantine iconography of chastity took up pre-Christian iconic representations that contained a clear message; these messages live on in Christian imagery. In adopting the fixed canon of images, some artists were, of course, no longer able to grasp the meaning of the original contents, especially in the West, where there was no established theology of images. These artists deviated from the models and in doing so unintentionally altered their messages.

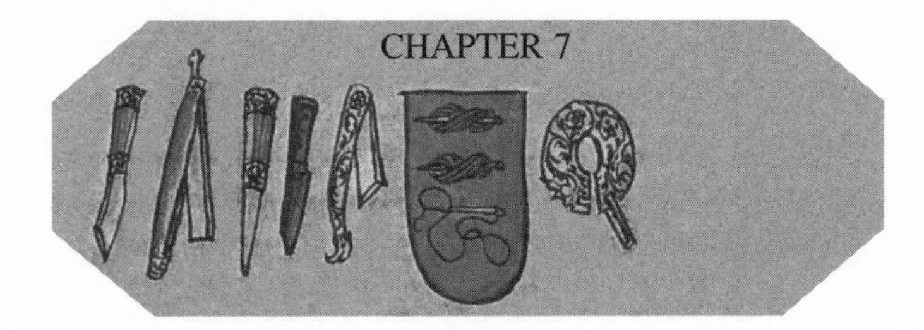

From the Origins of Islam to the Topkapi Seraglio

> "During my unconsciousness a barber was sent for, who castrated me completely and cauterised the wound with red-hot irons. I woke to find myself a eunuch for good and all . . . Later [my master] took me to the market and sold me for a much greater price than I had fetched before, because I was a eunuch."
>
> —*The Thousand and One Nights*, 39th night

The Thousand and One Nights, Harun al-Rashid, palaces of the caliphs, harems, and eunuchs . . . all of these names and terms have come to be synonymous in the Western imagination with Arabic-Islamic culture. Most of us are more likely to associate them with folktales and fantasy than with historical reality. This imagery set the stage for our western notions of the East. A widespread current of orientalism also ensued in the late 18th century and throughout the 19th century; historicizing, fantastic images of the orient were popularized by such painters as Jean-Auguste-Dominique Ingres (1780–1867), Théodore Gericault (1791–1824), Eugène Delacroix (1798–1863), Léon Gérôme (1824–1904), Sir Lawrence Alma-Tadema (1836–1912), Hans Makart (1840–1884), and Edmond Dulac (1882–1953). Their works also shaped the literature of the day, particularly the works of Alphonse de Lamartine, Victor Hugo, Gérard de Nerval, Théophile Gautier, Gustave Flaubert, Henryk Sienkiewicz, Edward William Lane, Sir Richard Francis Burton (1821–1890), and Karl May (1842–1912). These writers succeeded in popularizing in the West the effect of foreign, cruel, exotic, incomprehensible—and thus also fascinating and compelling—illusions and visions. Afterwards, these transposed visions were featured not only in libraries and museums, but also in opera houses, for example in works by Gioacchino Rossini (*The Caliph of Baghdad*, 1818; *Moses in Egypt*, 1818; *Semiramide*, 1823) and Giuseppe Verdi (*Nabucco*, 1842; *Aida*, 1871), and even in upper-class homes (servants, objects, pictures, etc.). These trends, greatly in vogue in the 19th century, had flourished with encounters with the Orient and the contemporary interest in foreign cultures and their legacies. The first French translation of the stories of the *Thousand and One Nights* (1704–1708) by Antoine Galland (1646–1715), which featured harem and eunuch stories, thus found an avid readership. These stories lived on in the literature of cultures around the world, from Proust's *Remembrance of Things Past* to the writings of Jorge Luis Borges, and have enriched western literature until the present day. Behind these visible phenomena, however, stood the growing field of orientalism, which had found one of its first representatives in Antoine Galland. It experienced a

Ingres: Odalisque, with a black eunuch in the background

strong upsurge with Napoleon's campaign in Egypt (1798–1799), which drew in scholars as well as military personnel.

Certainly the attraction of the Orient was also shaped by the expansion of colonialism during this period, to the detriment of the Ottoman Empire. The Industrial Revolution, which offered rapid communication and improved means of travel, intensified the confrontation of East and West and had far-reaching consequences for the East, in which western-style social and revolutionary movements began to predominate. These movements ultimately hastened the decline of romantic visions of the Orient, although orientalizing mythology did flare up again briefly with Lawrence of Arabia and his *Seven Pillars of Wisdom* (1926).

Political upheavals in the wake of the revolution of 1911 in China and after Mustafa Kemal's 1920 seizure of power in Turkey signalled the end of state-sanctioned eunuchism. The harem disappeared along with the Ottoman court, the "liberated" women and eunuchs were displayed in the capitals of the world, the fairy-tale imagery of Ingres and T. Chassériau (1819–1856) faded away.

This period of revolutionary changes did not open the portals of locked palaces in the "forbidden cities," but confronted the public with "memoirs" of harem women of the bygone oriental world. These books were most often written by western women who had become the wives of Muslim rulers, such as the memoirs of the Princess Djavidan Hanum, the former wife of the last khedive of Egypt, ousted by the British in 1914. Although the eunuchs were inextricably linked with the harems, they were often viewed as a mere marginal phenomenon, unworthy of discussion. They were considered neuter gender, the "third sex," as Princess Hanum (1877–1968), an Austrian, reported:

> The eunuchs established a connection to the outside world; they were, so to speak, the spokesmen of the harems . . . Their lives were played out both within the harem and outside its confines. Eunuchs were not slaves as they had been in earlier times. They could be brought in and let go, and had the right to leave their "job" if it did not suit them. The eunuch was more like a representative figure without specified duties. He was therefore only found in well-to-do harems. He accompanied the Hanums and the Kalfas when they went shopping. He haggled and paid for the purchases. He also bought their travel tickets, stowed away the veiled women as well as the innumerable packages wrapped in cloth, calmed the children, was rushed around and lost his head just like the Kalfas, who were of no use whatsoever once they were outside the harem.[120]

The oriental system of dignitaries was testimony to the magnificence of the ruler, the state, and the fortuitous destiny (*kismet*) to afford luxury and maintain a group of people in comfortable circumstances without really needing to occupy them. Remuneration of the eunuchs varied according to the financial circumstances of the harem. In the wealthiest harems, eunuchs wore silk-lined coats, patent leather shoes, fashionable clothing, and a tarboosh on their heads.

A glance back to the origin and basic values of Islam reveals that castration of human beings and animals was just as despised by the prophet Muhammed (ca. 570–632) as it was by the Jews. Emasculation was a punishable offense. This prohibition also prevailed during the Umayyad dynasty (661–750); apparent confirmation can be found in the architecture of the desert castles, which did not provide for harems. After a series of Islamic invasions into lands and empires in which harems with eunuchs were an essential component of a court, however, the situation began to change. The influence of Persia, which combined local customs and models from the Far East, was paramount in initiating this change. The nomadic Arabs, unfamiliar with courtly life, were overwhelmed by the luxury in the conquered territories.

Because castration was forbidden for Muslims, the eunuchs in the Islamic world generally came as slaves from Byzantium, where they had been castrated for psalmody, and from France, Africa—especially Nubia and Ethiopia—and, in later times, India and China. They were usually given new names and converted to Islam, which facilitated their position at the court.

According to the Arab historian Mukaddasi, white eunuchs were of two kinds:

> (a) The Slavs whose homeland was behind Khwarizm. They were imported to Spain, where they were castrated and exported thence to Egypt.
>
> (b) The Greeks who came to Syria and Armenia. But this source was exhausted owing to the devastation of the frontier.
>
> I questioned a number of them regarding castration, and learnt that the Greeks remove the testicles of boys, intended for dedication to the church. This they do so that they may not run after women or be assailed by lustful passions. When the faithful made their incursions

> they attacked the churches and carried away the boys.[121]

The "black" and "Chinese" eunuchs were usually brought to the courts as a result of slave trade or as diplomatic gifts.

Eunuchs were bought and sold not only by Muslims, but also by Jews and Christians. One of the few European pilgrims to Mecca, Heinrich Karl Eckard Helmuth von Maltzan (1826–1874), described this process in a report composed in 1854:

> At Assiut, Sheik Mustafa took the opportunity to inveigh against the dreadful Gipti [Copts]. Some Copts of Assiut make a business out of buying young black slaves and subjecting them to castration, in the course of which many of them die; however, the survivors are sold for twenty times more than the price they could formerly command. Are the Muslims wrong to despise oriental Christians?[122]

Von Maltzan thus confirms the earlier account provided by the 17th-century French traveler Chardin, who, regarding the same region of Upper Egypt, told of "large factories," which supplied Turkey with guardians of female virtue, and of two Coptic monks who proved more skillful at castrations than all of their predecessors.[123] All reports concur that thousands of children in the Coptic monasteries of Egypt, who had been obtained as spoils of war or bought from poor people, were castrated in a very primitive manner at a tender age, generally between seven and ten. The number of fatalities often exceeded 60 percent—a horrifying statistic, especially if we consider that in China the mortality rate for the same procedure was about 2 percent. From year to year, the demand for castrati grew, in direct proportion to the increasing number of women who wound up in the harems of the rulers, governors, and high dignitaries.

Mukaddasi provides details about the two major types of castration. In one procedure, the testicles were ablated simultaneously with the penis; in the other, an incision in the scrotum was made first, to remove the testicles, then, with a piece of wood under the penis, it was cut off at the root.[124] According to *The Encyclopedia of Islam*, however, "this horrible mutilation was not general, and it is probable that the majority of eunuchs were not actually *madjabib* [complete eunuchs], but *khisyan* properly so-called, who had undergone a *khisa* consisting, for the operator (*khasi*), of incising and at the same time cauterizing the scrotum by means of a red-hot blade of iron and removing the testicles."[125]

Eunuchism tends to be considered only in the context of harems. However, right from the beginning of the caliphate, eunuchism had a much broader dimension. Eunuchs were omnipresent. They were barred only from official religious positions, but it would have been inconceivable for anyone else to carry out their cult function as guardians of the holy sites. Even today, there are black eunuchs functioning as "guardians" in Mecca and Medina, at the Dome of the Rock in Jerusalem, and at the grave of Abraham in Hebron. The 14th-century traveler Ibn Batutta describes their wealth and power in Medina. "The servitors of this noble mosque and its custodians are eunuchs from among the Ethiopians and such like. They present a handsome appearance, they have a clean, meticulous look, and their clothes are elegant. Their chief is known as the *shaykh al-khuddam*, and he has the position of one of the grand amirs. They have stipends in the lands of Egypt and Syria which are brought to them every year."[126]

The earliest widely-known report in Europe is by Johann Wild, who traveled to Mecca and Medina in 1607. Wild describes seeing emasculated men, who were held in high esteem in Islamic society, at the grave of the prophet. The practice of using eunuchs as guardians was later chronicled by other travelers such as J.L. Burckhardt and Ch. Snouck Hurgronje. These reports were recently compiled by F.E. Peters. One report by Hurgronje included the following information:

> The great abuse condemned even by Islam but still maintained, we will not leave here unmentioned, the castration of such slaves as are to attend on the women of people of very high position, or have to keep order in the mosques of the holy town. In Mecca most of the eunuchs are of the latter class. These eunuchs are called *aghas* or more rarely *tawashis*, and so when a man exceptionally allows a young unmarried man to have conversation with female members of his family, he says to people who might be scandalized that the young man is like an *agha*. Very few eunuchs are kept by private persons. All are imported already castrated, but the demand for this article for the mosque makes Mecca an accomplice in this evil. Among the *aghas*—eunuch attendants in the mosques—are found Nubians, negroes, and Abyssinians, often strongly built but seldom amiable people.[127]

Burckhardt added the following details:

> I enquired at Shendi whether any of the slaves were eunuchs, but I was informed that no eunuchs were

> imported into that place during my stay, and that Borgho, to the west of Darfour, is the only country in eastern Sudan where slaves are thus mutilated for exploitation. Their number however is very small; a few are carried to Egypt from Darfour, and the remainder are sent as presents by the Negro sovereigns to the great mosques at Mecca and Medina, by way of Suwakin.[128]

The importance of this institution is confirmed by the fact that the Mamluks in Fustat had their graves guarded by black eunuchs. One can recognize in this custom the continuity of the sacral kingdom. Thereby the presence of the ruler, who was hardly visible to the outside world, is manifested by the guardians. The idea of the sacral kingdom continues; not only the grave of the prophet in Medina but also sacred locations in Morocco are protected by emasculated guards and are off limits to non-Muslims. Shaun Marmon reports that

> In 1990 the Saudi magazine *al-Yamama* published an interview with Salim Farid, the official in charge of the "affairs of the *aghawat*" of Mecca. According to this interview, fourteen eunuchs still served at the sanctuary of Mecca and seventeen at the sanctuary in Madina. Much of the interview is devoted to a discussion of the great wealth of the eunuchs. "Yes, they are very rich," says Salim Farid. "God has deprived them of sensual pleasure in the world but he has enriched them with material possessions and, before that, with the honor of serving the Sacred House."[129]

As the new ruling class, the Muslims took possession of the achievements of the peoples they conquered, especially since as a minority they had little choice but to adapt to existing structures. Many of the conquered converted to Islam, particularly the Persians, who, after the Arabs, soon constituted the largest Muslim ethnic group. This group shaped the future customs (such as harems guarded by eunuchs) and cultures of the Islamic world from East Asia to the Iberian Peninsula. Harun al-Rashid (786–809), the Caliph of Baghdad and contemporary of Charlemagne, had in his palace of Mutawakkil a harem with two hundred women and an unknown number of eunuchs—a remarkable development in view of the fact that his predecessor, the founder of the Abbasid dynasty, al-Mansur (754–775), had been the very first to establish a harem and al-Mahdi (775–786) was the first to benefit from this luxury. Fifty years later, oriental sources report that twelve thousand women from all parts of the globe populated the harem palaces of the caliph. Caring for them and organizing their palaces required an army of slaves and eunuchs who, just like their charges, hailed from many different countries. They came to the court as the spoils of victory in war or as gifts from abroad or from neighboring areas. Others were obtained at slave markets, which for centuries provided a steady supply of female slaves and eunuchs for the harems.

Even the four wives that were permitted and the ever-changing number of female slaves became ongoing source of intrigues, in part because of the preferential treatment and future status of sons born to them. This was certainly true of Harun al-Rashid's harem. His successor was not his son with the legitimate wife Zubaidah, but al-Mamun (813–833), the son of his union with Marajil, a Persian slave. This son eliminated his half-brother Amin, the co-pretender to the throne, who was seven months younger, just as his father had done when he had ascended the throne. These battles for succession, which occur in the Islamic world even today, gradually crystallized because no successor was specified by Muhammed and Arab tradition did not provide any detail as to how succession would take place. The caliphs had always seen themselves as charismatic rulers, which ultimately explains the heretical notion of the return of the prophet Madhi. These caliphs always tried to select their successors. The story of Jaffar and Abbasah has inspired writers even in modern times and contributes to our understanding of the caliph Harun al-Rashid's justifiable fear of additional pretenders to the throne:

> Both Tabari and Masudi tell us that Harun al-Rashid held his sister Abbasah in great affection and loved to spend his evenings in her company. But his favorite companion was Jaffar. It was quite unsuitable for a man from outside the family to be admitted to the company of a young woman, but Harun found a way to arrange things: he decided to marry them to each other but with the proviso, he explained to Jaffar, "that you see her only in my company, that your body never approaches hers and you have no conjugal relations with her. You may thus share our evenings of pleasure without risk." Jaffar accepted and swore solemnly before witnesses never to visit his young wife, stay alone with her, or even spend a minute under the same roof unless Harun was present. Thus, whenever Jaffar saw his wife, "he avoided looking at her and lowered his eyes."
>
> Jaffar was handsome, however, and according to Tabari, "There was no woman in Harun's palace, either among the free-born or among the slaves, more beautiful than Abbasah." . . . [Jaffar was tricked into consummat-

> ing the marriage, and Abbasah became pregnant and] gave birth to a son, who was whisked to Mecca in the care of a eunuch and a maidservant . . . . [When Harun learned of the child's existence, he] had the child tracked down, then did away with both him and his sister.[130]

Danger lurked everywhere, owing to the rising number of pretenders to rule, as a result of the familial and political courtly cross-connections between royal wives (family of the caliph) and high dignitaries (influential viziers). Harun al-Rashid recognized that the castrati could be used to ensure safety. For this reason, they were able to attain positions in his empire that were previously beyond their reach. The stories about Harun al-Rashid's nightly walks through the city, accompaned by his eunuch and sword-bearer Masrur, were later also attributed to the heretical Fatimid al-Hakim (996–1026), the persecutor of Jews and Christians, depicted centuries later in Gérard de Nerval's *Voyage en Orient* (1851).[131]

The sources provide a realistic impression of the time. Some are based on what is known about the Ottoman situation, which unfortunately does not concur with sources on the early Islamic period. Very few of the latter are extant, and even those few do not necessarily provide reliable information concerning the matter of the number of the harem women. It is, however, clearly established that their number was a symbol of power and prosperity, even back in the time of King Solomon (ca. 1000 B.C.). In the ruling families, the choice of official wives—from whom it was relatively simple to obtain a divorce—was determined mainly by political considerations. Female slaves were carefully selected by the ruler or the eunuch he entrusted with the task. All of this does not explain the necessity of a harem as a sanctuary of the master and of his wives. In the course of time, following the model of Muhammed, whose wives were not allowed to be touched by anyone after his death, an especially pronounced patriarchal view developed, according to which the mothers had to be shielded from the outside world and all men other than their husband to guarantee the paternity of the children. In this situation, only castrati could function as guards. They also had the special role of liaison between the wife or wives and the master. Many eunuchs maintained impeccable order in the harems, even when they did not hold a rank that obliged them to do so. If a eunuch fell in love platonically with a woman, his devotion knew no bounds. As an intimate confidant of the women, who lived in seclusion, he shared their dreams and sorrows, their anger and despair. Not always were the eunuchs assigned pleasant tasks. They often had to carry out unpleasant duties for their masters, such as speaking to the harem women about matters that would involve awkward confrontations and weepy encounters. The eunuch had to endure the onslaught of emotions in his master's stead; the master waited for the dust to settle before reappearing in the harem. This duty resulted in an especially intimate bond between rulers and eunuchs, who bore their secrets.

Eunuchs were sometimes the object of homoerotic desire for the Abbasids, as they had been in the cultures of antiquity. Evidently Amin, the son of Zubaidah and Harun al-Rashid, had pronounced leanings of this sort. Al-Tabari, one of the most prominent Persian historians, related that his mother Zubaidah tried to dissuade her son Amin from these leanings by supplying him with pretty girls disguised as boys, hoping thereby to cure him of his aberrant predisposition. It is not known whether her attempts succeeded.

Changes since that time were not limited to fashion, which was hailed by Abu Nuwas: "You see figures that are female in behavior, but in men's clothes. Their hands and feet are bare, their ears and necks unadorned. They are as slim as the reins of a horse, sword sheaths, or belts. But they have ample bottoms in their tunics and daggers at their waists. Their curls are coiled like a scorpion, and their mustaches are perfumed."[132] The ideal of feminine beauty also underwent a transformation. The preference was for "boy-girls." One can assume that stories about eunuchs became a standard feature of popular theater, shadow plays, and other spectacles (*hakija*), and paved the way for the early phases of tranvestism.

According to Abu Nuwas, whose verses are alleged to have appeared in some versions of the *Thousand and One Nights*, we may assume that the rise of eunuchism in high positions of administration and government was the work of al-Amin. He was consciously continuing a Sassanid tradition (Fatih 3774, fol. 269b–270a) and he loved eunuchs: "He has introduced the eunuchs; he has ushered in the cult of impotence. And the world follows the practice of the Prince of the faithful."[133]

After the time of the Abbasids, the world of Islam was pervaded with eunuchism. Eunuchs were found in all newly-established Islamic nations in Central Asia and India, as well as in Northern Africa and on the Iberian Peninsula. Their role as confidants provided them access to very influential positions even under the first caliphs. They were advisors, generals, administrators, and regents. Sometimes they even usurped power; one example is Mi'nis, the "Emir of emirs" (commander-in-chief), the eunuch of the caliph Muktadir (908–933). Over a course of decades, he governed policy, appointed viziers, administrators, and officers, and even the caliph Qahir (931–933). He eventually had the latter put to death after declaring him an unfit ruler. His own confidants and agents were also eunuchs and were even Christian. Stephen, one of these eunuchs, who died in 935, is said to have been the manager of the private treasury of the caliph. The status of the eunuchs, which was based on a pre-Islamic administrative innovation, had been typical for both the Abbasids and the Fatimids for a long time. But even before the Ismailites in Egypt under the dynastic name of the Fatimids seized rule, there was already among the Tulunids (868–905)—under whom the Turkish mercenaries achieved ever greater power—a black eunuch, Kafur, who came into power as a "master." The eunuchs, who were not necessarily castrati in the earliest phase of Islamization, seem to have carried on the tradition of antiquity. In this respect, comparison with the situation in Byzantium is warranted. The Muslims waged war with the Byzantine Empire over the course of centuries and captured men who then often entered the service of the court. It is altogether possible that the triumphant flotilla commanders who were recruited from their ranks included eunuchs, one notable example being Thamil of Tarsus, the victor over Niketas (919).

According to some sources, there were 11,000 castrati as early as the beginning of the 10th century; other sources claim only 7,000, and still others keep the number as low as 700. By all accounts, however, they were indispensable and influential at the court of the caliphs. In *Spanish Islam: A History of the*

Moslems in Spain, written in 1874, the Dutch orientalist Reinhart Dozy evaluated materials and chronicles that substantially enhance our understanding of influential eunuchs. The Umayyads, who had had to cede their rule in the East to the Abbasids, reached the Iberian Peninsula in 711 and founded in the place of the conquered Gothic empire their Cordovan caliphate, the formal end of which coincided with the fall of Granada in 1492. Six hundred years earlier, the situation had been quite different. Ibn al-Kutia's account of how the successor of Abd al-Rahman II (822–852) was selected sheds light on the machinations of the eunuchs at all Islamic courts:

> Abd er-Rahman II died suddenly . . . Since Abd er-Rahman had not decided which of his sons, Mohammed and Abdallah, was to succeed him, and both aspirants to the throne were ignorant of their father's death, all depended on the choice made by the eunuchs of the palace. Those who had attended Abd er-Rahman during his last moments promptly locked the gates of the castle, in order to prevent any rumor of the Sultan's death escaping, and summoned their colleagues. One of the most influential eunuchs addressed the assembly. "Comrades," he said, "an event of the deepest importance to us all has happened. Our master is no more." Thereupon the eunuchs began to weep and lament. "This is no time for tears," he continued, "our lamentations can be postponed. The moments are precious. Let us first guard our own interests and those of our fellow Moslems. To whom do ye award the throne?" "To our lord, the son of our benefactress the Sultana!" they cried with one voice.
>
> Tarub's intrigues seemed, therefore, to have borne fruit; by dint of bribery and promises she had won over

the eunuchs, and thanks to them, her son Abdallah would ascend the throne. But would the nation approve the choice of the eunuchs? It was doubtful, for Abdallah was chiefly distinguished for the laxity of his morals; his orthodoxy was more than suspect, and the people detested him. The eunuch Abu 'l-Mofrih, a pious Moslem who had made pilgrimage to Mecca, was conscious of these drawbacks. "Is the opinion just given that of you all?" he asked. "It is!" was the unanimous reply. "In that case, it is mine also," he went on, "I have a better reason than any of you to show my gratitude towards the Sultana, for she has lavished more favors upon me than on others. Nevertheless this is a matter which calls for our mature consideration; for if we elect Abdallah, our power in Spain is at an end. Henceforth, when we walk in the streets we shall be reviled. "Accursed be these eunuchs, who, when they might have conferred the throne upon the best of princes, chose the worst!" Such is the accusation which will assail our ears. Ye know Abdallah, and ye know his associates. If he ascends the throne what dangerous innovations must not Moslems look for! Religion will be imperiled! Remember that ye will be called to account for your choice, not only by men, but by God Himself!"

These words, which were indisputably true, made a profound impression upon the assembly. Already half convinced, they asked Abu 'l-Mofrih to nominate his candidate. "I propose Mohammed," he said, "a devout man of irreproachable morality." "That may be," replied the eunuchs, "but he is niggardly and austere." "You call him niggardly," said Abu 'l-Mofrih, "but how can he who hath naught to give show his liberality? When he reigns, and is master of the public treasury, he will show you his gratitude; be well assured of that!"

Abu 'l-Mofrih's counsel having prevailed, all present swore upon the Koran to acknowledge Mohammed; and the two eunuchs Sadun and Kasim, who to curry favor with Tarub had been hitherto the most ardent supporters of Abdallah's candidature, henceforth thought of nothing except how to make peace with his rival. Kasim begged his colleagues to intercede for him, and this they promised to do; while Sadun was given the privilege of announcing to Mohammed his accession to the throne.

. . . . The Prince had already risen, and was at the bath, when he was informed that Sadun desired to speak with him. Quitting the bath, he dressed and ordered the eunuch to be introduced. "What brings you here so early, Sadun?" he asked. "I come," replied Sadun, "to announce that we, the eunuchs of the palace, have elected you as your father's successor. He is dead; may his soul rest with God! Behold his ring!"

Mohammed could not credit Sadun's words. He suspected that his brother was already on the throne, and had sent the eunuch to assassinate him. Intent only on saving his life, he cried: "Sadun, spare me, as you fear God! I know that you are my enemy; but will you shed my blood? If needs be, I will quit Spain: the world is wide: I will seek some place afar off, where I may live without giving umbrage to my brother." Sadun found great difficulty in reassuring the Prince and persuading him that he had spoken the simple truth. At length his solemn protestations prevailed, and he added: "You are astonished that I have been chosen to bring you these tidings; but I entreated my comrades to make me their messenger, in the hope that you would pardon my past conduct." "May God pardon thee as I do!" cried Mohammed: "and now I will summon my chamberlain, Mohammed ibn Musa, and we will concert measures together."[134]

The accession of Muhammed I (852–886) to the caliphate, which is described in epic scope by Dozy, provides a sense of how a history of Islamic eunuchism that undertook to illustrate the character and the numerous facets of this phenomenon could be written. In the Umayyad caliphate of Cordova, which lasted into the 12th century and was then ruled by North African Almoravids (1067–1147), Slavic and Frankish eunuchs enjoyed an exalted status. Under Abd al-Rahman III (912–961), they gained access to all government offices. He thereby hoped to weaken the influence of the aristocracy. The castrati who came from Central and Northern Europe were in very high demand. Castration centers were operated in Verdun (as reported by Liudprand, the Bishop of Cremona [ca. 922–ca. 972]), in the south of the Iberian peninsula, and in Pechina, the former capital of Almeria. In addition to the eunuchs that are generally called Slavs, there were also members of other ethnicities, as many sources compiled by Dozy also document.

Originally the name of *Slavs* (Ar. *Sagaliba*) was applied to prisoners captured by Germanic tribes in their wars against Slavonic tribes, and sold by them to the Saracens of Spain; but in course of time, a multitude of men belonging to other races began to be classified as Slavs, and the name was applied to all foreigners who served in the harem, or in the army, whatever their origin. An Arab

> traveler of the tenth century explicitly states that the Slavs who were the retainers of the Khalif of Spain included Galicians, Franks (French and German), Lombards, Calabrians, and natives of the northern coasts of the Black Sea. Some of them had been captured by Andalusian pirates; others had been purchased in Italian ports . . . Another class, namely the eunuchs destined to be attendants in the harem, were imported from France. . .[135]

At the court of Abd al-Rahman III, their number was considerable. Some sources estimate 3,750, others 6,087; some even conclude that there must have been 13,750. Eunuchs were everywhere; they held very high offices, were rewarded with landed property, and in some cases became local princes. Their popularity continued under the Fatimids. Even the initial years of the caliphate of al-Hakim were accompanied by the eunuch Bardjawan, appointed regent by al-Hakim's father, the caliph al-Azis (975–996). Bardjawan is said to have amassed a great fortune and was allegedly murdered by his insane master, who thought he was God. As in the empires of antiquity, the rulers in the Islamic world were also the heirs to the great fortunes of their eunuchs, who in some cases were even allowed to marry. In this context, a report about Arabic customs published by the Swiss orientalist Adam Mez (1869–1917) merits special attention:

> I said to the eunuch Arib, a truth-loving savant: "Master, tell me about the eunuchs, for the learned are at variance on that subject. Even Abu Hanifa speaks of their marital capacity and credits them with children, born to their wives. On this question you are, therefore, the one to

> consult." He replied: "Abu Hanifa is right. In the process of castration the scrota are opened up and the testicles removed. Often, indeed, the patient takes a fright and one of his testicles disappears in the body, is looked for but is not instantly found. Eventually it reverts to its proper place after the incision has been cicatrized. Should it happen to be the left testicle—the eunuch recovers his passion and semen—should it be the right, he grows a beard like a normal man. Abu Hanifa has stood by the word of God: The child belongs to the husband, and that is possible with those eunuchs who retain one of their testicles." (I related this to Abu Sa'id at Nisabur. It is, indeed, possible. One of my testicles is small and the hair on it is light and scanty.) When castration is over, they insert a leaden peg in the urinal passage so that the passage may not be closed up in the process of healing.[136]

These opinions are confirmed by modern medicine, even if we can assume that such cases were the exception and later, especially among Turks and the Islamicized peoples of Asia, the entire organ was removed according to the Chinese model. The Islamic world has always attempted to cultivate the common culture of the *umma* (of the Islamic community) in the name of the prophet. Nonetheless, it was not possible to obliterate all distinctive features of the conquered ethnic groups, given the immense geographical expanse. Thus, beyond linguistic differences between Muslims who speak Arabic, Persian, Turkish, and Urdu, there are also varied outlooks concerning harems and eunuchs even today, as examples from Central Asian empires, the South Asian, Caucasian, Arabic emirates and sultanates of the Black African, Berber, and

Ethiopian kingdoms demonstrate.

The following descriptions of the situation in the Mughal and Ottoman empires should clarify and enhance *pars pro toto* our grasp of the basic contours of the situation of eunuchs under the Muslims. The situation in the Ottoman empire, which began to threaten Europe in late antiquity and helped determine historical events for centuries, also shaped beliefs about court castrati. The Turks, who in 1453 had conquered the visible symbol of the world of antiquity, namely Constantinople, and who became the terror of the occident for the following three centuries, subsequently built up an empire unlike any other in the history of the world. The power of the last caliphs, who were the nominal rulers of Islam until 1924, extended from the Carpathians in Northern Europe to the Bab el-Mandeb at the Horn of Africa, and from the northern coast of Africa to Central Asia and India. When besieging Vienna in 1683, Kara Mustafa, the grand vizier of the caliphs from 1676 to 1683, is said to have brought along a harem with 1,500 women and 700 black eunuchs. The Ottoman empire, the history of which can be traced back to the time of the early Asiatic migrations, formed a special bridge between orient and occident, in the historical as well as the geographical sense. This predestined Turkey to become what Europe considered a typical example of the orient or Islam. The European image of the orient, conceived in the art and literature of the 18th and 19th centuries, drew on Europe's fascination with Turkey. One need only think of Lady Mary Wortley Montagu (1689–1762), immortalized by the English painter Jonathan Richardson (1665–1745) in an orientalized portrait in the company of a black eunuch. Her letters, which were long considered the most popular depictions of the orient, are limited to the courtly life of the Ottomans, since the writer, in her capacity as wife of a diplomat, had only traveled in the European part of Turkey. Lady Montagu, who had even been granted permission to enter harems, provides an insightful view into this mysterious world. She mentions the eunuchs as a fixed component of the Seraglio, in which they had to carry out various tasks in their capacity as servants. Her report, however, understandably fails to distinguish between Seraglio and harem.

> I went to see the Sultana Hafise, favourite of the last Emperor Mustafa, who, you know (or perhaps you don't know), was deposed by his brother, the reigning Sultan, and died a few weeks after, being poisoned, as it was generally believed. This lady was immediately after his death saluted with an absolute order to leave the Seraglio and choose herself a husband from the great men at the Porte. I suppose you imagine her overjoyed at this proposal. Quite contrary; these women, who are called and esteem themselves queens, look upon this liberty as the greatest disgrace and affront that can happen to them . . . She chose Ebubekir Efendi, then secretary of state, and above fourscore year old, to convince the world that she firmly intended to keep the vow she had made of never suffering a second husband to approach her bed, and since she must honour some subject so far as to be called his wife she would choose him as a mark of her gratitude, since it was he that had presented her at the age of ten year old to her lost lord. But she has never permitted him to pay her one visit, though it is now fifteen year she has been in his house, where she passes her time in uninterrupted mourning with a constancy very little known in

> Christendom, especially in a widow of twenty-one, for she is now but thirty-six. She has no black eunuchs for her guard, her husband being obliged to respect her as a queen and not enquire at all into what is done in her apartment . . . [137]

A more recent example indicates how difficult it is for westerners to picture the domain of the eunuchs in the Turkish harem. Rupprecht, Crown Prince of Bavaria (1869–1955), who traveled through the East at the end of the last century, includes in his chronicle some remarks on harems and eunuchs:

> The mother of the Sultan, the *sultana valide*, who enjoys great prestige within the palace, was alleged to be among the ladies traveling to the *selamlik* [the domain of the husband] in closed carriages. Just below her in status was one of the four *kadins* or legitimate wives of the Sultan who bore him the first son. Of the remaining women, those with whom the Sultan has conceived children are designated as *gediklik* or favorites. There are three at this time. I was unsuccessful in learning how many other women the Sultan owns. Usually the other women remain in the imperial harem for only a brief time and are then given as gifts to pashas and minions. Gifts of this sort are considered a lofty gesture of goodwill. Since there is a separate household complete with servants for each of the women and concubines, the number of women residing in the imperial harem must be considerable. The supervision of the harem is incumbent on His Majesty, the Kislar Aga, the Chief Eunuch.
>
> At the colossal annual festival of the bayram, the

Sultan receives a tribute of Vilayet maidens, of whom he chooses one by throwing a cloth for the night in question. However, this act of throwing the cloth has become a meaningless ceremony in the past few years. Besides by the tribute of the Vilayets, the imperial harem is replenished by arrangements with the parents of the girls who have been selected for him as well as with business people who conduct trade in Top-Hané, at the entrance of the Bosporus, especially with young Circassians. This trading must take place under the veil of secrecy; otherwise the embassies would call it slave trade and protest against it. Trade in eunuchs is kept even more covert. They have become quite costly, especially the white eunuchs, of whom there are fewer and fewer in the old Seraglio. Ahmed Ali euphemistically called them eunuchs from birth. The black eunuchs usually come from Egypt, and it is claimed that the Coptic monks from Lake Natron engage in this infamous trade. Thin as a rail in youth, the eunuchs become unwieldy masses of fat as they age. Their beardless faces are wrinkled, their noses lack points, their teeth jut out, and their chins are stunted. They have long, flabby arms and legs, but disproportionately short torsos.

The Sultan has a considerable number of children from his wives and concubines. I would like to emphasize this expressly, because in general the number of children in the large harems is in marked disproportion to the number of women. This phenomenon is explained by the jealousy of the women of the harem, which often causes the midwives to do away with the children of their rivals either before or during childbirth. But those are abuses that occur only in the large harems in which the

> major preoccupations of their inhabitants are intrigues and grooming.[138]

It is obvious from this report that the issues concerning harems and eunuchs are closely related. To get a picture of the Ottoman eunuchs we must glance over to the harem of the sultan who referred to himself as *emperor* after conquering Constantinople and even had himself called *padishah* in accordance with Persian hierarchical terminology. Most depictions of harems focus their evaluations of this oriental institution, which has existed for millennia, on the late Ottoman period.

Before turning to our examination of the everyday life in harems and of eunuchs, it is advisable for us to note the Islamization of the Turkish peoples who in the course of history lost their ethnic unity and were Europeanized to the extent that they are viewed today in the orient as European (since they adopted the Latin alphabet, separated Church and State, etc.) and in Europe as oriental.

The history of the Turks, who themselves prefer to date their beginning from the time of the Ottomans, commenced in the Central Asian steppes. The oldest document of Turkish history dates back to 732, but there are strong indications that the Turkish people had entered the arena of history significantly earlier; they made their presence felt as far as China in the East, Persia in the South, and the Byzantine empire in the West, although initially in the form of nomadic tribes who turned up here and there and left their mark, although they had yet to develop a stable political structure. Early on they came into close contact with Arabs, who used them as mercenaries to defend the northern borders, but by whom they were soon themselves displaced. They became Islamicized quite rapidly and founded Central Asian khanates between Kashgar and Samarkand, which after the year 1000 entered the sphere of influence of the forerunners of the Ottomans, the Seljuks. The latter, who had already become Muslim, took over the power of the earlier caliphs and rose rapidly from the middle of the 11th century; in the West, they reached to the shore of the Bosporus and in the east to the mouth of the Ganges. In the 14th century, they had to yield their power to the Ottomans, who took over the heritage of the Seljuks and also soon conquered Byzantium, thus clearing the way for attacks on Europe.

It is evident that the contact between these rulers and the highly developed cultures they either conquered or constantly attacked left behind a distinct influence on political organization. They adopted government institutions and symbols. All spheres of life were affected, including harems and castrati. Castrati were a crucial component of the courts of the expanding Turkish peoples. Inquiries into the earliest Turkish societies reveal, however, that these customs of the conquered peoples were initially alien to the Turks. Like many other nomadic peoples, they evidently were not acquainted with polygamy. The result was a high status of wives and mothers in the earliest Turkish societies because the men were perpetually at war or hunting. As long as the Turks remained tied to their pre-Islamic, archaic, and shamanistic beliefs, familial customs and ceremonies were still matriarchal in nature. The influential position of the mother of the sultan, the *valide sultana*, may have originated in her position in the harem. She was the true ruler over the harem, which in the heyday of the Ottoman

Acemglan, a eunuch in Turkish service.
From Thomas Artus et al., *Histoire des Turcs* (Paris, 1662).

empire accommodated thousands of people. Its unusual structure was difficult to identify from the outside. The pre-Islamic customs of the Turkish peoples, some of whom lived on in Central Asia into the 19th century, diverged fundamentally from our stereotypical view of the harem as a restricted domicile of women who serve one man. Franz von Schwarz, who spent fifteen years as an astronomer in Turkestan in the late 19th century, wrote that among the Central Asian nomads, "virgin purity and conjugal fidelity are rather uncommon virtues. Circassian women in particular were sometimes quite open with foreigners and other men, often with the approval of their husbands. Among the Circassians there is virtually no trace of jealousy, which elsewhere constitutes a prominent characteristic of the Muslims."[139] He went on to explore the more tenuous link to Islam of this population, which had retained shamanistic ceremonies. Von Schwarz concluded that there were no eunuchs in Turkestan, although women lived in harems there as well. Ármin Vámbéry (1832–1913), a pioneer of Central Asian scholarship from Hungary, who visited Bukhara in 1863 under very peculiar circumstances, described harems in his travel account, but eunuchs are nowhere mentioned. Vámbéry emphasized the special role of the mother of the ruler, which strongly resembled the role of the mother of the sultan in the harems of Constantinople: "Mozaffar-ed-din Khan has . . . four legitimate wives and about twenty others, the former natives of Bokhara, the latter slaves . . . employed to tend upon the children, of whom there are sixteen, ten girls . . . and six boys. . . . The harem is presided over by the sovereign's mother, formerly a Persian slave . . . and by his grandmother, Hakim Ayim. It bears a high character for chastity and orderly training."[140] Eunuchism flourished only where it had a pre-Islamic tradition, notably where Chinese, Persian, or Byzantine culture had firm roots. There is nothing to indicate that even the male dancers were castrati. In fact, it is reported that these boys, who also appeared in women's clothing and played women's roles, because these were forbidden to men, gave up their lucrative profession and led a normal life once again as soon as they reached puberty.

The long confrontations between the empire at the Bosporus and the occident, punctuated by attempts at peaceful coexistence, resulted in a treasure trove of reports, stories, and letters. One notable example is the *Kaiserliche Gesandschaften ans Goldene Horn*, compiled by Karl Teply. This anthology provides telling detail regarding the daily life of eunuchs, including the following information:

> The Turks arrange to have the reproductive organs of the white and black Moors who guard the women cut off in their youth. Consequently, they remain beardless. They look like old, disfigured women. They guard the court and the entrance so well that no one can either enter nor leave in their presence, unless the emperor desires one or another of the women. In this instance, they are brought in covered coaches so that they cannot be seen by anyone. And on both sides of the coaches, as well as in front of and behind them, some of the aforementioned Moors ride along.[141]

Never had there been such an elaborate and multifarious hierarchy of court castrati as at the Ottoman court. At their head stood the "Kislar Aga," the Chief Eunuch, whose powers were greater than those of all other officials of the ruler. The

Chief Eunuch functioned as the liaison between the ruler and the women of the harem. He determined the course of the women's life and death, selecting them for trysts with the sultan and eliminating them on command. These women were generally done away with by drowning them in the sea.

The aforementioned instance of sacral power of the Ottoman ruler was expressed in these customs. He considered himself caliph of the entire Islamic world. His "majestic holiness" could not be viewed, only a select circle had direct access to him, and in the harem, where he wore silver sandals to document his presence audibly, hardly anyone was allowed to come in contact with him. The head chamberlain, the Kislar Aga, was among those privileged few who could come to him day and night.

Among the miniatures on view in the Topkapi Seraglio are representations of dark-skinned masters of ceremonies from the southern provinces of the empire or acquired on the slave market, including Ethiopians and Indians. The path to the most exalted position in the empire was long and arduous, reserved for only a select few. Sources indicate that castrati, who were the most expensive slaves, were employed at court only in special functions. Before they were accepted into the inner circle of the eunuchs, they had to pass numerous aptitude tests, including an initiation rite (*falaki*) in which they were bound and had their heels flogged, whereupon they were assigned a new name. They were usually given names of flowers, such as hyacinth, narcissus, or gillyflower, and underwent strict courtly instruction in all subjects required to carry out the demands of service in the harem and at court. Only then were they placed in the care of the Agas or the *valide sultana* (Sultan

Chief Black Eunuch of a Turkish harem,
Mouradgea d'Ohsson, *Tableau général de l'empire Othoman* (Paris. 1820)

mother), who ruled over the harem. The harem was not only the sanctuary of the sultan and the palace of his influential mother, but comprised the households of his numerous wives with all their slaves, the odalisques, and was the residence of his children, their domestics, and the eunuchs.

The residents of harems often numbered in the thousands. According to sources, 18,000 individuals were employed in the harem under Beyazid II (1481–1512), and as many as 35,000 under Süleyman the Magnificent (1518–1566). The *Eski-Saray*, the old palace, in which the harem was housed, was a small city in itself with individual houses, gardens, and kiosks; it served the private life of the sultan, who could enter the Seraglio at any time from his palace through a small gate guarded by eunuchs. Eunuchs were engaged there as superintendents of gardens, kitchens, and stables, and were responsible for the care of the harem women, for acquiring female slaves, for the preparation of ceremonies, such as weddings and circumcisions, as well as burials. Their presence was also indispensable at official receptions, and their influence rose in direct proportion to that of the women.

Roxelana, the favorite wife of Süleyman the Magnificent, attained an especially high status. Presumably of Slavic origin, she rose up from the ranks of the slaves. She clearly had a substantial influence on politics because she succeeded in making Süleyman the Magnificent her nearly exclusive husband, so that she could have her son Selim (1566–1574) occupy the favored position as the future successor. The ruler is said to have lived a monogamous life in order to please her and even to have agreed not to marry his female slaves to his courtiers. Her status was so elevated that all three of her sons succes-

18th-century miniature depicting the Turkish court.
The *kislar agasi*, the chief black eunuchs, are in the background near the top of the picture. (Topkapi Saray Library, Istanbul)

sively ruled over the Ottoman empire. During Roxelana's time, Slavic slaves received preferential treatment in obtaining high offices and honors, although hardly anybody could feel altogether secure in light of the constant courtly intrigues. Violent murders, including those committed by eunuchs, were common. And frequently the eunuchs themselves fell victim to crime, as did Jussuf and the Armenian Mohammed.

Intrigues were rampant at the court. The more eunuchs were recruited from captured Christians and members of enemy groups, the more the plots thickened. Several Venetian eunuchs are known to have engaged in covert negotiations in which Christians from Pera also took part as mediators.

Since the destinies of the eunuchs and the empire under the Ottomans were closely allied, eunuchs were subject to repeated public scrutiny and held responsible for grievances. They were even considered the cause of the downfall of the empire because of their conflicts with the janissaries, Turkish elite troops recruited from groups of captured boys who were trained in special military institutes as qualified warriors and had steered the expansion policies of the "last caliphate."

Under the Ottoman sultans, many eunuchs were generals and conquerors, and some were killed in action battling the enemy. Often they also held the office of a governor or grand vizier. Prosperous sultans even married their daughters to eunuchs, who were fully capable of satisfying them sexually. In Ottoman history, the long-lived Kislar Aga, the black Beshir, was examplary of the power a eunuch was able to attain. He usurped this power in 1731 after having thousands of janissaries, who were ill-disposed to him, secretly eliminated. The council of viziers was convened by him and had to comply with what the almighty "Moor" (as he was called) ordered in the name of the sultan, who was in reality dominated by the eunuch. He controlled the finances, which worked to the advantage of the economy, although the country had suffered large territorial losses in the aftermath of Russian policies in Asia. Despite the losses and strenuous military conflicts, he succeeded in achieving the best possible outcome for his country with shrewd peace negotiations in 1741. When he died in 1747 at the age of 96, he left behind not only an enormous fortune, but also a well-constructed bureaucracy with outstanding barristers and administrators. His successor, who bore the same name as he, was similarly involved in affairs of state, but was not spared the standard inglorious demise; like other reformers, he was murdered in 1752 and his head was impaled on the wall of the Seraglio. With these two Beshirs, the era of the influential great eunuchs who shaped the policies of the empire had come to an end.

Eunuchs did not vanish from the scene altogether. If we look back to the onset of the modern era, which began with the discovery of America and the water route to India that would bypass the Orient—which had devastating consequences for the Mamluk sultanate in Egypt—we recognize previously neglected reasons for the rise of the *khasi*. It is entirely possible that syphilis, which was rampant after the end of the 15th century and afflicted not only entire Mamluk regiments, but also emirs and sultans, spared the *khasi* for obvious reasons and thereby paved their way for their access to power. This development appears to be confirmed by the fact that more offices were taken over by eunuchs at this time. The result was that previously neutral official positions were now identified with eunuchs (the *khisyan*). For a local historian like al-Jabarti (1753–1825), best known for his chronicles of the French and Napoleon in Egypt, it went without saying that a particular *agha* or even *kathoda* was a *khasi*.

Eunuchs were also active in palaces and harems after the first victories of the revolution (1908), which ultimately forbade castration and harems. Kenizé Mourad, a granddaughter of the last sultana, glorifies courtly life in *Regards from the Dead Princess: Novel of a Life*:

> She sent for Zeynel, her favourite eunuch, a tall Albanian with very white skin. Zeynel was nearing forty, and she noted with amusement that a recent tendency to stoutness had lent him the dignified appearance of a pasha.
>
> She could well remember the timid youth who had arrived at Çergan Palace twenty-five years ago, when she and her sisters were sharing their father's captivity there. Zeynel had been sent by Sultan Abdul Hamid's chief eunuch, who found it a convenient way to get rid of him. Although he was a lively, talented youngster who had distinguished himself at the palace school attended by children being groomed for service in the imperial court, Zeynel later had shown himself ill-suited to the strict discipline of the harem.
>
> Çeragan soon tamed him. Did he feel freer among those prisoners? The Svetana remembered that he used to follow her everywhere, attentive to her smallest wish, and ignored her two sisters. It was she whom he had chosen to serve.
>
> Touched by Zeynel's devotion, she came to rely on him more and more. She valued the tact and discretion

> that set him apart from other eunuchs, most of whom were as garrulous as old women.[142]

Before modernity raises the curtain on the harem customs of the Arab empires, which were long shrouded in mystery, let us cast one final glance back to the Mughals of India, whose quantity and quality of artworks portraying life at the courts and in the harems are unparalleled. Their illustrations can be admired in many editions of the *Thousand and One Nights*.

There is a distinct affinity between the two large Islamic empires of the modern period, the Mughals and the Ottomans (ca. 1280–1924). The founder of the Indian Mughal empire, Babur (1480–1530), who took on the title "Emperor of Hindustan," was descended from Timur on his father's side and from Genghis Khan on his mother's side. He founded an empire that has taken its place in history in the figure of the Great Mughal Akbar (1556–1605). Akbar, whose propensity for self-deification was indisputable, achieved an especially good reputation as a Muslim ruler. This reputation owes more to the writings of his biographer and friend Abu'l Fazl than to his actual historical significance. In his *Akbarnama*, Abu'l Fazl depicts not only the emperor's victories and campaigns, but also his private life and his architectural monuments in Agra and Fathpur Sikri. These buildings provide some indication of the size of his court, in which eunuchs and harems had a prominent role that can be traced back to Persian influences. These same Persian influences also shaped Islamic kingdoms from the 10th century. Five thousand women are said to have lived in Akbar's harem; however, only his mother and one of his wives had any influence on the emperor. The women of this harem enjoyed far greater liberties than was the case in other Islamic empires. They were also assigned administrative tasks and were even employed as armed guardians (*urdubegis*) of the harem. These women were permitted to retain the religion of their birth; consequently, the harems displayed an abundance of shrines. The women were allowed to receive female guests and lodge them for periods of up to one month. Dance, song, music, and parlor games were cultivated to an unusual degree. The sources tell us that when Akbar played chess, he used the women as living chess figures. Eunuchs were chiefly found in the service of the emperor as chamberlains and guards, and only less commonly in the harem, in which the women performed most servant duties. The eunuch became the *maior domus* (master of the house), for which castration was not strictly requisite. Extant illuminations reveal more on this subject than the scanty written sources, which document the existence of eunuchs but provide no detailed information.

In the religious and cultural melting pot that is India, there are castrati even today. The dark-skinned Kojas in the South and the *hijra*s are eunuchs who typically engage in prostitution as transvestites in Bombay, Bangalore, and other urban centers. Castrati are said to continue playing a major role in insuring good luck and fertility at traditional weddings. This ritual tradition follows old archaic beliefs and mirrors royal customs.

In the multicultural Islamic world, there are various forms of and views on eunuchism that relate not only to the harems, but above all to forms of power that are local and generally sacral in nature. The Islamic religion never opposed this phenomenon. There are eunuchs in Saudi Arabia, in the Gulf States, in Brunei, and wherever oriental royal courts and harems are found. Today, of course, they are no longer sub-

Eunuchs at a Mongol court.

jected to the tormenting procedures and dangers of earlier times; the medical technology of emasculation has been virtually perfected. Some who consider themselves transsexuals in the West, although they have actually become castrati, extol this operation as a liberation. We might therefore also claim that there are still eunuchs in the West.

Emasculated Heroes of the Western Middle Ages

Radix omnium malorum cupiditas
(Lust is the root of all evil)

Christianity in late antiquity and in the Byzantine Empire constituted a cultural unit that lived on into the early centuries of Islam. It took some time until differences between West and East crystallized. The subsequent estrangement of the two worlds resulted not only from religious divergences, but also from differing languages and customs. However, reciprocal influences between West and East continued.

The Middle East, which had continued to embrace the post-Hellenic tradition, increasingly succumbed to Islam, which had become the third power in the Mediterranean region. Conflicts with the caliphate of Cordova in particular had a stimulating effect on the High Middle Ages.

The Christian world considered the Middle East, which was the birthplace of Jesus, the very center of the world. This focus was reflected in medieval cartography, notably the Ebstorf map of the world (ca. 1235), and shaped a worldview consistent with the syncretic tradition of an *imago mundi*. The universality of this world lay in its interpretation and history of the idea of salvation. There was a concerted effort to realize Augustine's vision of a *civitas dei*. To understand the mentality of the time, we would have to project ourselves into another framework beyond the here and now. The homogeneity of a world anchored in the hereafter unraveled with the Reformation, which clearly demarcated the Renaissance from the Middle Ages.

After the wave of migrations and invasions, which shaped historical events in East and West between the 4th and 6th centuries, belief in the afterworld under the sign of the Cross was the order of the day. This belief was manifested in ardent piety and ecstatic yearning for paradise, which the Gospel of John depicted as the locus of Christian fulfillment. In the East the new religion of Islam, which had spread rapidly since the 7th century, also cultivated profound devoutness. Fear of God and the "Judgment Day" ruled medieval society. In discussing *De contemptu mundi*, Curtius concludes that the Cluniac monk Bernard of Morlaix "not only inveighs against impiety, sodomy, and other vices of the age, but curses love and womankind."[143]

The empires between the Jordan and the Euphrates had garnered the strength they needed to become a new world power, having gained a foothold under the green banner of the Prophet. The Iberian Peninsula and Sicily were occupied by Muslim troops. Many Mediterranean coastal cities flourished as a result of trade between East and West, including the trade of slaves and eunuchs. This fusion of political, economic, and cultural currents left its mark on every aspect of the European Middle Ages, from the literature of Dante and Boccaccio to the fine arts and science.

Within this amalgam of orient and occident, the history of the emasculated representatives of an era with very diverse views on sexuality was unfolding inexorably. Emasculation was both an aspect of conscious transcendence of sexuality and a common punishment; it was one of the widely practiced cruelties that was better left unmentioned, in the view of Gregory of Tours (538–595). His *History of the Franks* reports about the incredible barbarism of kings and clergymen as the migration of nations was drawing to a close. This Gallic historian tells of the malicious wife of Badegisil, Bishop of Le Mans, who "on more than one occasion . . . cut off a man's penis with part of the skin of his stomach."[144]

Sexuality came in many guises in the Middle Ages: it was damned, praised, feared, and associated with sorcery, but also extolled and venerated. Its taboo status found outlets in the encoded language of legends and frightful visions of hell, including witches, magicians, and devils, as well as guardian angels to appeal to for protection. It is therefore not surprising that magicians distributed some potions to bolster potency and others to render the enemy impotent.

In the last years of the Late Middle Ages, people in cities and villages were seized by a collective fear of castration. Voices from the pulpit inveighed against castration, at the same time that religious doctrines and exegesis of the Holy Scriptures encouraged fear of women, who were condemned as the source of all evil and were considered unclean and therefore menacing. The following statement is attributed to Odo, the Abbot of Cluny (ca. 879–942): "Beauty is only skin deep. If people saw underneath the skin . . . they would be repelled by the sight of women. Every charming creature is composed of mucus and blood, of dankness and bile. If you think about the contents of the nostrils and the throat and the stomach, you find nothing but filth. And if we cannot even bring ourselves to touch mucus or putrefaction with our fingertips, how then can we wish to embrace a bundle of filth?"[145]

These views, disseminated by itinerant priests, monks, and father confessors as well as by Cathari and other sects that were considered heretical, could not fail to wield influence. Drawing on early Christian gnostic and other beliefs about the healing powers of chastity, sexual abstinence came to be seen as the path to paradise. The ideal was complete abstinence, which was equated with virginity. Marriage was tolerated only as a legitimate bond to secure progeny. The impulse behind lust and fornication was attributed to the carnality of human nature tainted by original sin. Biblical exegesis fostered this view, which Augustine (354–430), the Bishop of Hippo, pronounced the central principle of Church doctrine.

Against this backdrop, discourse on Hell and Purgatory specified loci of punishment and atonement for the sins of earthly life. Recognizing and avoiding particular vices, namely lust (*luxuria*), the essence of the sinful nature of sexuality, pride (*superbia*), covetousness (*avaritia*), envy (*invidia*), gluttony (*gula*), anger (*ira*), and sloth (*acedia*) (in sequence essentially according to St. Thomas Aquinas), afforded individuals some degree of control over their fate in the afterworld. Anyone who succumbed to one of these seven deadly sins was condemned to the torments of Hell after death. The devil, whose primary instruments of temptation were women and sexuality, played a leading role as the seducer of man in medieval ideology. This ideology later took the form of hunting down heretics and witches.

Medieval descriptions of the torments of Hell were horrifying, anticipating Dante's terrifying fantasies and hyperbolic representations of punishments for worldly transgressions. For this reason, fleeting earthly torments, for instance castration, were considered reasonable if one wished to escape hellish suffering.

Notions of hell and purgatory had a regulatory effect in a society that had just begun to set its ethical norms. To judge by the catalogues of sins, this society was not as pious and high-minded as the image the lives of the saints sought to convey. The visions of Hell that prevailed at the time were not purely Christian; on the contrary, they harked back to existing pagan and Jewish traditions. But not everyone thought like the theoreticians of Hell and most certainly did not act accordingly. Peter Abelard, for one, a renowned philosopher who taught philosophy and dialectics at the cathedral school in Paris, did not subscribe to their view.

Sustained research on the intellectual history of the Middle Ages has afforded us a more nuanced understanding of the medieval view of sexuality. During this period, the lives of the saints were read and imitated, but brutality and debauchery were also the order of the day. People seemed to revel in cruelty and obscenity. Their lack of compassion and essential crudeness are evidenced in the brutish punishments that were meted out: hacking off limbs, cutting off testicles, noses, and ears, putting out eyes, and ripping off eyelids. No one appeared shocked by these measures. Kings took pleasure in attending the execution of brutal sentences. Philip II (1180–1223), the ruler of France, made a point of witnessing executions of inconceivable barbarism together with his wife. These atrocities served to reinforce visions of Hell, but in doing so sealed the dire fate of many innocent people. Suffering and torture were described not only in chronicles and legends (for example, in the legend of the temptation of St. Anthony), but also visually represented in the scenes of martyrdom and hell that have been passed down to us by many anonymous painters and wood-carvers as well as the great masters at the threshold of the modern era, notably Stefan Lochner (ca. 1410–1451), Hieronymus Bosch (ca. 1450–1516), Martin Schongauer (ca. 1450–1491), and Matthias Grünewald (ca. 1480–1528).

When we picture the Middle Ages, we envision monks and monasteries, knights, castles, and troubadours as well as the Inquisition, alchemists, witches, and jongleurs. However, we must bear in mind that emasculated men, who had been mutilated either voluntarily or by force, also belonged in this group. It is the rare operagoer who is aware that the prototype for Klingsor, the lord of the opulent castle in Wagner's *Parsifal*, which is sung as a bass role, was in fact a castrato in its medieval epic source, *Parzival*, by Wolfram von Eschenbach (1170–1220). This Arthurian legend recounts the king's revenge against Klingsor, here called Clinschor:

> Clinschor the Duke was in the mouths of all, both men and women, until he fell into disgrace. Sicily had a noble king called Ibert, and Iblis was his wife, the loveliest

> woman ever weaned from a mother's breast. Clinschor served her until she rewarded him with love. For this the king robbed him of his honor. If I am to tell you his secret, I must ask your forgiveness, for it is unseemly for me to say such things. One cut of the knife, and Clinschor became a eunuch. . . .The king found Clinschor with his wife, sleeping in her arms. If he found a warm bed there, he had to pay the heavy price that by the hand of the king he was made smooth between his legs. The king thought that was his right. He clipped him in such a way that he can never more give pleasure to any woman.[146]

Klingsor's emasculation had unintended consequences, however. He was also a great magician, and the state of chastity that was thrust upon him bolstered his magical powers.

Medieval epic literature still carries many traces of traditions from antiquity and the orient as well as from the pre-Christian Celts and Teutons. Klingsor's story exemplifies the courtly custom of employing castration as a legitimate punishment for adultery. This punishment was designed to act as a deterrent. Men discovered *in flagrante delicto* often had to pay with their lives, and castration was considered the lenient alternative. The Annals of Worcester (1230) report the revenge of Llewellyn, who suspected a man named William of adultery with his wife: "At Easter Llewellyn deceitfully invited William of Braose . . . then cut off his members and hung him from the gallows."[147]

Aside from the Klingsor episode in Wolfram's *Parzival*, castration was rarely mentioned overtly, particularly in the late Middle Ages. Communications concerning emasculations were generally encoded, as in the legend of the Holy Grail. Anfortas, the wounded Grail King, sustains an injury on his thigh, which can only indicate a wound to his sexual organs. A physical connection is thus established between Klingsor and the holy keeper of the Grail. Chastity and virginity were required of the Grail knights and the ladies of their castle: "Maidens are appointed to care for the Grail. . . . That was God's decree, and these maidens performed their service before it. The Grail selects only noble company. Knights, devout and good, are chosen to guard it."[148] Wolfram emphasizes the fact that in the Grail castle, only the king was entitled to marry: "Any man who has pledged himself to serve the Grail must renounce the love of women. Only the king may have a wife, and she must be pure and his in lawful marriage."[149] This custom resembled the Byzantine and oriental tradition of the sacred kingdom.

Chivalry did not assert itself as a counterforce to monasticism, but rather affirmed monastic values and advocated chastity and asceticism, which were to become the ideals of the Crusaders. The knights presupposed that their tasks complemented those of the monks. While the knights fought against the external opponents of Christianity, the monks strove to preserve and shape morals within Christian society. Castration was seen in the framework of medieval ideals of chastity.

Renouncing the pleasures of life was tantamount to victory over *luxuria*. In the Middle Ages, the German verb *mönchen* (to make into a monk) denoted castration, because monks would castrate themselves to comply with the precept of sexual purity. As appalling as this self-mutilation might appear, it was voluntary and ethically motivated, since it affirmed the priority of the hereafter. The purpose of repairing to the desert was not to seek solitude, but to resist temptation. However, since young men followed their masters, those who were not emasculated found it easy to succumb to homosexuality.

In addition to the stories of King Arthur and his Round Table, a series of historical sources provides information, however equivocal, as to the nature and institution of eunuchism. At the itinerant court of Charlemagne (742/768–814), there were eunuchs among the numerous courtiers, following the oriental model. There is much to indicate that in the time of the Ottonians, when contacts with Byzantium were frequent, Greek monks came to the Rhine who distinguished themselves by their exceptional asceticism. Among them were St. Simeon (990–1035), whose *Vita* stressed his sexual abstinence. The epoch of the Ottonians merits examination not only for this reason, but also because the justification of the empress' claim to regency was directly determined by eunuchism.

Claims to regency by women were possible in the West, but more problematic than in Byzantium. Theophano, a Byzantine princess and the mother of Otto III (980–1002), is a classic example. Her regency had a theological and biblical prototype in the figure of Esther, who directed the affairs of state in the name of her husband. She was active at the Persian court, surrounded by eunuchs, whose names, Bigthan and Teresh, appear in the text (Esther 2:21). They are depicted in negative terms, but their function is courtly. Eunuchs were often priests in Persia, which establishes an interesting analogy to the court chaplains. Eunuchs at the Byzantine court appear to have shaped the royal household of Theophano, particularly John

Philagathus, who became the Italian chancellor in 980 and the Abbot of Nonantola in 982. This learned man, widely held to be chaste, sober, and wise, was godfather and teacher of Otto III, in whose records he even bears the title of *protovestiar*, which was used for eunuchs in Constantinople. Philagathus is said to have had a close bond with Theophano, which accords with the Byzantine tradition of rulers using their eunuchs as confidants. In the aftermath of intrigues between Aix-la-Chapelle, Constantinople, and Rome, Philagathus briefly became antipope (997–998). The synod deposed him and ordered him dragged through the streets of Rome after blinding him and mutilating his nose, ears, and tongue. It is not altogether clear whether he was castrated, but references by his compatriot, the holy Nilus the Younger (ca. 910–1005), indicate that he was.

Courtly splendor in the oriental style featuring eunuchs continued under the rule of the German Hohenstaufens in Sicily. Wolfram von Eschenbach and historical chronicles provide information about palace eunuchs even in pre-Hohenstaufen Sicily. Frederick II adopted many existing traditions. The Sicilian courts in Palermo included many eunuchs, who converted to Catholicism in order to remain in office. As castrati, they were devoted exclusively to the ruler and the state, as had been the case in Byzantium and the Islamic empires. After his death, a castrato's accumulated wealth would revert to the State, since castrati had no natural heirs. Most admirals were Greeks and Saracens; many of them were eunuchs. Extraordinary stories circulated about these eunuchs, especially about Philip of Mahdia, who led a victorious expedition by order of Roger II in the summer of 1153 on the North African coast, occupied by the Normans. According to later reports, he was burned alive under appalling circumstances despite his success. It may be assumed that he met this fate because he had joined another religious group and expressed too much sympathy for the Muslims.

The phenomenon of eunuchism has been linked to the idea of chastity since early Christianity. The Council of Nicaea (325), as we saw earlier in this chapter, rejected self-castration, although emasculation as such was tolerated under particular circumstances.

Despite this ruling of the Council, there were some who in literal exegesis of biblical passages (Isaiah 56:4f.; Matthew 19:12) preached the advantages of eunuchism, such as the adherents of the monastic reform movement with their militant distaste for the body. Peter Damian (ca. 1007–1072) was prior of the hermitage in Fonte Avellana beginning in 1043. This hermitage lived according to Benedictine rule. Peter Damian was elevated against his will to be the cardinal-archbishop of Ostia. His *Liber Gomorrhianus* advocated emasculation to liberate oneself from sin. This view was also adopted by the Regensburg Circle of the Reformers. Ulrich von Zell (1029–1091), who is said to have pierced his genitals with a glowing iron in furious reaction to his carnal desire, served as a model for his fellow friars Wilhelm von Hirsau (ca. 1030–1091) and Otloh von St. Emmeram (1010–1070). The latter, an exceptionally strict advocate of asceticism and renunciation, reports in his *Liber de temptationibus* that angels assisted in carrying out the liberating castration of the saints while they slept. Even today we do not know whether he meant this castration to be of a spiritual or physical nature.

The castration best known to us from the Middle Ages is that of Peter Abelard (1079–1142). As a result of his passionate love for the beautiful Heloïse (ca. 1100–1164), Abelard was assaulted and emasculated at the orders of Canon Fulbert, the uncle of his lover. Wounded and dishonored, he withdrew into a monastery and compelled Heloïse to do the same. However, the bond between the two lovers lasted a lifetime, as we know from their famous correspondence, which movingly depicts their attachment.

Abelard's autobiography conveys to modern readers the mentality and the societal and cultural mores of the twelfth century, which informed subsequent European intellectual history:

> Inasmuch as prosperity ever puffs up fools, and worldly tranquillity enervates the vigour of the mind, and easily loosens it by carnal allurements. . . . Seeing in [Heloïse] all those things which are wont to attract lovers, I thought it suitable to join her with myself in love, and believed that I could effect this most easily. For such renown had I then, and so excelled in grace of youth and form, that I feared no refusal from whatever woman I might deem worthy of my love. All the more easily did I believe that this girl would consent to me in that I knew her both to possess and to delight in the knowledge of letters; even in absence it would be possible for us to reach one another's presence by written intermediaries, and to express many things more boldly in writing than in speech, and so ever to indulge in pleasing discussions.[150]

Abelard inveigled his way into Heloïse's household as her tutor. The two soon became lovers. Their affair culminated in the birth of a son, which drove Heloïse's uncle to extremes of grief, humiliation, and rage. Abelard's subsequent marriage to Heloïse failed to placate the infuriated Fulbert, especially after Abelard brought Heloïse to Argenteuil to join the nuns at the abbey, whereupon Fulbert's men exacted a hideous revenge:

> . . . amputating, to wit, those parts of my body wherewith I had committed that of which they complained. Who presently taking flight, two of them who could be caught were deprived of their eyes and genitals. . . . But day coming the whole town congregating round about me, with what amazement they were transfixed, with what an outcry they lamented. . . . I was hurt far more by their compassion than by the passion of my wound, felt more occasion to blush than to bleed, and was troubled rather by modesty than by pain. It occurred to my mind with what glory I had but recently shone, how easily and in a moment this had been brought low, nay, utterly extinguished. By how just a judgment of God was I stricken in that portion of my body wherein I had sinned. . . . What way would lie open to me thereafter, with what face would I appear in public, to be pointed out by every finger, scarified by every tongue, doomed to be a monstrous spectacle to all.
>
> Nor did it less confound me that, according to the letter of the Law, that killeth, there is so great abomination of eunuchs before God that men who have been made eunuchs by the amputation or bruising of their stones are forbidden to enter the Church, as though they were stinking and unclean, and that in the sacrifice even animals of that sort are utterly rejected. As it is written in Leviticus, the twenty-second chapter and twenty-fourth verse: "Ye

> shall not offer unto the Lord that which is bruised, or crushed, or broken, or cut"; and in Deuteronomy, the twenty-third chapter and first verse: "He that is wounded in the stones, or hath his privy member cut off, shall not enter into the congregation of the Lord." Plunged in so wretched a contrition, it was the confusion of shame, I confess, rather than the devotion of conversion that drove me to the retirement of a monastic cloister. She, moreover, had already at my command willingly taken the veil and entered a convent. And so both the two of us at one time put on the sacred habit, I in the Abbey of Saint Denis and she in the Convent of Argenteuil aforesaid.[151]

Despite Abelard's relatively progressive outlook, he is also beset by a typical medieval fear of divine punishment. The disgrace he suffered was soon known throughout Paris. His self-recriminating letters to Heloïse reflect a medieval view of sexuality, imbedded in the theological discourse of 12th-century society:

> Thous knowest to what great infamies my immoderate lust had sacrificed our bodies, until no reverence for honour, nor for God even, for the days of Our Lord's Passion or of any solemnity soever could recall me from wallowing in that filth. And thee also unwilling and to the utmost of thy power resisting and dissuading me, being weaker by nature, often with threats and blows I drew to consent. For with such ardour of concupiscence I was attached to thee that those wretched and most obscene pleasures which even to name confounds us, I preferred both to God and to myself; nor could divine clemency seemingly decide otherwise than by forbidding me those

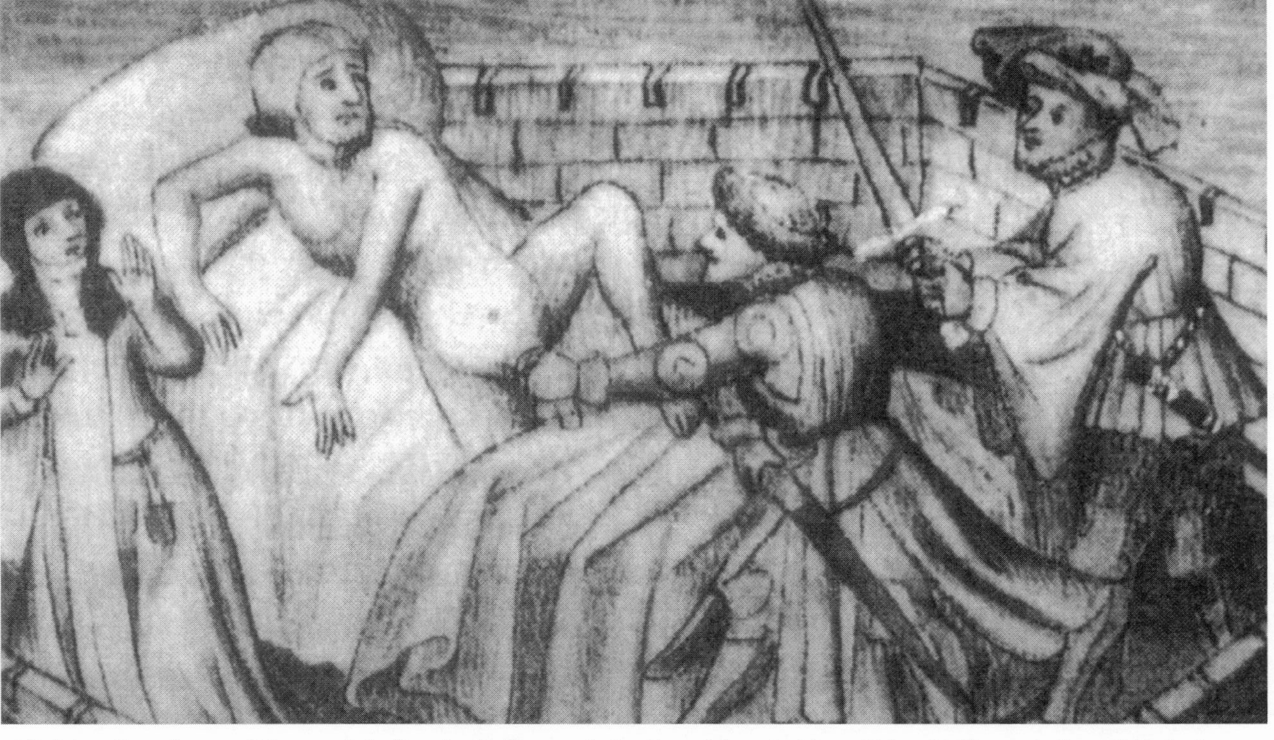

Miniature from the novel *Roman de la Rose* by Guillaume de Lorris and Jean de Meun, Valencia. The castration of Abelard was not only a literary theme, but was often used in paintings and drawings.

> pleasures utterly, without any hope. Wherefore most justly and most clemently, albeit with the supreme treachery of thine uncle, that I might grow in many things, of that part of my body have I been diminished wherein was the seat of lust, and the whole cause of his concupiscence consisted, that rightly that member might mourn which had committed all in us, and might expiate in suffering what it had misdone in enjoyment, and might cut me off from those filthinesses wherein as in the mire I had immersed myself wholly, circumcising me in mind as in body; and so make me more fit to approach the holy altar, in that no contagion of carnal pollutions might ever again call me thence. With what clemency also did He wish me to suffer so greatly in that member, the privation of which would both aid the salvation of my soul and not degrade my body, nor prevent me in any ministration of mine office. Nay, it would make me so much more prompt to all things that are honourably done, the more wholly it set me free from the heavy yoke of concupiscence.
>
> When therefore of these vilest members which from their practice of the utmost filthiness are called shameful, nor bear their proper name, divine grace cleansed me rather than deprived me, what else did it do than, to preserve the purity of cleanness, remove the sordid and vicious?[152]

This perspective, which conforms to the ethics of the time, was not entirely shared by Heloïse. Her letters are among the most moving and rare testimonies of the response of a woman to the man she loves, the man who obligated her to a monastic life when he ruled out any form of conjugal relationship after his emasculation. Far from echoing Abelard's sentiments, Heloïse counters with her own view of the situation:

> Would that thy love, beloved, had less trust in me, that it might be more anxious! But the more confident I have made thee in the past, the more neglectful now I find thee. Remember, I beseech thee, what I have done, and pay heed to what thou owest me. While with thee I enjoyed carnal pleasures, many were uncertain whether I did so from love or from desire. But now the end shews in what spirit I began. I have forbidden myself all pleasures that I might obey thy will. I have reserved nothing for myself, save this, to be now entirely thine. Consider therefore how great is thine injustice, if to me who deserve more thou payest less, nay nothing at all, especially when it is a small thing that is demanded of thee, and right easy for thee to perform.[153]

The fate of Abelard reflects the then-common practice for emasculated men to seek protection and repose in monasteries. The miscreants hired by Fulbert had learned their "craft" from techniques used in castrating animals. Terms for animal castrations, which had a long-standing tradition, were routinely applied to castrated humans, especially the term *capon* for a rooster whose reproductive organs had been severed.

Emasculation was not considered the true path to chastity, as is certainly clear from the writings of Abelard and the theological literature, but in practice castration was the first or only impulse to seek chastity. Thus a distinction was made between emasculation by self-castration and by use of force. In the following passage, Abelard contrasts his fate with Origen's self-castration:

> This purity of cleanness indeed we have heard that sundry wise men most vehemently desiring have laid hands also upon themselves, that they might remove utterly from themselves this disgrace of concupiscence. . . . An example is that great philosopher of the Christians, Origen, who, that he might wholly extinguish this fire in himself, was not afraid to lay hands upon himself; as if he understood in the letter that they were truly blessed who for the Kingdom of Heaven's sake made themselves eunuchs, and believed such to be truthfully fulfilling what the Lord enjoins about the members by which offence cometh, that we should cut them off and cast them from us, and as if he interpreted that prophecy of Esaias as history rather than as mystery, wherein the Lord prefers eunuchs to the rest of the faithful, saying: "The eunuchs that keep my sabbaths, and choose the things that please me, and take hold of my covenant; even unto them will I give in mine house and within my walls a place and a name better than of sons and of daughters: I will give them an everlasting name, that shall not be cut off." And yet Origen incurs no small blame when in the punishment of his body he seeks a remedy for his fault. Having zeal, doubtless, for God, but not according to knowledge, he incurs the guilt of homicide, by laying a hand upon himself. By the suggestion of the devil or by the greatest of errors, plainly he wrought this upon himself, which through the mercy of God was perpetrated upon me by another.[154]

The comprehensive catalogue of deeds for which emasculation was one form of punishment and the many emasculations brutally carried out for personal revenge make evident that the victims of these emasculations were driven by shame, mockery, or ostracism to seek entrance to monasteries. Others found refuge on the margins of society, for example as jesters. Although intellectual historians have devoted studies to various peripheral groups, such as minstrels, executioners, barbers, midwives, alchemists, astrologers, and itinerant poets, until quite recently the status of emasculated men has generally been overlooked.

Sodomites, as people of the Middle Ages called anyone who was in some way associated with lewdness and sexual deviance, were threatened with severe punishment. Men who engaged in homosexual relations were publicly castrated or burned for their allegedly indecent acts. In 1426, Antonio Masi of Bologna, also known as Cantarino, was found guilty. He was led naked to a place of execution, with a hood covering his head, and castrated.[155] These and similar punishments were commonly exacted as a deterrent in the Late Middle Ages.

The persecution of the "Sodomites" was inexorable. Women seem to have taken vicious pleasure in libelously charging men who had spurned them with sodomy, thus insuring their conviction. Men could be castrated for this crime. Castration, a punishment used from the time of Roman law, was now applied in cases of rape and "abnormal" sex. The cruelty of the procedure was extreme. The culprit was hanged from his genitals (*suspendatur per virilia*) before the castration was carried out. This act was even captured in pictures, for example in the *Coutume de Toulouse* (ca. 1296), the caption of which reads: "Those men who are known to have engaged in sodomy must lose their c. [*couillers*/testicles]. And a second offense results in the loss of the sexual organ. After a third instance, they must be burned."[156]

Castrating one's enemies to humiliate them was a common practice, not only after battles against the infidels, as during the Crusades, but also among the Christians themselves. The events of the Sicilian Vespers are evidence of this practice. On March 30, 1282, over 2,000 French men and their sympathizers in Palermo were castrated and murdered in the most brutal fashion. The genitals of the representatives of the hated rule of the house of Anjou were displayed as trophies.

Albertus Magnus (ca. 1200–1280), the Scholastic scholar and Dominican who brought Arabic and Jewish wisdom to the Christian Middle Ages, discusses in *De animalibus libri* the nature and character of hermaphrodites and an *effeminatus* named Favorinus, to whom he attributes the power to use magic for poisoning and other nefarious ends. The physiognomic and character traits Albertus specifies are the characteristics typically ascribed to emasculated men ("et passum esse ab aliis etiam contra naturam"). The fact that this famous church father does not explicitly refer to eunuchs could owe to the semantic ambiguity of the concept, which accounts for the common medieval usage of the term *effeminati* in preference to *eunuchs*.

Emphasis on the hereafter determined the image and perception of sexuality in the Middle Ages. Dante and the painters of that time gave ample poetic and visual expression to the role of sexuality in the divine and secular spheres. Dante characterized his *Comedy* as "'l poema sacro / al quale ha posto mano e cielo e terra" ("the sacred song / To which both Heaven and Earth have set their hand"),[157] and sublimated the images of his surroundings into visionary images of ascension into the divine order of eternal harmony. The fulfillment of being should be a mystical rather than sensual ecstasy:

> Their blessedness, therefore, is shown to come
> From seeing, if thou reasonest aright,
> Not loving, which is subsequent. Their sum
>
> Of merit is the measure of their sight—
> Merit, which grace and righteousness beget;
> So does their bliss proceed from height to height.[158]

The "sight" of the angels who escort souls into the kingdom of heaven is the highest bliss man can achieve. It promises a release from all vices of earthly existence. Innumerable works of art from this period filled with angels, whose immateriality artists wanted to render visually, attest to how strongly this view had taken hold, and how normative it was for the Middle Ages. These visions achieved their sublime form in the Early Renaissance in the paintings of the Dominican Fra Angelico (ca. 1401/1402–1455). His depiction of sexless, angelic beauty shows that de facto those who rendered themselves genderless, that is to say the emasculated, also hoped to partake of the chastity of angels, an ecstatic vision to counter the horrors of this epoch, and at the same time a symbol of the enormous tension in the Middle Ages between ascetic isolation and lust for life and flight into sublime illusions, which was the hallmark of the waning of the Middle Ages from the aristocracy down to the lower classes.

CHAPTER 9

From the "Waning of the Middle Ages" to the Witch Trials of the Early Modern Period

> "So violent and motley was life, that it bore the mixed smell of blood and of roses."
>
> —Johan Huizinga,
> *The Waning of the Middle Ages*[159]

The declining Middle Ages can be captured less in theoretical abstractions than in visual observation, as Johan Huizinga's classic text *The Waning of the Middle Ages* ably demonstrates. Art occupied a central place in this epoch, and best reflected its patterns of thought.

The paintings of Hieronymus Bosch, which were filled with encoded messages, served as a public arena in which to assert the moral and theological engagement of a mystic determined to denounce the religious state of affairs of the eve of the Reformation. His visual language is the key to understanding the mental attitude of an epoch shaped by war, plague, death, torture, castration, and the burning of heretics.

The literature of this period similarly abounds in the singular imagery of moralizing churchmen. In *Malleus Maleficarum*, known also as the *Hammer of Witches* (1487), a witch (whose gender is not indicated) was alleged to have the power to tear male organs out of bodies. A detailed and long-winded passage in *Malleus Maleficarum* ponders the question:

> . . . whether witches can with the help of devils really and actually remove the member, or whether they only do so apparently by some glamour or illusion. And that they can actually do so is argued *a fortiori*; for since devils can do greater things than this, as killing them or carrying them from place to place. . . therefore they can also truly and actually remove men's members. . .
>
> It may be said that this is done with the Divine permission. And in that case, as it has already been said that God allows more power of witchcraft over the genital functions, on account of the first corruption of sin which came to us from the act of generation, so also He allows greater power over the actual genital organ, even to its total removal. . .
>
> There is no doubt that certain witches can do marvellous things with regard to male organs, for this agrees with what has been seen and heard by many, and with the general account of what has been known concerning that member through the senses of sight and touch. . .
>
> From this it may be said that there is a true abstraction of the member in imagination, although not in fact. . .[160]

This passage reflects a superstition according to which demonic powers cause all kinds of metamorphoses. It was believed that people could be bewitched into animals, plants, or any type of matter.

Manicheism, a gnostic movement of the 3rd and 4th centuries with a dualist worldview rooted in Judaism and Iranian doctrines, had a major role in confrontations with ever new heresies, which developed along with Christianity. This movement extended as far as China and the Mediterranean. Manicheism, which was still widespread in the Early Middle Ages, adopted a radical form of dualism, according to which the king of darkness, the devil, stood in opposition to the ruler of the kingdom of light. This concept later appeared again among the Paulicians, Bogomils, and Cathari, and was the cause of persecutions, to which these movements eventually succumbed.

Since these sects discounted the possibility of a positive influence of man on the world, the world itself, which was held to be the creation of the devil, had to end. Thus, celibacy and renunciation, which entailed forswearing or sublimating eros, were the highest precept for all who wished to be one with God. These views found expression in written and visual documents.

The lives of the saints are replete with images of the battles of the protagonists against evil, aberration, and temptation. An especially impressive example is the triptych of the *Temptation of St. Anthony* by Hieronymus Bosch, which depicts a victory over earthly eros. The two outer panels of the closed triptych show the arrest and crucifixion of Christ with the symbols of death, suffering, and infertility in a wasteland setting. On the inner three panels, a visionary world of cosmic dimension unfolds, in which all four elements—fire, earth, air, and water—are visible. On the middle panel, St. Anthony, who had resisted all temptations, is kneeling before the ruins of a chapel, inside of which Christ is visible. The "temptations" surround him in their personifications and symbols. On the right inner wing we see an emasculated giant, whose mighty body seems to form a cell housing several people. His head is pierced by an arrow. As interpreted by Wilhelm Fraenger, head wounds are a sign of castration, revealing a symbolism that is further indicated by the absence of genitalia on the giant and by the grating, which forms the entrance to the cell and at the same time the buttocks of the giant. Elements of sodomy are here linked with those of castration. The dried-up boughs, which seem to grow out of the legs of the giant, symbolize his infertility. This image is reinforced on the left inner wing by a dried up tree, against which a naked woman standing in water is leaning. On the middle panel we also see a withered bark covering the head of a demonic figure atop a gigantic rat cloaked in a red cloth. The sterility of the tree is emphasized by an apparently lifeless snake hanging from it. As a phallic symbol, the snake is a clear reference to repudiated eros.

The iconographic repertoire of the repudiation of eros, namely of emasculation, is even more multifaceted. Several figures on the triptych are wearing funnels on their heads. On another painting, *The Operation for the Stone*, the castrator wears a funnel as a helmet. It seems reasonable to assume that the same symbolism of rendering infertile applies here. Three naked male figures on the right inner wing of the triptych display evidence of an unusual reception of mystery cults, the expressive force of which is heightened by the cupolas visible from the background, which function as phallic symbols. One

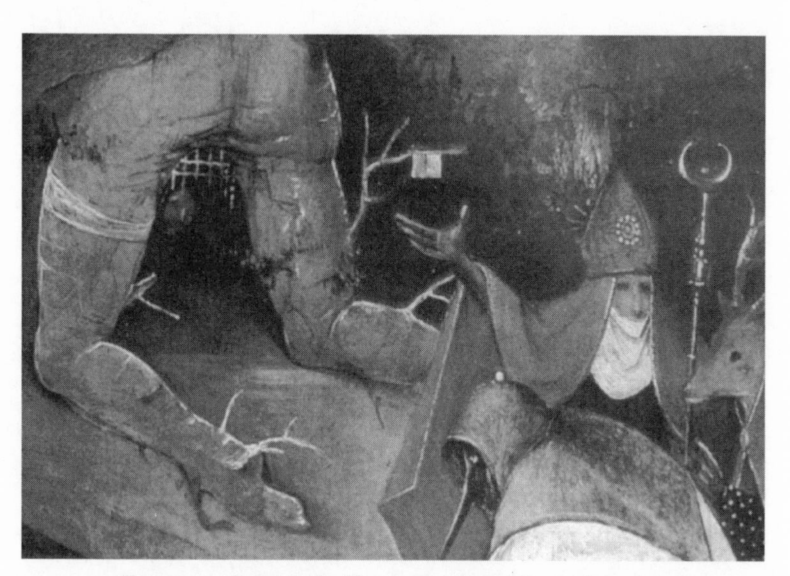

Fragment of a triptych: The temptation of St. Anthony by Hieromymus Bosch. Allusion to a castration, represented by a castrated giant. (National Museum, Lisbon)

of the men, wearing a Phrygian-style cap, is blowing a trombone-like instrument, which recalls the Cybele cults; another, to all appearances castrated, is lying on the ground with a sword in his hand, with his legs stretched upward to support the table.

On the middle panel, on the right at the shore, we see animals and fantastic beings that should be understood metaphorically. These include a beaver, which owed to a false etymological derivation of the verb *castrare* from the Latin *castor*, meaning beaver. The beaver came to be considered the symbol of a castrato. According to legend, this animal castrated itself to escape its pursuers. The harpist riding on a plucked goose is singing a dirge; the figure behind him in the hanging basket has a saber in his hands, which again makes evident his intention of severing. Carp, which are swimming in the water, were considered genderless or androgynous at that time. Also, an eel, which can be seen as a phallic symbol, is being swallowed by a bigger fish as a repudiation of carnality.

Art here reflects tensions between society and the Church, which inexorably persecuted heretics throughout the Christian West. Auto-da-fés, the burning of heretics in the Inquisition, occurred not only in Madrid, as shown in the panel of Pedro Berruguete (ca. 1450/1455–1503/1504), but in many other cities as well. In Florence, the Dominican moralizer Girolamo Savonarola (1452–1498) was hanged and burned as a heretic and schismatic on the Piazza della Signoria.

Alleged heretics were not only burned alive, but subjected to unbelievable torture and cruelty beforehand, including castration. Pedro Berruguete's painting captures the full brutality of this form of torture. Two victims bound to the stake are nailed to the poles with giant phallus-like nails that pierce their genitals. The graphic quality of this iconic statement mirrors not only the content of the tormenting sermons and the visionary literature about the hellish tortures and the Day of Judgment, but also the brutal reality of this period, which had its fill of pedophiles and murderers such as Gilles de Rais (1404–1440), whose sadistic murders of children, mutilations, and horrendous crimes fill extensive case records.

Other evils were also tackled with castration. Even Erasmus of Rotterdam (1466–1536), the humanist who preached tolerance, declared that all syphilitics should be castrated and burned because of the increase in this venereal disease. Men reacted to this epidemic with panic; some even emasculated themselves for fear of catching syphilis. Evidently this was a

An example of the cruel castrations of heretics in Spain. Autodafé by Pedro Berrguete.
(Prado Museum, Madrid)

popular prophylactic measure of the time!

During the Renaissance, motifs of castrations of Greek gods became the object of philosophical discourse and were frequently depicted in sculpture and painting, especially the mythological castration of Uranus by his son Cronos/Saturn.

The recently-discovered New World opened up new dimensions of discourse. Not only had the horizons of knowledge *per se* been expanded, but also the dimensions of the cruel subjugation of the people in the conquered lands. The Spanish are said to have murdered the *effeminati* among the Native Americans after their conquest of America. One extant depiction from that period shows the Spanish throwing these victims to the dogs to eat. The inhumanity of the Spanish conquerors was indescribable. Castration seems to have been the least of the evils in their repertoire of cruelty.

After the Turkish conquest of Constantinople and the subsequent flight of many Byzantines to the West, the prospect of further Islamic expansion became greater. The Byzantines, who had escaped primarily to Italy, brought with them not only many treasures of Greek art and literature, but also customs and practices that spread quickly. Byzantine music and vocal styles, including the voices of castrati, now became familiar in Italy and played a significant role in the further development of music. Music was no longer fostered exclusively in churches and monasteries, but also became a part of everyday courtly life.

Contacts with the Islamic enemy inevitably intensified, and the stories of harems and eunuchs began to lend wings to the fantasy of the Europeans. Their fascination with this new exoticism failed to open up their minds to the plight of those persecuted within their own societies, however. Witch trials reached new highs in the Renaissance and the early years of the Enlightenment.

Sexuality, beauty, and eroticism enjoyed an especially lofty status in these centuries. The fine arts blossomed, and popes had a significant role as patrons of the artists. It is noteworthy in investigating the often problematic relationship of the Church to sexuality that when choosing a pope it was a legal requirement that a candidate's virility be ascertained. Most likely this custom goes back to the medieval legend about Pope Joan, who was allegedly female. It is, however, certain that some churchmen had been castrated for various reasons but nonetheless achieved honors in the Pontifical State, for instance in the Cappella Guilia or the Cappella Sistina.

The princely courts of Italy gave rise to the modern courtier, who recalled the models of the court eunuchs of late antiquity and the Byzantine empire, serving an authoritarian prince, as Machiavelli (1469–1527) described in *The Prince*. Although the *cortigiano* was more accessible to the public, he depended on the mercy and benevolence of the ruler.

The comedy *Volpone, or The Fox* (1605) by Ben Jonson (ca. 1572–1637) vividly rendered the Italian court. Courtiers with unambiguous names such as Castrone (castrato) and Androgyno reveal the true cause of their identification with negative characteristics of flatterers, which court eunuchs were said to be. The hermaphrodite, depicted by Antonio Panormita Beccadeli (1393–1471) in the work of the same name (1410) as an object of homoerotic desire, was another aspect that often went unmentioned, although statues by Donatello (1386–1466), such as *David* and *Atys-Amorino*,

Copper engraving after a painting by Pieter Bruegel the Elder, in which human vices, according to Hieronymus Bosch, are iconographically represented. The eye stuck with a knife held up in the foreground symbolizes castration.

show an unmistakable tendency to idealize hermaphrodites. David is a youth of almost feminine grace, and Atys-Amor in a pose with bared genitals recalls the ancient representations of Atys, who emasculated himself for Cybele. All of these tendencies accord with examples from antiquity and ancient Rome. Beauty could be born only from the genitals of Uranos, which fell into the ocean after his castration and blended with the ocean, as immortalized in Botticelli's "Venus" (1485). The great masters of the Italian Renaissance expressed and embellished the dynamic potency of spiritualized sexual power.

In picaresque literature and folk culture, notably in the works of Rabelais (*Gargantua and Pantagruel*) and Sebastian Brant (*The Ship of Fools*) as well as in the popular German storybook *Till Eulenspiegel* and in Netherlandish painting, especially the works of Pieter Bruegel and his school, late medieval symbolism continued. The language became more explicit, sometimes even obscene; proverbs were transformed into images or parables. In Bruegel's works we find specific allusions to castration. His pictures reveal the vices and joys of the peasants, without idealizing and mythologizing. The loss of the male organ is shown not only metaphorically, but quite graphically. The testicles, hanging over a basket, are about to be cut off with a knife. On the basis of Bruegel's pictorial representations and a small number of literary imitations, we can form some idea of the dimensions of folk and peasant culture, although it is hardly conceivable that Pantagruel could have been the product solely of a folk fantasy. Although the number of popular poets was limited, the resonance of their popular culture was considerable. Knowledge about God and the world was casually proclaimed at church festivals, passion plays, and fairs. Shakespeare reworked these sources to create immortal characters.

Shakespeare's works meld the Italian love for antiquity and the folk culture of Bruegel and others in his reworking of historical characters, mythical dreams, and fantastic visions. The theme of sexuality appears in innumerable guises, including the dilemma of castration. The myth of Cybele and Attis unfolds anew in Shakespeare's *Venus and Adonis* (1593). Drawing on Ovid's *Metamorphoses*, the story revolves around the inexhaustible theme of passion. During a boar hunt, Venus falls in love with Adonis, who spurns her advances:

> Even as poor birds, deceiv'd with painted grapes,
> Do surfeit by the eye, and pine the maw,
> Even so she languisheth in her mishaps,
> As those poor birds that helpless berries saw:
> The warm effects which she in him finds missing,
> She seeks to kindle with continual kissing.

Adonis, the darling of the earth, attempts to flee from her:

> But all in vain; good queen, it will not be;
> She hath assay'd as much as may be prov'd;
> Her pleading hath deserv'd a greater fee;
> She's Love, she loves, and yet she is not lov'd.
> "Fie, fie," he says, "you crush me; let me go;
> You have no reason to withhold me so."

> "But if thou fall, O then imagine this,
> The earth in love with thee thy footing trips,
> And all is but to rob thee of a kiss.
> Rich preys make true men thieves; so do thy lips
> Make modest Dian cloudy and forlorn,
> Lest she should steal a kiss, and die forsworn."

Having fled the embrace of Venus, Adonis seems not to have heard the warning:

> "Therefore, despite of fruitless chastity,
> Love-lacking vestals, and self-loving nuns,
> That on the earth would breed a scarcity
> And barren dearth of daughters and of sons,
>   Be prodigal: the lamp that burns by night
>   Dries up his oil to lend the world his light."

The hunt and the flight come to a tragic end:

> "'Tis true, 'tis true; thus was Adonis slain;
> He ran upon the boar with his sharp spear,
> Who did not whet his teeth at him again,
> But by a kiss thought to persuade him there;
>   And nuzzling in his flank the loving swine
>   Sheath'd, unaware, the tusk in his soft groin."
>
> "Since thou art dead, lo! here I prophesy,
> Sorrow on love hereafter shall attend;
> It shall be waited on with jealousy,
> Find sweet beginning but unsavoury end;
>   Ne'er settled equally, but high or low;
>   That all love's pleasure shall not match his woe."
>
> By this, the boy that by her side lay kill'd
> Was melted like a vapour from her sight,
> And in his blood that on the ground lay spill'd,
> A purple flower sprung up, chequer'd with white.
>   Resembling well his pale cheeks, and the blood
>   Which in round drops upon their whiteness stood.[161]

In this poem, subtle allusions can be found to the Cybele-Attis/Venus-Adonis myth, which was quite popular in Elizabethan England with its constant fluctuation between hermaphroditic and chaste ideas.

Shakespeare was well acquainted with the notion of transvestism, and incorporated it into his plays, giving androgynous characteristics to Rosalind in *As You Like It*. Woman, man. . . both are possible for a single individual. In a related idea in *Twelfth Night*, Viola goes under the guise of a eunuch named Cesario. This gender switch and that of Portia in *The Merchant of Venice* might appear to be forerunners of modern views of the "third sex," but they also typify the theater of the time, which, like the dramas of antiquity, was accustomed to gender switches on stage.

The positive view of eunuchism in the early modern period created favorable conditions for the appearance of castrati in the Italian conservatories and in opera.

CHAPTER 10

Voices of the Angels: The Papal Castrati and the Birth of Opera

> "I was born in Naples . . . there they castrate two or three thousand boys every year; some die as a result, others acquire a voice finer than that of women, and others still go off and govern countries."
>
> —Voltaire, *Candide*

With their high male voices, castrati were the superstars of the music scene in the 17th and 18th centuries. Farinelli, Caffarelli, Matteuccio, and other renowned castrati appeared on all the great opera stages of Europe, received exorbitant pay, and enjoyed celebrity status, although they faced perpetual discrimination in their private lives. Today, the Baroque arias that were composed for castrati are sung by countertenors such as René Jacobs, Jochen Kowalski, Paul Esswood, Charles Brett, and Andreas Scholl, who achieve the requisite high pitch using special techniques. The vocal castrati of the European opera stages were almost exclusively Italian;

Padua, Bologna, and Naples were the centers of this art. No composers of note, from Monteverdi to Palestrina, Lully, Handel, and Mozart, failed to write music for the voices of castrati.

The tradition of angelic voices produced by castration goes back to the beginnings of church music, which was highly developed in the East and in Byzantine ceremonies. This sacred music used no instrumentation, which was prohibited at that time, but exclusively male soloists and choral singers. Women were not allowed to sing church music; thus, high male voices resulting from castration were indispensable. Only castrations that took place at an early boyhood age yielded the desired vocal range.

High angelic voices were a pivotal component of sacred music for centuries, and their ability to mesmerize listeners can be traced back to antiquity. However, Christian attacks on pagan festivals and their music consigned the art of Christian singing exclusively to monasteries and churches, a state of affairs that lasted for many centuries.

Psalmody and liturgical practice in synagogues developed from biblical traditions. The leading Byzantine churches had outstanding conservatories to train choral singers and soloists, led by renowned castrati. Even church architecture stood in the service of the euphony of this music. The vaulted ceiling, which was designed to symbolize the sky as a cosmic principle, created a space in which the sound and vibration of songs produced, as it were, a fourth dimension in the total harmony of the sacred church microcosm. The human senses were engaged from several directions at once. The liturgy, coupled with the sound of the music, colors of the artwork, and fragrance of the incense, combined to bring on ecstatic exaltation. The art of sacred music flourished in imperial Constantinople, where it was an important component of courtly life. Syrian and Coptic forms of Oriental Christianity in particular had a decisive influence on song. The art of song with prominent solo parts was highly developed in Egyptian monastic communities as far back as the 4th century.

Byzantine notations and the sparse chronicles confirm that the number of castrated singers—mostly monks—must have been high, because the notations indicated pitches and coloratura that could be sung only by castrati. The significance of music in the Byzantine and oriental churches extended to the Armenian and Georgian churches as well. In the course of Christian missionary work, masters of song had also come to these countries. Some even traveled as far as Russia. Manuel Castratus and his followers settled in Smolensk in 1137 and taught church song. The influence of Byzantine music and song also spread to the West, especially to southern Italy and Sicily, where castrato voices are documented as far back as the third century. Bishop Ambrose of Milan (340–397) introduced antiphonal singing based on the eastern model.

The conservatories that were launched by Popes Sylvester (314–335) and Hilarus (461–468) demonstrate the central importance of music and song. The renowned *schola cantorum* originated in the church of St. John Lateran; it still exists today. The western centers trained primarily boys as choral singers and clerics. An incisive reform of church music that shaped the course of European musical life for centuries to come began with Pope Gregory the Great (ca. 540–604), who spent six years in Byzantium as an envoy of his predecessor and there learned a great deal about music and song.

In the Carolingian empire, the monastery schools in Fulda, Metz, Hirsau, Reichenau, and St. Gall fervently cultivated the development of Ambrosian hymns. The singers of the royal conservatories came from these schools. The royal conservatories were in great need of voices, since women were not allowed to sing in the western churches until the 17th century. Castrati were therefore indispensable as singers. It is an established fact that even the monastery of Monte Cassino had a castration center.

A similar situation prevailed in the Iberian Peninsula. The Spanish preference for vocal castrati was still quite pronounced during the period of Philip V (1701–1746) and his successor Ferdinand VI (1746–1759). Both took such delight in Farinelli's singing that in 1737 they engaged him at their court for a full 24 years with exorbitant pay, gifts, and privileges of a *criado familiar.*

People went to great lengths to engage the best castrati voices for the Papal Chapel. Early in the 20th century, castrati were still singing in St. Peter's. Pius X (1835–1914) was the first to enact legislation designed to reform Church music by banning castrati from the Papal Chapel. The artistic director of the Sistine Chapel of the time was the castrato Alessandro Moreschi (1858–1922). At the age of 15, he became a member of the Papal Chapel at the Lateran church as a soprano, and was soon singing solo parts. Moreschi performed outside St. Peter's as well and gave guest performances abroad.

The papal conservatory was directed by a prior and six additional subdeacons. This type of school, which originated as a charitable institution to educate orphans and abandoned children, gradually began to specialize in training choirboys, who earned their livelihood by singing in church choirs. The choral director, who was called the *primicier* or the *archicantor* or *armarius*, accompanied the boys by singing in their musical register, which indicates that he was either a castrato himself or was singing falsetto, most likely in the range of a countertenor.

The composers were themselves the singers; the manuscripts therefore required no specific singing notations. The Spanish and Dutch were the first to use codified, polyphonic, and figural song. The composer and conductor Giovanni Pierluigi da Palestrina (1525–1594) was only in the Sistine Choir for one year because Pope Paul IV did not allow married singers. The number of singers increased with the splendor of the pontificate. In the 15th century, the Papal Chapel numbered only nine singers; by the time of Urban VIII (1623–1644) it was up to 32. After this time, soprano parts were invariably sung by castrati.

The choirs expanded in the 16th century. In addition to the private Papal Chapel and the choirs of St. John Lateran and St. Mary the Great, various conservatories were established, notably in Venice (St. Mark's), Bologna (St. Peter's), and at the Milan Cathedral. All of them were in competition; none could survive without castrati. The Vatican, however, tried to avoid using the expression "castrato" and spoke of these singers only as sopranos and falsettos or as "Spanish voices," the "Spagnoletti."

The celibate circle of the Sistine Chapel had elements of a secret covenant; admission required an oath never to reveal its secrets, which explains the difficulties we encounter in tracing the history of the vocal castrati in the Catholic church choirs. After the decree of Pope Clement VIII (1592–1602), the Sistine was also open to Italian castrati, *ad honorem Dei* (for the glory of God). The churches of Rome included approximately one hundred vocal castrati in 1694; by 1780 the number had doubled. They were designated as sopranos in the Vatican lists. Some castrati also worked as actors in the theater.

At the end of the 16th century, opera was born from efforts to revive the spirit of Greek tragedy by setting the dialogue of dramas to music rather than just including choral interludes as in earlier pastoral plays. Poetry, vocal and instrumental music, dramatic art, and, frequently, dance were brought together in opera. In Venetian Baroque opera, song in particular was highly developed and thus marked the transition from church to secular song. Opera opened up a new avenue for the castrati of the Papal Chapel and the conservatories to display their singing ability. The public reacted with frenetic acclaim, and the castrati were all the rage. Of every ten voices in an opera, there were generally seven castrati, two tenors, and one bass. Opera houses sprang up in many Italian cities; some cities, such as Venice, had several. By appearing on these opera stages, the castrati attained international prominence.

The vocal range of the opera castrati varied considerably. In some instances, their range exceeded three octaves. Farinelli, for example, could reach from C2 up to the D above C5.[162] Other castrati barely commanded a single octave, such as Senesino, who was esteemed by Handel. Senesino actually had only an alto voice. The peerless connoisseur of singers and voices of his day was the traveling musician Charles Burney

(1726–1814), who reports on a memorable test of stamina between Farinelli and a famous trumpeter:

> The trumpeter, wholly spent, gave it up, thinking, however, his antagonist as much tired as himself, and that it would be a drawn battle; when Farinelli, with a smile on his countenance, shewing he had only been sporting with him all the time, broke out all at once in the same breath, with fresh vigour, and not only swelled and shook the note, but ran the most rapid and difficult divisions, and was at last silenced only by the acclamations of the audience. From this period may be dated that superiority which he ever maintained over all his cotemporaries [sic] . . . In the year 1734, he came into England, where every one knows who heard, or has heard of him, what an effect his surprising talents had upon the audience: it was extacy [sic]! rapture! enchantment![163]

Special arias or roles were composed for the unique voices of renowned castrati, much as they were for solo instrumentalists. From these notations we can conjecture as to the range of the singers in their various timbres.

Audiences of that time were dazzled by the vocal castrati, as Franz Haböck has exhaustively documented in *Die Kastraten und ihre Gesangskunst* (1927).[164] Castration experienced a veritable boom, although the procedure was certainly not harmless. Charles d'Ancillon provides graphic details in his *Eunuchism Display'd*:

> [One method of castration involved the] Testicles, [which] by a detestable Art have been made so frigid, as at last quite to disappear and vanish . . . this is done by cutting the Vein that conveyed their proper Aliment and

> Support, which makes them grow lank and flabby, till at last they dry up and come to nothing. Another Method was, to take the Testicles quite away at once, and this Operation was commonly effected, by putting the Patient in a Bath of warm water, to soften and supple the Parts, and make them more tractable; some small time after, they pressed the Jugular Veins, which made the Party so stupid, and insensible, that he fell into a kind of Apoplexy, and then the Action could be performed with scarce any Pain at all to the Patient; and this was generally done by the Mother or Nurse in the most tender Infancy. Sometimes they used to give a certain quantity of Opium to the Persons designated for Castration, whom they cut while they were in their dead Sleep, and took from them those Parts which Nature took so great care to form; but as it was observed, that most of those that had been cut after this manner, died by this Narcotick; It was thought more adviseable to practise the Method I just before mentioned.[165]

The dangers of infection and hemorrhage were great, the methods of castration diverse. For children, the operation was performed between the ages of eight and twelve. It was by no means certain that these boys would retain their crystalline voices in the process. After the surgery their voices sometimes became hoarse and shrill. These risks were eagerly assumed, however, for a chance at fame and fortune. Agencies formed to procure future castrati—a profitable business. Most Italian castrati came from the lower classes in southern Italy. By having their sons castrated, parents hoped to raise the living standard of their own large families. This practice expanded when a Neapolitan law was passed permitting castration of peasant

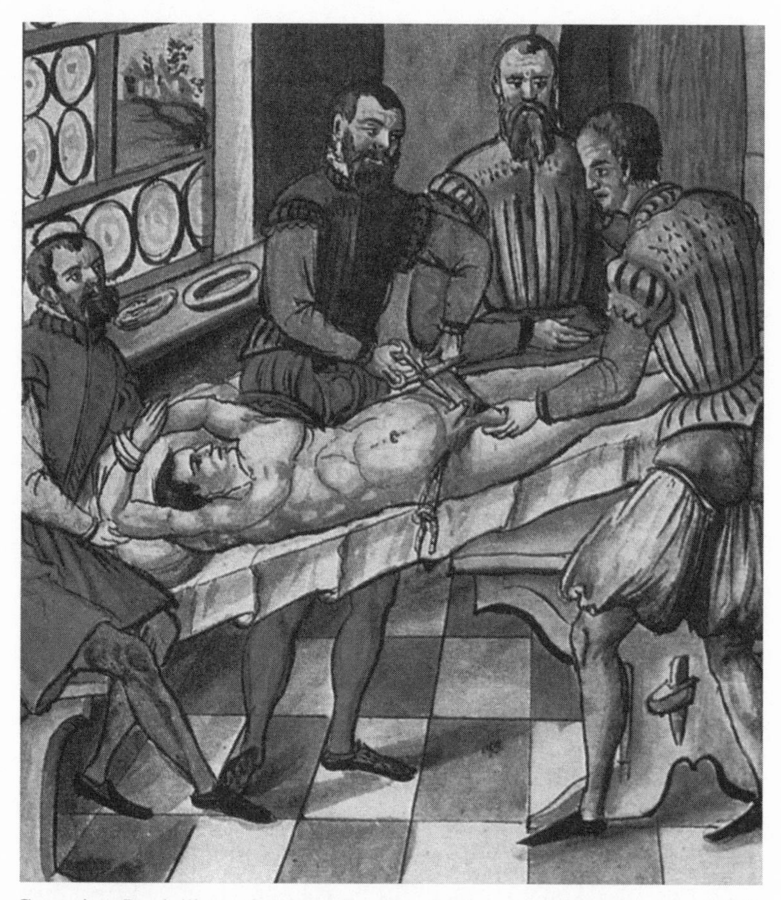

Castration. Book illustration from *Practica Copiosa* by Caspar Stromayr (1559).

children above the age of four.

In 1586, Pope Sixtus V not only issued a ban on marriage for castrati, but also effectively prohibited any form of sexual relations for them, since sexuality outside of marriage was not permitted. However, the inventive Italians launched the institution of *cicisbeo*, the gallant companion. The institution of the *cicisbei* enabled a married woman, usually from aristocratic circles or from the grande bourgeoisie, to cultivate a "gallant relationship that enhanced marriage" in a socially acceptable form. This function was also fulfilled by the vocal castrati, who were in great demand as lovers!

As the popularity of the vocal castrati continued its swift ascent, castrati even influenced the course of political events. During the Thirty Years War, hostilities between Sweden and Poland were temporarily halted to allow Queen Christina to receive and hear Baldassarre Ferri (1610–1680), who then served at the Polish court. Other kings also jumped at the chance to hear his singing at their courts, and outdid one another with offers of money and gifts. The western world was enthralled by the music of castrati, who consequently became the richest artists of their time. Only France made some attempt to resist this trend, but to no avail. Jean-Baptiste Lully (1632–1687), the courtier of Louis XIV, composed a mythological opera requiring singing by castrati. His opera *Atys* (which premiered in 1676) reworks the Greek legend of Attis, who castrates himself and dies, and is then transformed into a pine tree by Cybele. Jean-Philippe Rameau (1683–1764) also featured vocal castrati in his operas (most notably in *Hyppolite et Aricie* and *Castor et Pollux*). Castrati also served at the royal French court. Queen Anne, the mother of Louis XIV, passionately loved the castrato Atto Melani (1626–1693), who paid his musical respects to her every second evening. He was also slated to sing the title role in the opera *L'Ercole amante* by Francesco Cavalli at the wedding of Louis XIV and the Spanish princess Maria Theresia, but he was forced to leave France in 1661 because of intrigues involving the detested

Minister and Cardinal Jules Mazarin.

Enthusiasm for the vocal prowess of the castrati knew no bounds. Some castrati sought engagements and societal recognition outside of Italy, because musical life north of the Alps was also dependent on castrati. They distinguished themselves as singers, composers, and dramatists owing to their outstanding extensive training in both song and instrumental music and their solid grasp of art and literature. For this reason, they often became teachers and conductors and were in high demand at court even apart from church music.

When Mozart was eight years old, he met Giovanni Manzuoli (1720–1782) in London; Mozart may even have taken singing lessons from Manzuoli. Six years later he wrote an opera for Manzuoli, *Mitridate re di Ponto.* The opera premiered in 1770 in Milan with great success, but did not feature Manzuoli, who had placed unreasonable demands on Mozart. Early in his career, Mozart composed a motet for Luigi Marchesi (1755–1829), and collaborated with the young and incalculable Venanzio Rauzzini (1746–1810) and Giusto Ferdinando Tenducci (1736–1790), whose voice dazzled audiences of his day. For Vincenzo dal Prato (1756–1828), he composed a role in *Idomeneo*, but their collaboration deteriorated during a strained rehearsal period. Mozart's enthusiasm for vocal castrati eventually waned, owing in part to their excessive monetary demands, and Mozart composed his subsequent great opera works without parts for the high voices of the castrati. Going back to his earlier works, he even rewrote them for tenors, including the part of Idamante in *Idomeneo*.

One of the most renowned castrati to come to Germany was Giovanni Andrea Bontempi, known as Angelini (1624–1705).

He served the Saxon elector, composed operas, wrote books on history and musicology, and worked together with two singers who made their mark on history apart from their achievements in music. One was the lover of the French Queen Anne, Atto Melani; the other, Bartolomeo de Sorlisi (1632–1672), even married into Protestant Saxony as a noble musician, which triggered a judicial dispute that seems strikingly modern. The views of the Leipzig theologians closely mirrored those of the Catholic theologians, and were based on the principle: “Quod impotens ad copulam sit impotens ad matrimonium” (He who is incapable of intercourse cannot marry). However, there was some attempt to weigh the human consequences of denying Sorlisi the right to marry. His marriage was ultimately approved as a lesser evil, in light of the fact that he was not altogether impotent and might otherwise succumb to impure desires.[166]

Many aspects of marriage that had never been debated before became the subject of open discussion. A set of debates was compiled in 1685 in the volume *Eunuchi conjugium, oder die Capaunen-Heyrath* (Halle) and published under the name Hieronymus Delphinus (most likely a pseudonym). The Königsberg theologians held an extreme view on this matter:

> The human race is so ample that we need not concern ourselves with propagation. Therefore the state of marriage nowadays is principally a remedy for fickle desire . . . In some cases, not only the testicles, but also the spermatic cords from which they are suspended are cut off; in other cases the sexual organs are removed altogether. Those who have only severed spermatic cords occasionally remain capable not only of coitus, but also of pro-

> creation. Men who are emasculated are incapable of either coitus or procreation. If, however, only the gonads are cut away and the spermatic cords are left intact, men can experience not only ejaculation, but also erections and can engage in intercourse with women. In fact, they are more potent and more suited to sexual intercourse than those who have not undergone these procedures.[167]

Although these arguments served to sanction the marriage of Sorlisi, his marriage was nonetheless denounced until his death.

Matters of this sort were less problematic in Germany than in Italy. The castrato and composer Filippo Finazzi (1706–1776), who had a singing engagement in Hamburg, had relatively little difficulty gaining Senate approval for his marriage to a German widow. He was also granted permission to adopt her son.

Cultural life in the 17th and 18th centuries was unthinkable without vocal castrati. People went to the opera less to experience the dramatic plot than to hear castrati singing, as Handel learned in London, when he quarreled with Francesco Senesino (1680–1759) and sent him back to Italy. London audiences shunned the opera once their beloved castrato was gone. Every single eminent composer of the era incorporated castrato voices. Claudio Monteverdi, Alessandro Scarlatti, Antonio Lotti, Christoph Willibald Gluck, and Joseph Haydn all created vocal roles that today are sung by female sopranos. Giacomo Meyerbeer (1791–1864) wrote his last opera *Il crociato in Egitto* (which premiered in 1824) for castrati. Even Wagner contemplated casting the role of Klingsor in *Parsifal* with a castrato, Domenico Mustafá (1829–1912), the last great figure in opera of this type.

Of all the singing court castrati, Farinelli was the most renowned "castrato of kings." He spent over 24 years in Madrid singing to royalty. Patrick Barbier's biography of Farinelli describes the first fateful encounter of the singer and King Philip V, the grandson of Louis XIV:

> It would be idle speculation to attempt to identify which arias Carlo Farinelli sang before the King on that August evening in 1737 . . . Only one single minute mattered: when the crystalline, velvety, and sensual notes of the best singer in the world succeeded in making the despondent face of Philip V glow with pleasure . . . The King summoned the strength to call Farinelli, to touch him, to ask him to sing additional songs, this time directly at his bedside . . .
>
> Five days after he had first heard Farinelli, Philip V signed the following decree on August 30, 1737: "For this reason I have decided that Don Carlo Broschi, known as Farinelo, shall remain in my royal service as a *criado familiar*, owing to his unique talent and his singing ability, and sing exclusively for me and the Queen, my dear and beloved wife. I grant him an annual salary of 1500 guineas in English coins, which is equivalent to 1300 reales de velon; a coach with two mules for his personal use, and a mule-drawn carriage to accompany the travels of the court; a coach for his family and his servants, and a suitable home for himself and his family both in the royal residences and in every place to which he follows me . . ."[168]

The promotion of a singer to a *criado familiar*, a chamber-

Caricature of a famous castrato

lain (in the original sense of a eunuch) at the court of one of the most powerful potentates of the time, was the talk of the land. The king, who was suffering from neurasthenia, commissioned Farinelli to sing before him nearly every night, usually between the hours of midnight and four in the morning. Farinelli won the trust of the ruler and wielded influence on his decisions. After the death of Philip V, the situation remained unchanged; his son Ferdinand VI (from his first marriage) also venerated Farinelli, decorated him with the Cross of the Order of Calatrava, an award bestowed on the highest dignitaries, and appointed him artistic director of the opera. Life in Madrid, then one of the dirtiest cities, was full of surprises for the talented Italian. Farinelli described them in his extensive correspondence, especially in letters to his old friend Metastasio.

Farinelli experienced deep satisfaction as well as recognition in serving the Spanish Crown. With the arrival of Ferdinand's successor Charles III, however, who was hostile to Italian influences in Madrid, Farinelli was summarily dismissed. He was forced to leave Spain, and could not even return to Naples because this city belonged to the dominion of Charles III. Farinelli moved back to Bologna, where he died.

No other epoch in the history of western music was as decisively shaped by castrati as the 17th and 18th centuries. Many oratories by Bach, Handel, and Haydn would have been inconceivable without castrati voices. But just as in the opera, women, who revolutionized song with their vocal range, eventually displaced the castrati.

However, singing by castrati lived on in church music throughout the 19th century and into the early 20th century.

Franz Haböck, the author of one of the classic works on castrati singing, was among those privileged to hear and speak with castrati. His 1927 book, *Die Kastraten und ihre Gesangkunst*, describes a music conference held in 1911 in Rome, where Haböck thrilled to the virtuosity of "the last angel of Rome," Alessandro Moreschi (1858–1922), when the latter sang at St. Peter's Church. Moreschi's voice has been captured on one of the earliest sound recordings and can still be heard today, but this recording cannot begin to convey the quality of what his audiences must have experienced. Haböck reported:

> Moreschi's voice can only be compared to the clarity and purity of crystal. The absolute balance of his notes, which sound uncommonly powerful, clear, lucid, sweet, yet different from both women's and boys' voices, the complete effortlessness that we physically feel along with his inexhaustible ability to hold a note, awakened in me a compelling vision of the most beautiful wind instrument that has ever been inspired by human breath . . . . After an accent on the peak of the 'messa di voce,' the tone fades and actually seems to shift to an endless, tranquil, barely discernible 'tenuta la voce,' which I have never heard from any other singer or instrumentalist. An oboist or a trumpeter might come closest to achieving this effect. I never have so genuinely, so intensively experienced the feeling that the voice is the most wonderful, most glorious of all instruments that the human breath commands.[169]

This praise from the pen of a connoisseur attests to the power of a phenomenon that ended with the pontificate of Pius

Caricature of the famous castrato Farinelli in a theater performance with Francesca Cuzzini and Jacob Heidegger in London. Drawing by Marco Ricci (about 1730).

X, but there is much to indicate that the dream of the voices of angels lives on. The operatic phenomenon of vocal castrati continues to capture the imagination of writers around the world. A recent novel, *The Virtuoso* (1993) by the Dutch writer Margriet de Moor, revisits this golden age of song and its wide-ranging impact on European society.

The Virtuoso, recently translated into English, describes the passion the narrator Contessa Carlotta feels for the castrato Gasparo Conti upon hearing his voice:

> God's Creation dissolved into a man-made brew. Gasparo started his aria on a high note. Soft, long-sustained and ever-swelling, it was a high F-sharp at the very least. . . . We want the sound of passion to be high, high and of extreme virtuosity. We want artfully elaborated ecstasy. Then we can weep, not on account of the story, but on account of ourselves. Then we will be filled with joy. May virtue and love assail us from on high! . . .
>
> The singer embarked on his final cadence. Without apparent effort, without the slightest flutter on the lungs, with that Indian garden behind him and that red sky overhead, he emitted a flow of tempestuous triads and then launched into a string of hammered-out triplets so prodigious that the audience, bursting with pent-up love, went wild . . . Shouts rang out even before his feat had been accomplished. . . .
>
> . . . heaven help me, that single interval encapsulated all I knew about love, and yes, also his journey in a carriage to a medical clinic in Norcia.[170]

The protagonist's realization that she had fallen for a castrato, which is indicated by the phrase "a clinic in Norcia" (then a synonym for Italy's best known castration center), did not stop her from craving his company. She found herself surrendering to a passion that dazzled her senses.

Epilogue

BY SHELLEY L. FRISCH

"Eunuchs in the twentieth century? Did the man really say eunuchs?"[171] Readers might well share author Zia Jaffrey's astonishment at learning that eunuchism is alive and well in our era.

At several junctures in history, eunuchism has seemed to reach a natural or a forced end, only to rise again in new guises. The largest community of eunuchs today is in India, where estimates range from 50,000 to over 4 million (no census figures are available). These eunuchs are referred to as *hijra*s, the Urdu word for "impotent ones." The hijras rank lower than the untouchables in India.

Zia Jaffrey, the daughter of actress and food critic Madhur Jaffrey, undertook her journey to India to study the culture of her maternal lineage and to attend the wedding of a relative, but almost immediately encountered what became the focus of her visit: men dressed in tattered saris, beating on tambourines and drums, singing in jarring cacophony, and hurling obscenities. The hijras earn a living wage by appearing uninvited at weddings and singing abominably until paid to leave. Whereas our main association with castrati is the legendary beauty of their singing voices, which the Italian castrati of the 18th century put to extraordinary professional advantage, the hijras employ screeching as a professional singing device.

In the past few years, hijras have begun to move from the margins of Indian society to its center. Several hijras have been making international news with their successful bids for political office. In 1998, the *Wall Street Journal* featured a report about a Ms. Shobha Nehru,[172] whose story both typifies and diverges from the standard profile of hijras. In typical fashion, she was kidnapped at a young age and brought to a succession of major cities in which she led the life of a societal and sexual outcast, dancing to eke out a paltry income. Ms. Nehru dresses in women's clothes and calls herself "she." Unlike most hijras, however, Ms. Nehru began lobbying for better conditions in her community, and was urged to run for the Hissar City Council in 1995, on which she has served ever since. She works hard to combat problems facing the poor and socially neglected citizenry, and intends eventually to run for Parliament, under the slogan: "You don't need genitals for politics. You need brains."

Another sizable community of eunuchs that flourished in modernity arose in Russia during the time of Catherine the Great and lasted into the Stalin era. The *skoptsi* ("self-castrators"), as this fellowship was called, were a community of Christians who engaged in ritual self-castration as a religious act in the quest for spiritual purity and eternal life. It has been speculated that at its peak, the number of skoptsi may have exceeded ten million.[173]

Skoptsi males could opt for a "minor seal," in which the testicles were removed by slicing through the scrotum and cauterizing the wound while the operator cried out: "Christ is risen!" To attain an even higher level of purity, the penis was removed altogether in a "major seal."[174] Women also submitted to various excisions to assert their dedication to spiritual salvation. Their ersatz castration entailed the extraordinary pain and disfigurement of having their nipples, breasts, and/or outer vaginal parts cut to signal the permanence of their commitment.[175] Because these procedures were specifically outlawed, skoptsi often claimed to have been castrated by strangers or by individuals who were now deceased, so as to shield themselves and their accomplices from prosecution.[176]

Emasculations undertaken out of ideological conviction are quite rare in our age, but not unheard of. When the members of Heaven's Gate made headlines with their mass suicide in 1997 outside of San Diego, it was learned that some of this movement's adherents had submitted to castration in search of salvation.

Castration is currently being employed to treat an increasingly broad range of medical conditions. New developments in cancer research, for example, indicate that chemical or surgical castration after the removal of the prostate increases the survival rate of patients with prostate cancer. The procedure deprives the tumor of testosterone, which it needs to grow.[177]

The most highly publicized type of castration is treatment for "gender dysphoria," unhappiness with one's birth gender. People who suffer from this condition can now seek surgical modification of their gender. One of the first MTF (male to female transgender) operations was performed on Christine Jorgensen (née George William Jorgensen, Jr.) in 1950. Jorgensen was an American who was regendered in Denmark, which pioneered the procedure. Jorgensen later became the object of merciless American media coverage. She published her memoirs,[178] which were followed in due course by a virtual flood of transsexual memoirs as the operation became more widespread.

The result was a new subgenre of autobiography in both the MTF category, such as the memoirs of Jan Morris,[179] and the FTM category, notably the autobiography of Mario Martino.[180] An especially high-profile transgendering operation was that of professional tennis player Renée Richards, who transformed him/herself from a man into a woman in 1975, and chronicled this extraordinary journey of identity in *Second Serve: The Renée Richards Story.*[181] By the 1990s, the genre had evolved from a narrative of the agonies and ecstasies of assuming a new gender, and turned to activism. One notable example, written by MTF Kate Bornstein, with the provocative title *Gender Outlaw: On Men, Women and the Rest of Us,*[182] argues that gender is an issue not only for transsexuals, but for everyone.

A recent book by John Colapinto, *As Nature Made Him: The Boy Who Was Raised As a Girl,*[183] has meticulously chronicled the case of Bruce/Brenda/David Reimer. Reimer, now a married man with three children and an ordinary suburban life, switched genders not once, but twice. Born Bruce, he suffered the catastrophic effects of a botched circumcision in 1966. His parents were counseled, astonishingly, to have him castrated, given hormonal treatments, and be brought up as a girl instead. Renamed Brenda, s/he spent the next decade attempting to lead the life of a girl, until his parents fully realized what a devastating toll this gender switch had taken on their son, and allowed him to take the long and difficult road back to his original gender, with the new name of David. The book even suggests a triumph of good over evil, the evil embodied by Dr. John Money of Johns Hopkins University, who had advocated the castration.[184]

The transgender community has expanded so greatly that it has even suffered at least one epidemic disease specific to that community. Since 1998, transgendered individuals living in social groups known as "houses" that participate in drag balls have been testing positive for a particular strain of tuberculosis. The Center for Disease Control and Prevention first identified cases of this strain in Baltimore, then in New York City among young men who were born male, but live predominantly as women. As of April 2000, dozens of cases had been diagnosed, and it is expected that the numbers will continue to grow.[185]

Transsexuals have banded together in organized support groups, and use the Internet as an important resource for information exchange and communication. Among the popular websites are the following: www.tgforum.com and www.transgender.org/tg/ifge. A more specialized website is www.eunuch.org, a site that Netscape describes as "a friendly home for eunuchs on the net."

Scholarly studies of eunuchism, castration, transsexualism, and the "Third Sex" are burgeoning as well. At the January 2000 convention of the American Historical Association, an entire session was devoted to discussions of the perception and social construction of eunuchs in late antiquity and the Middle Ages. This session considered the gender politics of Christian self-castration in late antiquity, the fashioning of children into eunuchs in Byzantium, and the "good" eunuch in Mamluk sources. Many recent book-length studies[186] are beginning to contribute significant new dimensions to our understanding of eunuchs and castrati, as does the present volume.

The term "eunuch" has gained metaphorical currency in scholarship as well. The best-known application of the term in the social sciences is Germaine Greer's *The Female Eunuch*,[187] which argues that women are deformed and desexualized into eunuchs by men who subscribe to the Freudian theory that the defining feature of females is their lack of a sexual organ.

Cinematic portrayals of transgendering have ranged from the frivolous (*Tootsie, Mrs. Doubtfire*) to the provocative (*The Crying Game*) to the documentary (*Boys Don't Cry*). In April 2000, Hilary Swank received an Academy Award for Best Actress for the 1999 film *Boys Don't Cry*, which tells the true story of Brandon Teena, born Teena Brandon, whose tragic brief life was dominated by the desire to switch genders and live life as a man, a desire that catapulted his/her life into a downward spiral of mockery and hatred, culminating in Brandon's homicidal death.

However, it is castrati who have made the most indelible mark on aesthetic history with their sublime performances in Italian opera. Their achievements have proven their perpetual ability to fascinate us and engage our imaginations, even long after the end of the era in which they flourished. Modern technology has allowed listeners to capture a sense of the exquisite acoustic beauty that singing castrati communicated to their audiences. A 1994 film by Gérard Corbiau, *Farinelli, Il Castrato*, employed computer technology to blend the voices of a soprano and a countertenor to convey the breathtaking range of Farinelli's voice. There is even one extant sound recording made by the the last of the great singing castrati, the renowned Alessandro Moreschi.[188]

Literature returns again and again to the theme of the transcendental beauty of operatic castrati. An outstanding example is Anne Rice's *Cry to Heaven,*[189] which recreates the operatic world of 18th-century Italy with two fictional castrati protagonists, Tonio Treschi and Guido Maffeo and their historical counterparts Nicolino, Farinelli, and Caffarelli. The novel depicts the rise to stardom of Tonio, who is under the tutelage of Guido. Because Guido's own voice has soured, he must experience acclaim vicariously through his pupil. Tonio, who was castrated as a young teenager, years beyond the typical age for this surgery, at first refuses to sing, and devotes his energies instead to avenging his mutilation. In a tense performance toward the end of the novel, Guido fears that his disciple will be outsung by a renowned rival, Bettichino, whose "show of tremolos and trills ... seemed to defy human explanation," and brings the audience to its feet.[190] Then it is Tonio's turn. Now reconciled to his fate as social pariah, he takes the stage, and, in a magnificent aria, proves with bittersweet triumph that his castration has endowed him with the voice of angels:

> Tonio . . . ascended in the most exquisite passage, rising and rising until he found that very same note again, only a full octave higher. Slowly, slowly he swelled it, slowly he let it pulse from his throat, this very limit of what the human voice could attain, yet so velvet smooth and soft it seemed the loveliest sigh of grief drawn out and out until one could not endure it.[191]

Notes

1. The *Reallexikon für Antike und Christentum*—as against *Paulys Realencyclopädie der classischen Altertumswissenschaft* edited by Pauly and Wissowa—contains an entry only under the heading *gallos* and none under the term *eunouchos*. In fact, the general information pertaining to eunuchs in the *Reallexikon* is even subsumed under the heading *effeminatus*.
2. Berlin: Henschel, 1993.
3. The term *Sitz im Leben* is used in English and derives from biblical form criticism. It is part of the method used by the form-criticism school in analyzing literary forms in order to offer a genetic explanation for the accomplished fact of the Gospels as the result of earlier oral traditions. To attain this objective, the method requires that the following three steps must be taken: (1) the literary units must be isolated; (2) they must be classified according to type; (3) their place of origin and transmission must be determined. "There is no intention or even possibility of drawing from the form conclusions regarding the date, place, or author of the analyzed form. Rather, it is in the activity of the community that the literary type has its situation in life—the community's worship, catechesis, and apologetics." *New Catholic Encyclopedia* (New York: McGraw-Hill, 1967), vol. 5, pp. 1017–18.—Trans.
4. John Irving, *A Son of the Circus* (New York: Random House, 1994), p. 263.
5. Roger Caillois, *Man and the Sacred*, trans. Meyer Barash (Westport, Conn.: Greenwood Press, 1959; repr. 1980), p. 140.
6. Plato, *Symposium*, trans. Alexander Nehamas and Paul Woodruff (Indianapolis and Cambridge: Hackett Pub. Co., 1989), 206b ff.
7. Flavius Philostratus, *Vitae soph.*, 2.4.2.
8. Rainer Maria Rilke, *Duino Elegies*, trans. J. B. Leishman and Stephen Spender (New York: W. W. Norton, 1939), 1.1–14 (p. 25).
9. Andreas Lommel, *Schamanen und Medizinmänner* (Munich, 1980), pp. 109f.
10. Petronius Arbiter, *Satyrica* [*Satyricon*], ed. and trans. R. Bracht Branham and Daniel Kinney (London: J. M. Dent, 1996), 23.3.

11. *Anthologia Palatina*, ed. P. Waltz (Paris, 1928). English trans., W.R. Paton, *The Greek Anthology*, Loeb Classical Library (Cambridge, Mass., and London, 1916), 2.102.
12. Robert Musil, *The Man without Qualities*, trans. Sophie Wilkins (New York: Alfred A. Knopf, 1995), pp. 980ff.
13. *Diodorus of Sicily*, trans. C. H. Oldfather (Cambridge, Mass.: Harvard University Press, 1989), vol. 1, 1.78.4.
14. Terence, *The Eunuchs*, act 5, scene 4, trans. Douglass Parker, in *The Complete Comedies of Terence*, modern verse translations, by Palmer Bovie, Constance Carrier, and Douglass Parker, ed. Palmer Bovie (New Brunswick, N.J.: Rutgers University Press, 1974), p. 215.
15. Max Grühl, *Citadel of Ethiopia: The Empire of the Divine Emperor*, trans. Ian F.D. Morrow and L.M. Sieveking (New York: AMS, 1977), p. 15.
16. Herodotus, *The Histories of Herodotus*, trans. Henry Cary (New York: D. Appleton, 1904), book 8, 474–75.
17. Plutarch, *De Iside et Osiride*, trans. and ed. J. Gwyn Griffiths (Swansea: University of Wales Press, 1970), 12ff.
18. Plutarch, 18.
19. Plutarch, 19.
20. *The Ancient Pyramid Texts*, trans. R.O. Faulkner (Oxford: Clarendon Press, 1969), Teti 185/192.
21. *Texte aus der Umwelt des Alten Testaments*, vol. 3, ed. Otto Kaiser (Gütersloh: G. Mohn, 1982), 944f.
22. Plutarch, 55.
23. *Das Totenbuch der Ägypter*, trans. with commentary by Erik Hornung (Zürich/Munich, 1979), 125.
24. Volkert Haas, *Hethitische Berggötter und hurritische Steindämonen: Riten, Kulte und Mythen* (Munich, 1982), p. 132.
25. Gustave Flaubert, *Salammbo,* trans. J. C. Chartres (New York, Dutton, 1931), pp. 60ff.
26. Flaubert, pp. 40–41.
27. Flaubert, p. 158.
28. Hesiod, *Theogony*, in *Hesiod: The Works and Days; Theogony; The Shield of Herakles*, trans. Richmond Lattimore (Ann Arbor: University of Michigan Press, 1959), 173ff.

29. Ovid, *Fasti: Roman Holidays*, trans. Betty Rose Nagle (Bloomington: Indiana University Press, 1995), 4.341f.
30. Johann Wolfgang von Goethe, *Schriften zur Kunst* (Munich), 13.2, 120 and 131.
31. Homer, *The Iliad*, trans. Richmond Lattimore (Chicago: University of Chicago Press, 1951), 22.75f.
32. Clement of Alexandria, *Protrepticus*, 2.19.4.
33. Walter F. Otto, *Beiträge zur Hierodulie im hellenistischen Ägypten* (Munich: Bayerische Akademie der Wissenschaften, 1949), p.152f.
34. C. [Karl] Kerényi, *Dionysos: Archetypal Image of Indestructible Life*, trans. Ralph Manheim (Princeton, N.J.: Princeton University Press, 1976), p. 277, quoting *Protrepticus* 2.19.4; ibid., p. 277.
35. *Roman und Mysterium in der Antike* (Munich: Beck, 1962).
36. Martin Nilsson, *Geschichte der griechischen Religion* (Munich: Beck, 1974), pp. 590f.
37. Euripides, *The Bacchae*, trans. William Arrowsmith, in *Euripides*, vol. 5 (Chicago: University of Chicago, 1968 [1959]), 1079–81.
38. Ibid., 453f.
39. Ibid., 1109f.
40. Ibid., 773f.
41. Friedrich Nietzsche, *The Birth of Tragedy out of the Spirit of Music and the Genealogy of Morals*, trans. Francis Golffing (Garden City, N.Y.: Doubleday, 1956), p. 78.
42. Martial, *Epigrams* XIII, ed. and trans. D. R. Shackleton Bailey (Cambridge, Mass.: Harvard University Press, 1993), 3.63. Untranslatable play on two meanings of *gallus*: (a) a cockerel; (b) a Gaul or Galatian. Hence a priest of Cybele, hence a eunuch.
43. Paul Veyne, *Bread and Circuses.*, trans. Oswyn Murray (London: Penguin, 1990), pp. 468ff.
44. Ernst Cassirer, *Philosophie der Symbolischen Formen*, part 2, Das mythische Denken (Darmstadt: Wissenschaftliche Buchgesellschaft, 1964 [1924]), esp. pp. 78ff.
45. Ernst Bloch, *Geist der Utopie* (Frankfurt a.M.: Suhrkamp, 1964 [1918, 1923].
46. Max Weber, *Wirtschaft und Gesellschaft* (Tübingen, 1922), p. 832.
47. Theologisches Worterbuch zum alten Testament.

48. Ernst H. Kantorowicz, *The King's Two Bodies: A Study in Mediaeval Political Theology* (Princeton, N.J.: Princeton University Press, 1957).
49. Cited in Giovanni Pettinato, *Semiramis* (Zurich/Munich, 1989), p. 213.
50. All Biblical quotations are taken from the *The New Oxford Annotated Bible, with the Apocryphal/deuterocanonical Books, New Revised Standard Version*, ed. Bruce M. Metzger and Roland E. Murphy (New York: Oxford University Press, 1994).
51. Cited in Pettinato, p. 244.
52. *Ammianus Marcellinus*, trans. John C. Rolfe (Cambridge, Mass.: Harvard University Press, 1935), vol. 1, 14.6.17.
53. This dignitary of the Ethiopian Church, the *'aqabe sa'at*, is known variously in English translation as the keeper of the watch, the guardian of the hours, and the guardian of the [canonical] times. He used to be the third dignitary of the church and the first religious officer in the palace.—Trans.
54. Eike Haberland, *Untersuchungen zum äthiopischen Königtum* (Wiesbaden: F. Steiner, 1965), p. 160, quoting J. Perruchon, *Les chroniques de Zar'a Ja`eqob et de Ba'eda Maryam*, Bibliothèque de l'Ecole des Hautes Etudes, fasc. 93 (Paris), pp. 8f.
55. Hesiod, *Works and Days*, in *Hesiod: The Works and Days; Theogony; The Shield of Herakles*, trans. Richmond Lattimore (Ann Arbor: University of Michigan Press, 1959), 5.785ff.
56. Pompey married Caesar's daughter Julia.
57. Livy, *The War with Hannibal. Books xxi–xxx of the History of Rome from Its Foundation*, trans. Aubrey de Sélincourt and ed. Betty Radice (Baltimore: Penguin Books, 1965), 39.14.10ff.
58. Ovid, *Fasti* 4.179ff.; 212ff.
59. Catullus, *Carmina,* in *The Poems of Catullus,* trans. Charles Martin (Baltimore: Johns Hopkins University Press, 1990), 63.1–49, 62–72, 91–93.
60. Pausanias, *Pausanias's Description of Greece*, trans. J. G. Frazer (New York: Biblo and Tannen, 1965), 7.17.10ff.
61. Arnobius, *Adversus Nationes* (Padova: Draghi, 1929), 5.5ff.
62 Volkert Haas, *Hethitische Berggötter*, pp. 186–90.
63. *Scriptores Historiae Augustae,* trans. David Magie (London:

William Heinemann, 1924), 17.7.

64. Apuleius, *Metamorphoses*, ed. and trans. J. Arthur Hanson (Cambridge: Harvard University Press, 1989), vol. 2, 11.23 (p. 341).
65. *Codex Justinianus*, selected and ed. Gottfried Härtel/Frank-Michael Kaufmann (Leipzig: Reclam, 1991), 4.42.2.
66. Pliny the Elder, *The Natural History of Pliny*, trans. John Bostock and H. T. Riley (London: George Bell & Sons, 1890), 7.128f.
67. Daldianus Artemidorus, *The Interpretation of Dreams*, trans. Robert J. White (Park Ridge, N.J.: Noyes Press, 1975), 2.69; 4.37.
68. Josephus Flavius, *Vita*, 429, in vol. 1 of the works of Josephus, trans. H. St. J. Thackeray *The Life; Against Apion* (Cambridge, Mass.: Harvard University Press, 1956 [1926]).
69. Petronius, *Satyricon*, 119.19–24.
70. Cassius Dio, *Dio's Roman History,* with an English translation by Ernest Cary, on the basis of the version of Herbert Baldwin Foster (Cambridge: Harvard University Press, 1925; 1955), 62.28.2–3.
71. Tranquillus Gaius Suetonius, "Nero," in *The Twelve Caesars*, trans. Robert Graves, revised by Michael Grant (London: Penguin Press, 1989), 28.1f.
72. Dio, 64.10.1.
73. *Historia Augusta*, 17.5.5ff.
74. *Historia Augusta*, 18.23.4ff.
75. *Historia Augusta*, 6.67.
76. Juvenal, *Satires*, 6.366ff.
77. Tacitus, *Annals*, trans. John Jackson (London: William Heinemann, 1937), 14.3.
78. Martial, *Epigrams*, 6.2.
79. Sun Yao-ting, *Der letzte Eunuch,* trans. Uwe Frankenhauser (Leipzig: G. Kiepenhauer, 1993).
80. Wolfgang Bauer, *Das Antlitz Chinas* (Munich: C. Hanser, 1971), pp. 84ff.
81. Sun Yao-ting, *Der letzte Eunuch*, p. 468.
82. Li Chi, *Book of Rites*, trans. James Legge and ed. Ch'u Chai and Winberg Chai (New Hyde Park, N.Y.: University Books, 1967), xxxviii, 1, 5–7.
83. Ulrike Jugel, *Politische Funktion und soziale Stellung der Eunuchen zur späteren Hanzeit (25–220 n. Chr.)* (Wiesbaden:

Steiner, 1976).

84. Albany, N.Y.: SUNY Press, 1995.
85. Sun Yao-ting, *Der letzte Eunuch,* pp. 44ff.
86. Ce Shaozhen, *Flaneur im alten Peking. Ein Leben zwischen Kaiserreich und Revolution* (Munich, 1987/90), p. 27.
87. Bauer, pp. 228ff.
88. Bauer, pp. 132ff.
89. Cited in Ulrike Jugel, *Politische Funktion und soziale Stellung der Eunuchen zur Späteren Hanzeit*, p. 306.
90. Ce Shaozhen, p. 28.
91. Bauer, p. 479.
92. Ce Shaozhen, p. 28.
93. Clement of Alexandria, *Christ the Educator*, translated by Simon P. Wood, vol. 23 of *The Fathers of the Church* (New York: Fathers of the Church, Inc, 1954), III, 4.26.221.
94. Eugen Fehrle, *Die kultische Keuschheit in Altertum,* vol. 6 of *Religionsgeschichtliche Versuche und Vorarbeiten* (Gießen, 1910).
95. Swami Nikhilananda, *The Upanishads* (New York: Harper & Row, 1963), p. 235.
96. Uta Ranke-Heinemann, *Eunuchs for the Kingdom of Heaven: Women, Sexuality, and the Catholic Church*, trans. Peter Heinegg (New York: Doubleday, 1990), chapter 4.
97. Clement of Alexandria, *Stromateis*, bks. 1–3, trans. John Ferguson (Washington, D.C.: The Catholic University of America Press, 1991), 3.91(1)–92(2).
98. *The Gospel According to Thomas,* in *The Gnostic Scriptures*, trans. and ed. Bentley Layton (Garden City, N.Y.: Doubleday, 1987), Logion 22, p. 384.
99. Ibid., Logion 37, p. 387.
100. Adolf von Harnack, *Marcion*, trans. John E. Steely and Lyle D. Bierma (Durham, N.C.: Labyrinth Press, 1990), pp. 96–97.
101. *Nag Hammadi Codices IX and X*, trans. Søren Giverson and Birger A. Pearson and ed. Birger A. Pearson (Leiden: E. J. Brill, 1981), 9.3, "The Testimony of Truth," 29.26–30.16.
102. Jerome, *Adversus Jovinianus* I, 16.25.
103. Benjamin Walker, *Gnosticism: Its History and Influence* (Wellingborough: The Aquarian Press, 1983), p. 114.

104. *The Faith of the Early Fathers*, selected and translated by W. A. Jurgens (Collegeville, Minn.: The Liturgical Press, 1970), Canon 1 of the Council of Nicaea, p. 282.
105. Hans Jonas, *The Gnostic Religion* (Boston: Beacon Press, 1958), p. 231.
106. *The History of the Church from Christ to Constantine*, translated by G. A. Williamson (New York: Penguin, 1989 [1965]), 6.8, p. 186.
107. *The Sayings of the Desert Fathers: The Alphabetical Collection*, trans. by Benedicta Ward (Kalamazoo: Cistercian Publications, 1984 [1975), pp. 124–38.
108. *Select Works of S. Ephrem the Syrian*, trans. Rev. J. B. Morris (Oxford: John Henry Parker; London: F. and J. Rivington, 1847), 34th hymn, section 1, p. 213.
109. *The History of the Church*, 5.16, p. 161.
110. *The Odes of Solomon: The Syriac Texts*, edited and translated by James H. Charlesworth (Missoula, Mont.: Scholars Press, 1977), Ode 42, 8f.
111. New York: Columbia Univ. Press, 1988.
112. Ammianus Marcellinus, *The Later Roman Empire (A.D. 354–378)*, translated by Walter Hamilton (New York: Penguin, 1986), 22.4, p.238.
113. Ibid., 16.7, p. 95.
114. Peter Brown, *Power and Persuasion in Late Antiquity* (Madison: University of Wisconsin Press, 1992), p. 9.
115. *Collectio Casinensis*, ed. E. Schwartz, 224 in Acta Conciliorum Oecumenicorum 1.4, trans. John I. McEnerney, in St. Cyril of Alexandria: Letters 15–110, *Fathers of the Church*, pp. 151–52.
116. One biography that merits attention is *Narses: Hammer of the Goths* by L.H. Fauber (New York: St. Martin's Press, 1990
117. Wilhelm Schubart, *Justinian und Theodora* (Munich: F. Bruckmann, 1943), pp. 260f.
118. Ferdinand Gregorovius, *History of the City of Rome in the Middle Ages*, trans. Annie Hamilton (London: George Bell & Sons, 1894), vol. 1, 1.7.3, pp. 495–98.
119. *Imperial Byzantium* (Boston: Little, Brown and Co., 1938).
120. Princess Djavidan Hanum, *Harem. Erinnerungen der Prinzessin*

Djavidan Hanum (Berlin: Verlag für Kulturpolitik, 1930), 129ff.

121. Cited in Adam Mez, *The Renaissance of Islam*, translated by Salahuddin Khuda Bukhsh and D. S. Margoliouth (London: Luzac & Co., 1937), p. 354.
122. Heinrich von Maltzan, *Meine Wallfahrt nach Mekka* (Tübingen, 1982), p. 40.
123. Gérard de Nerval, *Reise in den Orient* (Werke I) (Munich, 1986), 6.42.
124. Mez, p. 354.
125. *Encyclopedia of Islam*, 2d ed., s.v. *khasi*, vol. .4, pp. 1087–88.
126. Ibn Battuta, p. 278, quoted in Shaun Marmon, *Eunuchs and Sacred Boundaries in Islamic Society* (New York: Oxford University Press, 1995), p. 34.
127. C. Snouck Hurgronje, *Mekka in the Nineteenth Century*, trans. J.H. Monahan (Leiden: E.J. Brill, 1931, repr. 1970), 20, quoted in F.E. Peters, *Mecca: A Literary History of the Muslim Holy Land* (Princeton, N.J.: Princeton University Press, 1994), 273–74.
128. John Lewis Burckhardt, *Travels in Nubia* (London: John Murray, 1819), 328, quoted in Peters, 274.
129. Shaun Marmon, *Eunuchs and Sacred Boundaries in Islamic Society*, p. 111, quoting interview by Tawfiq Nasr Allah in *al-Yamama*, February 7, 1990.
130. André Clot, *Harun al-Rashid and the World of the Thousand and One Nights*, trans. John Howe (New York: New Amsterdam Books, 1989), 90–91.
131. See n. 123 above.
132. Abu Nuwas, trans. E. Wagner, 177.
133. Abu Nuwas in Tabari, 3.956, quoted in Mez, 353.
134. Reinhart Dozy, *Spanish Islam: A History of the Moslems in Spain*, trans. Francis Griffin Stokes (London: Chatto & Windus, 1913), pp. 294–98.
135. Dozy, p. 430.
136. Mez, pp. 354–55.
137. *The Selected Letters of Lady Mary Wortley Montagu*, ed. Robert Halsband (New York: St. Martin's Press, 1970), p. 107.
138. Rupprecht von Bayern, *Reiseerinnerungen aus dem Süd-Osten Europas und dem Orient* (Munich, 1923), 183ff.

139. Franz von Schwarz, *Turkestan* (Freiburg i. Br.: Herder, 1900), p. 56.
140. Arminius [Armin] Vámbéry, *Travels in Central Asia* (London: John Murray, 1864), pp. 189–90.
141. *Kaiserliche Gesandtschaften ans Goldene Horn*, compiled by Karl Teply (Stuttgart: Steingrüben, 1968), pp. 268ff.
142. Kenizé Mourad, *Regards from the Dead Princess: Novel of a Life* (New York: Arcade Publishing/Little, Brown and Company, 1989), p. 12.
143. Ernst Robert Curtius, *European Literature and the Latin Middle Ages,* translated by Willard R. Trask (Princeton: Princeton University Press, 1973), p.122.
144. Gregory of Tours, *The History of the Franks*, trans. Lewis Thorpe (New York: Penguin, 1974), VIII,39, p. 471.
145. Odo, *Collationum libri III*, Migne Ph 133, 556.
146. Wolfram von Eschenbach, *Parzival*, trans. Helen M. Mustard and Charles E. Passage (New York: Vintage Books, 1961), 13.656–57.
147. Cited in Joachim Bumke, *Courtly Culture*, translated by Thomas Dunlap (Berkeley: University of California Press, 1991), p. 393. Bumke concludes that castration was a standard punishment in that era.
148. *Parzival,* 9.493.
149. Ibid., 9.495.
150. Peter Abelard, "The Calamities of Abelard," in *The Letters of Abelard and Heloïse*, trans. C.K. Scott Moncrieff (New York: Alfred A. Knopf, 1942 [1926]), pp. 10–12.
151. Ibid., pp. 20–21.
152. Ibid., pp. 97–98.
153. Ibid., pp. 60–61.
154. Ibid., pp. 98–99.
155. Bernd-Ulrich Hergemöller, *Krötenkuß und schwarzer Kater: Ketzerei, Götzendienst und Unzucht in der inquisitorischen Phantasie des 13. Jahrhunderts* (Warendorf: Fahlbusch Verlag, 1996), p. 373.
156. Cited in Hans Peter Duerr, *Der Mythos vom Zivilisationsprozeß, Nacktheit und Scham, Intimität, Obszönität, und Gewalt* (Frankfurt a. M.: Suhrkamp, 1993), vol. 3, p. 282.

157. *The Comedy of Dante Alighieri, Cantica III: Paradise*, trans. Dorothy L. Sayers and Barbara Reynolds (Baltimore: Penguin, 1973), 25.1–2.
158. Ibid., 28.109ff.
159. Johan Huizinga, *The Waning of the Middle Ages* (Garden City, New York: Doubleday, 1954), p. 27.
160. *The Malleus Maleficarum of Heinrich Kramer and James Sprenger*, trans. and ed. Reverend Montague Summers (New York: Dover, 1971 [1928, 1948]), part 1, question 9 (p. 58).
161. William Shakespeare, *The Norton Shakespeare*, ed. Stephen Greenblatt (New York: W.W. Norton & Co, 1997).
162. Patrick Barbier, *Histoire des castrats* (Paris: B. Grasset, 1989), p. 93.
163. Charles Burney, *The Present State of Music in France and Italy, or The Journal of a Tour through Those Countries, undertaken to Collect Materials for a General History of Music* (London, 1771), pp. 205–208.
164. Berlin/Leipzig, 1927.
165. Charles d'Ancillon, *Eunuchism Display'd. Describing all the Different Sorts of Eunuchs*, trans. Robert Samber (original French, 1707; English trans. London, 1718), pp. 15-16.
166. Hubert Ortkemper, *Engel wider Willen* (Berlin: Henschel, 1993), p. 194.
167. Hieronymus Delphinus, *Eunuchi conjugiu, oder die Capaunen-Heyrath*, cited in Ortkemper, p. 199.
168. Barbier, pp. 199ff.
169. Franz Haböck, *Die Kastraten und ihre Gesangkunst* (Stuttgart: Deutsche Verlags-Anstalt, 1927), pp. 206f.
170. Margriet de Moor, *The Virtuoso*, translated by Ina Rilke (Woodstock and New York: Overlook, 2000), pp. 26-27, 29.
171. Zia Jaffrey, *The Invisibles: A Tale of the Eunuchs of India* (New York: Pantheon Books, 1996), p. 18.
172. "And She's a Eunuch: Ms. Nehru Goes Far in Indian Politics; Lower than the Untouchables, 'Hijras' Begin to Change Some Popular Prejudices," *Wall Street Journal*, September 24, 1998.
173. This community is the subject of a recent comprehensive and fascinating study by Laura Engelstein, *Castration and the Heavenly*

Kingdom: A Russian Folktale (Ithaca: Cornell University Press, 1999). This population statistic appears on p. 11.

174. Engelstein, p. 13.
175. Engelstein, p. 5.
176. Engelstein, p. 49.
177. "Castration Found to Save Lives in Prostate Cancer," *New York Times*, December 9, 1999.
178. *Christine Jorgensen: A Personal Autobiography* (New York: Bantam, 1968).
179. *Conundrum: An Extraordinary Narrative of Transsexualism* (New York: Henry Holt & Co., 1974).
180. *Emergence: A Transsexual Autobiography* (New York: Crown, 1977).
181. with John Ames (New York: Stein & Day, 1983). Renée Richards later became the tennis coach of Hall-of-Famer Martina Navratilova.
182. New York: Routledge, 1994.
183. New York: HarperCollins, 2000.
184. John Money has himself written a 650+-page scholarly tome on transgendering, entitled *Venuses Penuses: Sexology, Sexosophy, and Exigency Theory* (Buffalo: Prometheus, 1986).
185. Jennifer Steinhauer, "TB Outbreak is Identified Among Transgender People," *New York Times*, Friday, April 21, 2000.
186. See in particular the following studies: Serena Nanda, *Neither Man nor Woman: The Hijras of India* (Belmont, Calif.: Wadsworth Publishing Company, 1990); Shaun Marmon, *Eunuchs and Sacred Boundaries in Islamic Society* (New York and Oxford: Oxford University Press, 1995); Bernice L. Hausman, *Changing Sex: Transsexualism, Technology, and the Idea of Gender* (Durham, N.C.: Duke University Press, 1995); *Women, Men and Eunuchs*, ed. Liz James (New York: Routledge, 1997); Sander Gilman, *Making the Body Beautiful* (Princeton: Princeton University Press, 1999), especially chapter 8, "The Wrong Body," on pp. 258–94; and Anne Fausto-Sterling, *Sexing the Body: Gender Politics and the Construction of Sexuality* (New York: Basic Books, 2000).
187. New York: McGraw-Hill, 1970.
188. Alessandro Moreschi, *The Last Castrato*, Pearl OPAL CD 9823.

189. New York: Alfred A. Knopf, 1982.
190. *Cry to Heaven*, p. 418.
191. *Cry to Heaven*, p. 420.

Bibliography

Ammianus Marcellinus. *The Later Roman Empire (A.D. 354-378).* Trans. Walter Hamilton. New York: Penguin, 1986.

d'Ancillon, Charles. *Eunuchism Display'd. Describing all the Different Sorts of Eunuchs.* 1707. Trans. Robert Samber. London, 1718.

Anthologia Palatina. Ed. P. Waltz. Paris, 1928. English trans., W.R. Paton, *The Greek Anthology*, Loeb Classical Library. Cambridge, Mass., and London, 1916.

Apuleius. *Metamorphoses.* 2 vols. Ed. and trans. J. Arthur Hanson. Cambridge: Harvard University Press, 1989.

Arnobius. *Adversus Nationes.* Padova: Draghi, 1929.

Artemidorus, Daldianus. *The Interpretation of Dreams.* Trans. Robert J. White. Park Ridge, N.J.: Noyes Press, 1975.

Barbier, Patrick. *Histoire des castrats.* Paris: B. Grasset, 1989.

Barbier, Patrick. *The World of the Castrati: The History of an Extraordinary Operatic Phenomenon.* Trans. Margaret Crosland. London: Souvenir, 1998.

Bauer, Wolfgang. *Das Antlitz Chinas.* Munich: C. Hanser, 1990.

Baumann, Hermann. *Das doppelte Geschlecht: Studien zur Bisexualität in Ritus und Mythos.* Berlin: D. Reimer, 1955.

Das Totenbuch der Ägypter [The Egyptian Book of the Dead]. Trans. with commentary by Erik Hornung. Zürich/Munich, 1969.

Bornstein, Kate. *Gender Outlaw: On Men, Women and the Rest of Us.* New York: Routledge, 1994.

Brown, Peter. *The Body and Society.* New York: Columbia University Press, 1988.

Brown, Peter. *Power and Persuasion in Late Antiquity.* Madison: University of Wisconsin Press, 1992.

Bumke, Joachim. *Courtly Culture.* Trans. Thomas Dunlap. Berkeley: University of California Press, 1991.

Burney, Charles. *The Present State of Music in France and Italy, or The Journal of a Tour through Those Countries, undertaken to Collect Materials for a General History of Music.* London, 1771.

Caillois, Roger. *Man and the Sacred.* 1959. Trans. Meyer Barash. Westport, Conn.: Greenwood Press, Publishers, 1980.

Catullus. *The Poems of Catullus.* Trans. Charles Martin. Baltimore: Johns Hopkins University Press, 1990.

Ce Shaozhen. *Flaneur im alten Peking.* Munich, 1987/90.

Clement of Alexandria. *Stromateis.* Trans. John Ferguson. Washington, D.C.: Catholic University of America Press, 1991.

Clement of Alexandria. *Christ the Educator.* Trans. Simon P. Wood. Vol. 23 of *The Fathers of the Church.* New York: Fathers of the Church, Inc., 1954.

Clot, André. *Harun al-Rashid and the World of the Thousand and One Nights.* Trans. John Howe. New York: New Amsterdam Books, 1989.

Codex Justinianus. Selected and ed. Gottfried Härtel/Frank-Michael Kaufmann. Leipzig: Reclam, 1991.

Collectio Casinensis. Ed. E. Schwartz, 224 in Acta Conciliorum Oecumenicorum 1.4. Trans. John I. McEnerney, in St. Cyril of Alexandria: Letters 15–110, *Fathers of the Church.*

Curtius, Ernst Robert. *European Literature and the Latin*

Middle Ages. Trans. Willard R. Trask. Princeton: Princeton University Press, 1973.

Dante. The *Comedy of Dante Alighieri, Cantica III: Paradise*. Trans. Dorothy L. Sayers and Barbara Reynolds. Baltimore: Penguin, 1973.

Dio, Cocceianus Cassius. *Dio's Roman History*. Trans. Ernest Cary, on the basis of the version of Herbert Baldwin Foster. Cambridge: Harvard University Press, 1925; 1955.

Diodorus of Sicily. Trans. C. H. Oldfather. Cambridge, Mass.: Harvard University Press, 1989.

Dozy, Reinhart. *Spanish Islam: A History of the Moslems in Spain*. Trans. Francis Griffin Stokes. London: Chatto & Windus, 1913.

Duerr, Hans Peter. *Der Mythos vom Zivilisationsprozeß, vol. 3 Nacktheit und Scham, Intimität, Obszönität, und Gewalt*. Frankfurt a. M., 1993.

Eckstein-Diener, Bertha. *Imperial Byzantium*. New York: Little, Brown and Co., 1938.

Ephrem the Syrian. *Select Works of S. Ephrem the Syrian*. Trans. Rev. J. B. Morris. Oxford: John Henry Parker, and London: F. and J. Rivington, 1847.

Erasmus of Rotterdam. *In Praise of Folly*. London: Reeves & Turner, 1876.

Eschenbach, Wolfram von. *Parzival*. Trans. Helen M. Mustard and Charles E. Passage. New York: Vintage Books, 1961.

Euripides. *The Bacchae*. Trans. William Arrowsmith, in *Euripides*, vol. 5. Chicago: University of Chicago, 1968.

Eusebius. *The History of the Church*. Trans. G. A. Williamson. New York: Penguin, 1989.

The Faith of the Early Fathers, selected and trans. W. A.

Jurgens. Collegeville, Minn.: The Liturgical Press, 1970.

Fauber, L. H. *Narses: Hammer of the Goths*. New York: St. Martin's Press, 1990.

Fehrle, Eugen. *Die kultische Keuschheit in Altertum*. Vol. 6 of *Religionsgeschichtliche Versuche und Vorarbeiten*. Gießen, 1910.

Flaubert, Gustave. *Salammbo*. Trans. J. C. Chartres. New York: Dutton, 1931.

The Gnostic Scriptures. Trans. and ed. Bentley Layton. New York: Doubleday, 1987.

Goethe, Johann Wolfgang von. *Schriften zur Kunst*. Munich.

Gregorovius, Ferdinand. *History of the City of Rome in the Middle Ages*. Trans. Annie Hamilton. London: George Bell & Sons, 1894.

Gregory of Tours. *The History of the Franks*. Trans. Lewis Thorpe. New York: Penguin, 1974.

Grühl, Max. *Citadel of Ethiopia: The Empire of the Divine Emperor*. Trans. Ian F.D. Morrow and L.M. Sieveking. New York: AMS, 1977.

Haas, Volkert. *Hethitische Berggötter und hurritische Steindämonen: Riten, Kulte und Mythen*. Munich, 1982.

Haberland, Eike. *Untersuchungen zum äthiopischen Königtum*. Wiesbaden: F. Steiner, 1965.

Haböck, Franz. *Die Kastraten und ihre Gesangkunst*. Berlin/Leipzig, 1927.

Hanum, Princess Djavidan. *Harem. Erinnerungen der Prinzessin Djavidan Hanum*. Berlin: Verlag für Kulturpolitik, 1930.

Harnack, Adolf von. *Marcion*. Trans. John E. Steely and Lyle D. Bierma. Durham, N.C.: Labyrinth Press, 1990.

Hathaway, Jane. *The Politics of Households in Ottoman Egypt*. New York: Cambridge University Press, 1997.

Hergemöller, Bernd-Ulrich. *Krötenkuß und schwarzer Kater.* Warendorf: Fahlbusch Verlag, 1996.

Herodotus. *The Histories of Herodotus.* Trans. Henry Cary, with a critical and biographical introduction by Basil L. Gildersleeve. New York: D. Appleton, 1904.

Hesiod. *The Works and Days; Theogony; The shield of Herakles.* Trans. Richmond Lattimore. Ann Arbor: University of Michigan Press, 1959.

Historia Augusta: see Scriptores Historiae Augustae.

Homer. *The Iliad of Homer.* Trans. Richmond Lattimore. Chicago: University of Chicago Press, 1951.

Huizinga, Johan. *The Waning of the Middle Ages.* Garden City, N.Y.: Doubleday, 1954.

Iorga, Nicolae. *Geschichte des osmanischen Reiches.* Ankara: Guney Matbaacilik ve Gazetecilik, 1908–13.

Irving, John. *A Son of the Circus.* New York: Random House, 1994.

Jaffrey, Zia. *The Invisibles. A Tale of the Eunuchs of India.* New York: Pantheon Books, 1996.

James, Liz, ed. *Women, Men and Eunuchs: Gender in Byzantium.* New York: Routledge, 1997.

Jonas, Hans. *The Gnostic Religion.* Boston: Beacon Press, 1958.

Jonson, Ben. *Volpone, or The Fox.* Ed. John W. Creaser. New York: New York University Press, 1978.

Jugel, Ulrike. *Politische Funktion und soziale Stellung der Eunuchen zur Späteren Hanzeit (25–220 n. Chr.).* Wiesbaden: Steiner, 1976.

Juvenal. *Sixteen Satires upon the Ancient Harlot.* Trans. Steven Robinson. Manchester, England: Carcanet New Press, 1983.

Kantorowicz, Ernst. *The king's two bodies: a study in medi-*

aeval political theology. Princeton, N.J.: Princeton University Press, 1957.

Kerényi, Karl [Carl]. *Dionysos: Archetypal Image of Indestructible Life*, trans. Ralph Manheim. Princeton, N.J.: Princeton University Press, 1976.

Koran. Trans. with notes by N. J. Dawood. 4th rev. ed. Hammondsworth, N.Y.: Penguin Books, 1974.

The Letters of Abelard and Heloïse. Trans. C.K. Scott Moncrieff. New York: Alfred A. Knopf, 1942.

Li Chi. *Book of Rites*. Trans. James Legge and ed. with introduction and study guide by Ch'u Chai and Winberg Chai. 2 vols. New Hyde Park, N.Y.: University Books, 1967.

Livius, Titus (Livy). *The War with Hannibal. Books xxi-xxx of the History of Rome from Its Foundation*. Trans. Aubrey de Sélincourt and ed. Betty Radice. Baltimore: Penguin Books, 1965.

Lommel, Andreas. *Schamanen und Medizinmänner*. Munich, 1980.

The Malleus Maleficarum of Heinrich Kramer and James Sprenger. Trans. and ed. Montague Summers. New York: Dover, 1971.

Heinrich von Maltzan. *Meine Wallfahrt nach Mekka*. Tübingen, 1982.

Marmon, Shaun. *Eunuchs and Sacred Boundaries in Islamic Society*. New York: Oxford University Press, 1995.

Martial. *Epigrams* XIII. Ed. and trans. D. R. Shackleton Bailey. Cambridge, Mass.: Harvard University Press, 1993.

Merkelbach, Reinhold. *Roman und Mysterium in der Antike*. Munich: Beck, 1962.

Mez, Adam. *The Renaissance of Islam*. Trans. Salahuddin Khuda Bukhsh and D. S. Margoliouth. London: Luzac & Co., 1937.

de Moor, Margriet. *The Virtuoso*. Trans. Ina Rilke. Woodstock and New York: Overlook, 2000.

Morris, Jan. *Conundrum: An Extraordinary Narrative of Transsexualism*. New York: Henry Holt and Company, 1974.

Mourad, Kenizé. *Regards from the Dead Princess: Novel of a Life*. New York: Arcade Publishing/Little, Brown and Company, 1989.

Musil, Robert. *The Man without Qualities*. Trans. from German by Sophie Wilkins. New York: Alfred A. Knopf, 1995.

de Nerval, Gérard. *Reise in den Orient* (Werke I). Munich, 1986.

New Catholic Encyclopedia. Vol. 5. New York: McGraw-Hill, 1967.

The New Oxford Annotated Bible, with the Apocryphal/deuterocanonical Books, New Revised Standard Version. Ed. Bruce M. Metzger and Roland E. Murphy. New York: Oxford University Press, 1994.

Nag Hammadi Codices, IX and X. Trans. Søren Giverson and Birger A. Pearson and ed. Birger A. Pearson. Leiden: E. J. Brill, 1981.

Nietzsche, Friedrich. *The Birth of Tragedy out of the Spirit of Music. and The Genealogy of Morals*. Trans. Francis Golffing. Garden City, N.Y.: Doubleday, 1956.

Nikhilananda, Swami. *The Upanishads*. New York: Harper & Row, 1963.

Nilsson, Martin. *Geschichte der griechischen Religion*. Munich: Beck, 1974.

The Odes of Solomon: The Syriac Texts. Ed. and trans. James H. Charlesworth. Missoula, Mont.: Scholars Press, 1977.

Ortkemper, Hubert. *Engel wider Willen: die Welt der*

Kastraten. Berlin: Henschel, 1993.

Otto, Walter F. *Beiträge zur Hierodulie im hellenistischen Ägypten*. Munich: Bayerische Akademie der Wissenschaften, 1949.

Ovid. *Fasti: Roman Holidays*. Trans. with notes and introduction by Betty Rose Nagle. Bloomington: Indiana University Press, 1995.

Pausanias. *Pausanias's Description of Greece*. 6 vols. Trans. J. G. Frazer. New York: Biblo and Tannen, 1965.

Peters, F. E. *Mecca: A Literary History of the Muslim Holy Land*. Princeton, N.J.: Princeton University Press, 1994.

Petronius Arbiter. *Satyrica [Satyricon]*. Ed. and trans. R. Bracht Branham and Daniel Kinney. London: J. M. Dent, 1996.

Pettinato, Giovanni. *Semiramis*. Zurich/Munich, 1989.

Plato. *Symposium*. Trans., with introduction & notes, by Alexander Nehamas and Paul Woodruff. Indianapolis, Ind. and Cambridge: Hackett Pub. Co., 1989.

Pliny the Elder. *The Natural History of Pliny*. Trans. John Bostock and H. T. Riley. London: George Bell & Sons, 1890.

Plutarch. *De Iside et Osiride*. Ed. with an introduction, translation, and commentary by J. Gwyn Griffiths. Swansea: University of Wales Press, 1970.

The Ancient Pyramid Texts. Trans. R. O. Faulkner. Oxford: Clarendon Press, 1969.

Ranke-Heinemann, Uta. *Eunuchs for the Kingdom of Heaven: Women, Sexuality, and the Catholic Church*. Trans. Peter Heinegg. New York: Doubleday, 1990.

Rice, Anne. *Cry to Heaven*. New York: Alfred Knopf, 1982.

Richards, Renée, with John Ames. *Second Serve*. New York: Stein and Day, 1983.

Rilke, Rainer Maria. *Duino Elegies*. Trans. J. B. Leishman and Stephen Spender. New York: W. W. Norton, 1939.

Rupprecht von Bayern. *Reiseerinnerungen aus dem Süd-Osten Europas und dem Orient*. Munich, 1923.

The Sayings of the Desert Fathers: The Alphabetical Collection. Trans. Benedicta Ward. London: Mowbrays, 1975.

Schubart, Wilhelm. *Justinian und Theodora*. Munich: F. Bruckmann, 1943.

Schwarz, Franz von. *Turkestan*. Freiburg i. Br., 1900.

Scriptores Historiae Augustae. 3 vols. Trans. David Magie. London: William Heinemann, 1924.

The Selected Letters of Lady Mary Wortley Montagu. Ed. Robert Halsband. New York: St. Martin's Press, 1970.

Shakespeare, William. *The Norton Shakespeare*. Ed. Stephen Greenblatt. New York: W.W. Norton & Co., 1997.

Suetonius, Tranquillus Gaius. *The Twelve Caesars*. Trans. Robert Graves. Revised with an introduction by Michael Grant. London: Penguin Press, 1989.

Sun Yao-ting. *Der letzte Eunuch*. Trans. Uwe Frankenhauser. Leipzig: G. Kiepenhauer, 1993.

Tacitus. *Annals*, vol. 4. Trans. John Jackson. London: William Heinemann, 1937.

Teply, Karl. *Kaiserliche Gesandtschaften ans Goldene Horn*. Stuttgart: Bibliothek Kleines Reisebuch, n.d.

Terence. *The Eunuch*. In *The Complete Comedies of Terence*. Trans. Palmer Bovie, Constance Carrier, and Douglass Parker. New Brunswick, N.J.: Rutgers University Press, 1974.

Tsai, Shih-shan H. *Eunuchs in the Ming Dynasty*. Albany, 1995.

Texte aus der Umwelt des Alten Testaments. Ed. Otto Kaiser.

Gütersloh: G. Mohn, 1982.
Vámbéry, Arminius [Armin]. *Travels in Central Asia.* London: John Murray, 1864.
Veyne, Paul. *Bread and Circuses.* Trans. Oswyn Murray. London: Penguin, 1990.
Walker, Benjamin. *Gnosticism: Its History and Influence.* Wellingborough: The Aquarian Press, 1983.
Zinkeisen, J. W. *Geschichte des osmanischen Reiches in Europa.* Hamburg: F. Perthes, 1840–63. 8 vols.

Index of Names